THERE'S ONLY ONE ARTHUR BOTTOM

FOOTBALL ICONS & CULT HEROES

© Haynes Publishing, 2013

The right of David Walker to be identified as the author of this Work has been asserted
by him in accordance with the Copyright, Designs & Patents Act 1988.

First published in 2013

A catalogue record for this book is available from the British Library

ISBN: 978-0-85733-201-1

Published by Haynes Publishing, Sparkford, Yeovil,
Somerset BA22 7JJ, UK
Tel: 01963 442030 Fax: 01963 440001
Int. tel: +44 1963 442030 Int. fax: +44 1963 440001
E-mail: sales@haynes.co.uk
Website: www.haynes.co.uk

Haynes North America Inc., 861 Lawrence Drive, Newbury Park, California 91320, USA

Images © Mirrorpix

Creative Director: Kevin Gardner
Designed for Haynes by BrainWave

Printed and bound in the UK

THERE'S ONLY ONE ARTHUR BOTTOM

FOOTBALL ICONS & CULT HEROES

DAVID WALKER

INTRODUCTION

It was a photograph of Sir Alex Ferguson, Bryan Robson and Bob Paisley together on the Manchester United team coach that proved the catalyst for this book.

All three had claims to being icons of their clubs: Ferguson and Robson with Manchester United; Paisley with Liverpool. When I met Sir Alex at United's training ground a few months ago I showed him a print of the picture from the Mirrorpix archive. Robbo and Bob were sitting together on the coach. The United boss was standing in the aisle and a happy band of sporting brothers they made, too, with broad smiles on their faces.

Fergie has an encyclopaedic memory but I could tell I had him struggling to remember the precise occasion and its significance. It was Boxing Day 1986 and after a previous attack on the United team as they arrived at Anfield the legendary former Liverpool manager had agreed to travel with the United team to ensure their safe passage. It was also significant because it was the first time a team managed by Ferguson had ever won at Anfield. It would not be the last.

Once Fergie's memory had latched onto the date and the game he virtually relived key moments, the winning goal and the fact that he played Robson, United's Captain Fantastic, at centre-half that day. He also remembered that the following day United followed up their epic win at Anfield by losing at home to Norwich. Oh, and Robbo sustained a hamstring injury in that defeat by standing on the ball. Those were difficult early days in the Ferguson regime.

But if the football legends featured on one photograph could spark so much debate the issue broadened to the fact that every club has its own iconic figures and cult heroes. The two categories are different. Icons tend to be a club's greatest star player. The cult heroes are the players who arrive at your club, make a spectacular impact but then move on. Yet such were their deeds – perhaps good, sometimes bad – that they will never be forgotten.

This book examines the very best players to represent the 92 clubs who were members of the Premier and Football Leagues at the start of the 2012–13 season. There are the incomparables, such as Liverpool's Kenny Dalglish and Nat Lofthouse at Bolton, who have emerged as beacons to illuminate the history of their clubs. There are other, less well-known icons like the late Arthur Bottom who has an electronic fanzine named in his honour: "There's Only One Arthur Bottom."

We accept, and actually hope, that this book will spark heated debate. We do not claim to have perfected a formula to ensure every choice is perfect. But football is all about opinions, and that's why we asked readers of the *Sunday Mirror* and the members of the Football Supporters' Federation to help us in our task. Their feedback provided the raw material that we were able to process. And by bringing together all the elements – information, opinion, knowledge and pictorial history – we've created *There's Only One Arthur Bottom*. We hope you enjoy it.

ACCRINGTON STANLEY

ⓘ George Stewart   **ⓗ Brett Ormerod**

Stanley fans have accepted for years that they're going to be the butt of jokes. Too many people still remember the old milk advert. Two little Scouse kids are raiding the fridge. As one pours himself a glass of milk he explains: "Ian Rush said that if I didn't drink lots of milk when I grow up I'll only be good enough to play for Accrington Stanley." His little mate replies: "Accrington Stanley, who are they?" And the one-word response is: "Exactly!"

Well, Stanley are the club that came back from the dead. After 44 years outside the Football League they managed to win promotion back as Conference champions in 2006. The original club was formed in 1891 and played in the League from 1921 to 1961. The collapse at that time saw Stanley become one of the few clubs to drop out of the Football League altogether – that's why the renaissance is even more remarkable.

A man who played a significant part in the rebirth is our Stanley cult hero, Brett Ormerod. The hard-running striker is arguably the club's finest player in their modern era. Ormerod was released by neighbours Blackburn and joined Accrington in 1995. He made 54 League appearances for the non-League club and scored 32 goals before moving to Blackpool to resume his full-time football career.

The Seasiders paid Stanley £50,000 for Ormerod in 1997 plus a lucrative sell-on agreement – they agreed to pay 25 per cent of any profit they received from Ormerod's future transfer. Ormerod blossomed at Bloomfield Road, got over the set-back of a double fracture to his leg, and then became a target for a string of Premier League clubs.

Blackpool insisted they didn't have to sell him, but eventually accepted Southampton's offer of £1.75million. At a stroke Stanley were around £400,000 better off and Ormerod's sale helped fund the club's successful assault on getting into the Football League. That's what makes a man a cult hero.

Our Accrington icon is from an earlier era. George Stewart signed for them in 1954 for £1,500 from St Mirren and went on to become Stanley's greatest ever marksman. He scored 136 goals in 182 games. The Scottish striker broke his club's goalscoring record by dispatching 35 goals in the 1955–56 season, including three hat-tricks. Stewart played in the team that is widely accepted as the best ever Stanley side. They were in the old Third Division and narrowly missed promotion. And in one game against Rochdale in 1955 the entire team was made up of Scotsmen, managed by a fellow member of the tartan army, Walter Galbraith.

Stewart's heading prowess was renowned. That's why it came as little surprise in his later years that George was diagnosed with dementia. His was a tragic fate that had befallen other fine centre-forwards, including Jeff Astle and Nat Lofthouse.

THE FAN'S VIEW

Neil McGuinness: *"I'd like to nominate Paul Mullin. He was pivotal in our rise to the Football League. Great target man and wonderful servant to the club."*

AFC WIMBLEDON

 **Their fans**    **Erik Samuelson**

AFC Wimbledon was formed in 2002, set up by a democratic, mutual supporters trust.

The FA's decision to allow Wimbledon FC to relocate to Buckinghamshire and become Milton Keynes Dons outraged most supporters of the Plough Lane club.

The independent panel set up by the FA who sanctioned the controversial move actually suggested in their report: "resurrecting the club from its ashes as, say, 'Wimbledon Town' is, with respect to those supporters who would rather that happened so that they could go back to the position the club started in 113 years ago, not in the wider interests of football."

Thankfully, hundreds of Wimbledon fans ignored that advice and AFC Wimbledon was born. The club held trials on Wimbledon Common to find new players. After all, the contracts of the established names had been transferred with the takeover to MK Dons.

It's a matter of justified pride that, having started at the foot of the football pyramid, AFC Wimbledon climbed through nine divisions and hit the Football League in 2011. It must have been a sweet moment for them. And the remarkable way they have built their club is the reason why we nominate the supporters as our AFC Wimbledon icons. This astonishing phoenix from the ashes story could not have happened but for their tenacity and commitment.

At the helm of the good ship Wimbledon is Chairman Erik Samuelson. He has been a formidable leader for the new club. And he recognizes what the sale of the old club was all about and why, rather than becoming bitter and twisted about the past, the new club must look towards the future.

Samuelson explained the land deals behind the move: "It was all about enabling Asda to build a supermarket."

He continued: "The right way is the way that AFC Wimbledon have done it – we were a bunch of people who knew nothing about running a football club and now we are a sustainable club, that has increasingly positive hopes about moving to a new stadium, which would be back to Plough Lane. If that happens then I will die happy."

Recapturing those heady days of the Wimbledon Crazy Gang playing in the top flight and winning the 1988 FA Cup final remain on distant horizons. At the moment, protecting their Football League status is a worthy goal. But Dons fans must never underestimate the size of their achievements. What they have done with their new club is truly unique.

ALDERSHOT TOWN

 **Jack Howarth**

 **John Dungworth**

Who is more valuable to a club? The man who scores the goals or the guy who keeps them out at the other end of the pitch?

It's a debate that will not rage stronger anywhere than at Aldershot when fans decide who deserves to be considered the club's greatest icon. Is it striker Jack Howarth, who in two stays at the Recreation Ground scored a club record 171 goals from 421 League games? Or is it goalkeeper Glen Johnson who spent more than a decade as the team's No. 1?

Both could lay claim to extraordinary feats, the most outstanding being Johnson who saved three penalties in a game against Newport in February 1977. A former Arsenal trainee, he had moved to Doncaster in search of first-team football before returning south in 1973 to join the Shots, initially as cover for Tony Godfrey. When Godfrey was injured before a game at Plymouth, Johnson got his chance and was rarely out of the team, until a back injury forced him to retire 10 years later. By then he'd played 424 League games plus another 43 in Cup competitions, a record no keeper in the club's history has come close to matching.

But for all those achievements, centre-forward will always be the glory position. And so it is Howarth who just about wins the vote.

Born in Crook in County Durham in February 1945, there was little sign of the good things to come when Howarth signed for the Shots as a raw 20-year-old. He had been at Chelsea for a while, but although he scored a lot of goals for the reserves, when he then moved to Swindon he had been picked only twice for their first team.

But, under the guidance of managers Dave Smith and then Tommy McAnearney, the six-footer blossomed. He was powerful in the air with natural timing to his leap, and the fans loved his old-fashioned centre-forward play, top scorer in every one of six seasons until a shock decision to sell him to Rochdale for £8,000 in 1972. He never settled there, and a year later was back to lead a promotion team with 25 goals in the season. He stayed until 1977, always the man to look to when the team were in need of a goal.

Yet it's the man who replaced him in the No. 9 shirt the following season, John Dungworth, who is the Shots' cult hero. The Rotherham-born striker represented another gamble by the club: when McAnearney signed him on a free transfer his record read just five goals from 44 League games at Huddersfield, Barnsley and Rochdale.

In his first season he scored 23 times and was voted Player of the Year, and the next campaign, 1978–79, brought 26 goals in Division Four. But it was in that year's FA Cup run that he became a special hero to the fans, scoring eight times as the club reached the fifth round, matching their best ever achievement in the competition and only going out after extra-time in a replay at Shrewsbury. Ironically that was the club he joined when he left the Recreation Ground in 1979 for a £100,000 fee set by a tribunal – and even at that price it was small compensation for the loss of a man who had scored 58 times in just 105 appearances.

THE FAN'S VIEW

William Young: *"I nominate Nikki Bull, a true Shots legend. The goalie signed for us as a teenager in 2002 and was immediately first choice. He stayed that way until he departed for Brentford at the end of the 2008–09 season having made 312 appearances for the club.*

"He had a strong affinity with the fans and gave an emotional interview straight after the vital win at Torquay in our promotion season that virtually secured the Conference title in which he spoke about how the fans had rebuilt the club since 1992."

ARSENAL

(i) **Thierry Henry**   (h) **George Armstrong**

Why do Arsenal, London's establishment club, wear red? Every Gunners fan should know of their club's links with Nottingham Forest.

Formed by workers at the Royal Arsenal at Woolwich in 1886, they began as Dial Square, the name of one of the workshops. Their team included two former Nottingham Forest players, Fred Beardsley and Morris Bates. When Beardsley wrote to his old club asking for help, Forest responded by sending the new club a set of red jerseys and a ball. The club became known as the Woolwich Reds, and soon after its formation their official title was changed to Woolwich Arsenal. It was the legendary manager Herbert Chapman who changed the kit to include white sleeves to brighten it up.

Such has been Arsenal's record at producing fine teams and winning trophies down the decades that any discussion of icons and cult heroes sparks ferocious debate, with names from the Twenties and Thirties being pitched alongside some more modern heroes.

Unfortunately, there is no television footage to capture the likes of David Jack, Joe Hulme and Cliff Bastin in their prime. There is some Pathé News footage of memorable days – such as Alex James skippering the Arsenal team to the 1936 FA Cup final win over Sheffield United – but we're deprived of the kind of video analysis and slow-motion replays that have enhanced our insight into modern Arsenal greats such as Thierry Henry and Dennis Bergkamp.

Suffice to say that some of the contemporary interview evidence about the impact the Gunners stars had on the game is compelling. For instance, as a youngster the great Tom Finney was in awe as he watched Alex James play for Preston before his move to Highbury. Finney, who can justifiably lay claim to being England's finest footballer, said: "James was the top star of his day, a genius. There wasn't much about him physically, but he had sublime skills and the knack of letting the ball do the work. He wore the baggiest of baggy shorts and his heavily gelled hair was parted down the centre. I was in awe of James. There was a magic and a mystery about James that mesmerised me."

With Arsenal, James was the creator par excellence. Alongside him in that Arsenal era of the Thirties were goalscoring wingers Bastin and Hulme. Today you can only speculate at their value for the 1933–34 season when, from wide attacking berths, they contributed 53 goals. Hulme on the right wing claimed 20 of them.

Bastin, on the left, was the club's top scorer with 33 goals – and Arsenal were champions. They retained their crown in 1934–35. Ted Drake was their goal king then, with 42 goals in 41 games including three hat-tricks and the astonishing feat of scoring four goals in four other matches. This was a golden era for the Gunners. During the Thirties they won the League title five times and twice lifted the FA Cup.

As well as these iconic figures the Gunners also had an early nomination for the club's cult hero. A fierce left-half who is often described as the game's original hard man – and Wilf Copping was hard. The boxer's face, a scowl that could make hell freeze over and physical commitment bordering on the insane, the Barnsley-born left-half intimidated opponents wherever he played. Copping joined Arsenal from Leeds United for £8,000 in June 1934. He was their enforcer.

In November 1934 Copping played for England against world champions Italy. It was a ferocious match that has gone down in history as the most brutal international England have played in. Stanley Matthews said: "For the first quarter of an hour there might just as well have not been a ball on the pitch as far as the Italians were concerned. They were like men possessed, kicking anything and everything that moved bar the referee. The game degenerated into nothing short of a brawl and it disgusted me."

Gunners colleague Eddie Hapgood later revealed: "Wilf enjoyed himself that afternoon. For the first time in their lives the Italians were given a sample of real honest shoulder charging, and Wilf's famous double-footed tackle was causing them furiously to re-think." Matthews added: "Just before half-time, Wilf Copping hit the Italian captain Monti with a tackle that he seemed to launch from somewhere just north of Leeds. Monti went up in the air like a rocket and down like a bag of hammers and had to leave the field with a splintered bone in his foot."

Just as Copping was tough, David Jack supplied silky skills. Jack was 29 when he moved to Highbury from Bolton in a world record £10,890 deal. FA President Sir Charles Clegg issued a statement claiming that no player was worth such a vast amount. Yet Jack produced some superb displays for the Gunners and manager Herbert Chapman, who had masterminded the club's emergence as a major power in the English game during the Twenties, always hailed Jack as one of his shrewdest buys. When Arsenal won the 1930 FA Cup final against Huddersfield Jack became the first player to win the trophy at Wembley with two different clubs.

Mention of Copping provides a link to one of the heroes of the Arsenal team that won the League and FA Cup Double in 1971 – Peter Storey. The Farnham-born midfielder built up his own fearsome reputation during an era when every team could boast their own enforcer. Storey was among the best. But, like many of the old destructive players, Storey could surprise you with moments of creativity, such as in the 1971 FA Cup semi-final against Stoke. Arsenal were losing 2-0 when Storey struck two priceless goals to force a replay. Until Storey's remarkable intervention, any suggestion that the Gunners were on course to create football history as Double winners seemed a tad fanciful.

Another prime contender to be Arsenal's all-time cult hero came from Bertie Mee's side of 1970–71. Like Storey, Charlie George was a home-grown player. Acclaimed as the King of the North Bank, he dispatched the extra-time winner in the 1971 FA Cup final victory over Liverpool. The long-haired lad from Islington had seen his rising 20-yard shot clinch the Double. His goal celebration, collapsing to the turf and lying flat on his back, is now part of FA Cup folklore.

But perhaps even the Double winners will accept that some of Arsenal's greatest creative talents have arrived on the scene in the modern era and, when deciding on the ultimate icon, it's hard to look beyond Thierry Henry and Dennis Bergkamp. Yes, there will be some Tony Adams loyalists who believe that the centre-back who reformed his chaotic, alcoholic lifestyle while skippering the club to glory deserves acknowledgment for his searing commitment to the Gunners' cause and brilliant insight into how to defend. Like many of the players alongside him, who had been so expertly tutored by manager George Graham, Adams appreciated the finer arts of defending. He would probably have been acclaimed even more vociferously if he'd been Italian and playing in Serie A.

But Bergkamp and Henry represent an era when Arsenal teams were vibrant, exciting, full of pace and flair. And that hasn't always been the case! Bergkamp's recruitment from Inter Milan in 1995 must surely rank as the best thing Bruce Rioch did in his brief reign as Arsenal manager. But the brilliant Dutch striker truly blossomed under Arsène Wenger's tutelage, especially when the French manager exploited his knowledge of unheralded talent from his homeland by signing Henry, Patrick Vieira and Robert Pirès for Arsenal.

Bergkamp was the antithesis of many Dutch footballers. Many are renowned as barrack room lawyers, outspoken in their tactical assessment of their colleagues and ever willing to express their opinions via the media. Bergkamp was different. He had a sharp, dry sense of humour, yet never courted publicity or controversy by declaring outspoken views. The fact he developed an aversion to flying, which made his contribution to European campaigns increasingly difficult, was a set-back. But on his best days the pasty-faced Dutchman was a class apart. He has in his personal locker a collection of stupendous goals few other players on the planet could imagine, never mind emulate.

Perhaps his greatest goal in an Arsenal shirt came against Newcastle. Pirès drilled a pass into his feet and with the most audacious of touches Bergkamp flicked the ball to one side of Nikos Dabizas, performing a pirouette to take his body around the other side of the defender. The ball spun into his path as if it was under his spell and he side-footed a clinical shot past Shay Given into the Newcastle goal. Sir Bobby Robson, the Newcastle manager that day, was old enough and wise enough to recognize that something special had happened. Robson said: "You can't blame anyone for that. You just have to accept that Bergkamp did a beautiful thing."

While Bergkamp was fleet-footed and revelled in the role of the withdrawn striker, working as a link between the midfield and strikers, Thierry Henry was a stunning predator. From being a Juventus cast-off when recruited by Wenger in 1999, Henry went on to become one of Europe's most feared marksmen. I remember seeing him in the dressing room area at Elland Road. He was stripped to the waist and you realized that here was a player who at 6ft 2ins was as tall as the old-fashioned Arsenal centre-forwards like Lee Chapman and Alan Smith, yet he was built like a middleweight boxer with incredible upper-body muscles and blessed with a turn of speed that was more akin to a flying winger like Marc Overmars. Henry was a brilliant athlete and the fact that at times he'd stand rooted to the spot, wide on the left flank before coming to life and leaving the mesmerized opposition defence flat-footed, simply added to his allure. He just recognized the importance of standing still.

So in our cast of Arsenal icons Henry emerges as the main man – just. But that status recognizes the fact he is the club's greatest goalscorer of all-time. He overtook Ian Wright to achieve that goal and eclipsed Cliff Bastin as Arsenal's top League marksman. He won the Footballer of the Year award a record three times.

As for the Arsenal cult hero, we're looking beyond some of the obvious names, such as Ian Wright, the late and much lamented David Rocastle and the more modern mavericks like Paul Merson. In fact, our cult hero epitomized an approach of quiet modesty, a player who could be totally relied on to give his all for the Arsenal cause. George Armstrong, known to everyone as Geordie because of his Durham roots, joined the Gunners as an apprentice, played a key role in their 1971 Double triumph and later returned to spend 10 years on the coaching staff as reserve coach. He set standards by his enthusiasm and commitment that young players warmed to. John Lukic, the goalie when Arsenal won the League title on a day of last-match drama in 1989, said: "Geordie was a real cult hero inside Arsenal. A fine man who gave his all for the club. He may not be the name that many people immediately think of as the Arsenal cult hero but when people who really know Arsenal think about him and his contribution to the cause nobody will resent any accolade heaped on his shoulders. He was a fine man."

Geordie Armstrong, our Arsenal cult hero, died in 2000, aged 56. He collapsed while taking a training session at the Arsenal training ground and died the following day in hospital.

THE FAN'S VIEW

Barry Purchese: *"No matter how badly the team were playing Geordie Armstrong never let his head drop and he stayed with the club all his life. He was Arsenal through and through and the fans loved him."*

ASTON VILLA

 **Paul McGrath**

 **Ian Taylor**

Aston Villa's greatest player? Well the trouble with making that judgement is that, arguably, the best of the lot could be lost in the mists of time. After all, it was in August 1878 that Archibald "Archie" Hunter moved from Scotland to Birmingham to become the Victorian game's first superstar.

It was his skill – records from the time said it was common for him to dribble the length of the field to score – that brought the crowds which later encouraged his fellow Scot William McGregor to found the Football League. He was the first to score in every round of the FA Cup when Villa won the trophy in 1887.

His tale was also tinged with tragedy. He was just 31 when he suffered a heart attack playing in a match against Everton in 1890, and was forced to retire on medical advice. He never recovered fully, losing his life to heart failure four years later.

Nobody is left alive to make a proper judgement on just how good he was – but more than 100 years later his record, 42 goals in 73 games at a pivotal time for the birth of professional football, earned him a place in the Football League's list of a hundred legends of the game.

Does that make him Villa's greatest icon? Well, there have been plenty more contenders. Tom "Pongo" Waring scored 49 goals in the 1930–31 season, and then there was the crowning glory of Tony Barton's European Cup winners in 1982. Many would argue that the midfield genius of Gordon Cowans in that side, and in later spells with the club, should be recognized. "Syd", as Cowans is widely known, remains one of the most friendly and self-effacing football men you could wish to meet. The openness and honesty he has displayed throughout his career as a player and coach has simply emphasized his value to Villa.

But the man most modern Villa fans hail as the greatest still has his name sung from the Holte End at every game: Paul McGrath. He joined for a £400,000 fee in August 1989, signed by Graham Taylor after Manchester United had tried but failed to persuade the troubled Irishman to take a package to retire from the game.

Crippled by an arthritic knee condition, and with personal demons that gave him issues with alcohol that have been well documented, it was a signing that seemed a gamble. In fact, Taylor tells the story of how, after having the Irishman at the club for just 48 hours, he went home to confess to his wife that he might have made the biggest mistake of his managerial career. The traits of lateness and drinking had immediately surfaced. The handicap of his arthritic knees was plain to see.

Paul was always a gentle soul. Shy in the company of strangers, even on football trips with Villa or the Republic of Ireland, he would quietly adjourn to his own room. Some fine players who've trained, played and socialized with him insist the performances McGrath produced against some of the toughest opponents in the world were unbelievable. There were days during his Villa career when McGrath was superhuman. He could read the game better than most, anticipate danger, and then make a tackle or interception that would leave world-class strikers shaking their heads in dismay at his pace, power and athleticism. And in possession there was no whacking the ball to row Z from big Paul. He was calmness personified as he picked out a team-mate and delivered an inch-perfect pass. You could see why Ireland boss Jack Charlton had insisted McGrath was the best holding midfielder in the world, never mind his performances when he played in his favoured role at centre-back.

Without doubt, the biggest transfer gamble of Graham Taylor's career turned into his finest coup. McGrath was magnificent for Taylor's team as they finished First Division runners up in 1990. McGrath went on to be the shining star of the adventurous side under Ron Atkinson, which missed out by a whisker on winning the first Premier League season in 1993, and then beat champions Manchester United in a thrilling League Cup final at Wembley in 1994.

McGrath, voted the PFA's Player of the Year in 1993, won yet another League Cup for Brian Little in 1996. There were great nights in Europe too, memorably knocking Inter Milan out of the UEFA Cup. He was the defensive rock on which everything was built – yet his 252 games were as much a triumph for the care of physio Jim Walker, who nursed him through weeks when his knees gave him so much pain he couldn't train, yet somehow got him on to the pitch on a Saturday for yet another man of the match display.

Walker was more than just the physio when it came to McGrath's care. He was dispatched to Dublin for every Ireland home game to chaperone the player after the match and ensure he was on the first available plane back to Birmingham. And such were Jim's values of care and consideration that his patient never quibbled at being supervised. Paul knew it made sense.

Ironically in that same team was the man who is Villa's cult hero. And when he wasn't in the team, or if he was injured, he was often in the crowd cheering on the team and singing songs with the fans. Cap pulled down in an attempt not to be recognized, he'd be with his mates, just one of the fans.

Ian Taylor grew up a Villa fan, played his first football part-time for Moor Green before joining Port Vale then Sheffield Wednesday before Brian Little gave him his dream move to the club he loved. Never the greatest technically, he made up for that with work rate, industry and sheer joy at wearing the claret and blue shirt. In nearly 10 years he played 234 games, scored in the 1996 League Cup final and was part of the team that went to the last FA Cup final played at the old Wembley in 2000.

But Taylor's status wasn't about statistics. It was because, most of all, he was one of the fans, the guy who got to play for his club, the guy everybody wished they could have been. A real Villa cult hero.

THE FAN'S VIEW

Paul Murphy: *"We wondered what was happening when Paul McGrath signed. Everyone knew Man United were trying to pension him off but what a signing. He was a sensational player for Villa."*

BARNET

 Ian Hendon  Jimmy Greaves

Ian Hendon was never one to grab the headlines, but he made a solid reputation for himself at Barnet as both a player and manager.

The defender began as a member of Tottenham's FA Youth Cup-winning side in 1990. He won seven England Under-21 caps – as many appearances as he made for the Spurs first team.

Hendon played for a variety of clubs after that, leaving White Hart Lane before linking up at Conference Barnet in 2003 with his mentor Peter Shreeves, who had coached him at Spurs and Sheffield Wednesday.

Hendon captained Barnet on their return to the Football League in his second season and made 143 League appearances in an impressive playing career at Underhill. He was invited to join Paul Fairclough's coaching staff in 2007 and eventually took over the reins when the manager was sacked. He was credited by Bees fans for keeping Barnet up that season, but was eventually dismissed in 2010. But his efforts at Underhill are still well appreciated.

It's difficult to believe that until this season the legendary Jimmy Greaves used to boast he was the only international ever to play for AC Milan and Barnet and that, on top of that, he was the Bees' most capped player.

Then along came veteran Holland superstar Edgar Davids in 2012 to steal Greavesie's thunder on two counts. But the former England striker still fondly recalls his twilight years at Barnet as some of the happiest days of his career. Greaves explained:

"I joined the Bees at the age of 37 and spent just about the most enjoyable two seasons of my career there. I was a recovering alcoholic, still on and off the booze, when I arrived at Barnet – but within a couple of months I had kicked it for good. The chairman Dave Underwood, a former Fulham goalkeeper, was a good friend during that time. After a long period out of the game, it was at Barnet where I really rediscovered my enthusiasm for the game. The place gave me a cause, a purpose and a sense of belonging. It was there where I solved my problems."

BARNSLEY

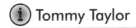 Tommy Taylor

 Ronnie Glavin

Many clubs can trace their formation back to a local church. In 1887 the Revd T T Preedy, curate at Barnsley's St Peter's, set up a team in that name. A decade later the club's name was shortened and Barnsley FC was formed. A year later they were admitted into the Football League.

A supporters' meeting at a Barnsley hotel in 2003 emphasized the status of the ultimate Oakwell icon. Patrick Cryne, a local boy turned millionaire businessman, had funded a takeover of a football club that was teetering on the brink of extinction. Barnsley were already in administration following a previous, ill-fated change of regime. Without doubt Cryne was seen as the club's saviour and his Barnsley pedigree made him a welcome benefactor. Cryne agreed to attend a supporters' get-together at the Ardsley House Hotel to share his vision for their club's future.

It was during this meeting that a fan asked who the new owner thought was Barnsley's greatest ever player. Knowing some of the legendary names of Barnsley's past I was slightly surprised by Cryne's answer. Yet his instant response provoked prolonged applause and shouts of "here, here." The player he named was Tommy Taylor. The tall, dark, centre-forward had only played for Barnsley for four years before being lured across the Pennines by Matt Busby and Manchester United. United paid a record £29,999 for the man Busby believed would be the focal point of his team's attack for the next decade or more. The wily manager insisted on the bizarre fee because, although it was still a record, he didn't want Taylor to be labelled the first £30,000 footballer.

Busby's long-term vision never came to fruition. Less than five years after signing Taylor, and witnessing his instant impact among the most gifted group of young players ever seen in English club football, his attacking talisman was one of the eight brilliant footballers who died in the Munich Air Disaster on 6th February 1958. He was only 26.

Football had not been Taylor's first job. Like most sons of Barnsley in the post-war years he worked at a colliery. Mining, the camaraderie of the pits, the town of Barnsley and their local football team are all interlinked with pride. Taylor, swarthy, brave and physically powerful, reflected intrinsic south Yorkshire values. So on one hand the history books starkly reflect that in 44 appearances for his home-town team the young striker scored 26 goals before joining the champions of England. Yet to this day Barnsley fans still see Taylor as one of their own. And he wasn't the only young man from Barnsley to perish on that snowbound Munich runway. Mark Jones, a pipe-smoking centre-back, had joined United as a 15-year-old apprentice.

Taylor was a brilliant goalscorer. Brave, athletic and lethal with his head and feet, his record of 16 international goals in 19 England appearances merely hints at the potential that the plane crash in Munich snuffed out. He was certainly good enough to spark a world record £65,000 bid from Internazionale the year before he perished. Busby had no hesitation in rejecting the approach.

So if Tommy Taylor is our Barnsley icon, who is their cult hero? Given the umbilical chord linking the football club with the local community, it may come as a bit of a surprise that our shortlist features not only two popular home-grown players but also an import from Scotland. The home-grown heroes are Sydney "Skinner" Normanton and Mick McCarthy. Thanks partly to Michael Parkinson's sports writing in the *Sunday Times* during the Seventies, Normanton undoubtedly enjoyed greater fame in his retirement than he'd ever seen during his playing days. Parky, also born and brought up in Barnsley, recalled the way he marvelled at Skinner's no-nonsense, some might say brutal, approach to the game. Certainly Danny Blanchflower, who went on to skipper Tottenham's Double-winning team of 1961, recalled: "It was my first practice match at Oakwell and I was against Skinner. As he ran towards me I thought will he go left or will he go right? He did neither. He ran straight over me! And that was in training."

Skinner wasn't a great player but in south Yorkshire parlance he took no prisoners. The same could be said for Mick McCarthy, who was a much more accomplished player and proved it with Manchester City, Celtic and the Republic of Ireland (he qualified to play for Ireland through his dad, Charlie). But Mick played more games for Barnsley than any other of his clubs and is still revered in the town. One day they hope he'll go home and be their manager.

Back in the late Seventies Mick was in a promotion-winning team that featured the man who wins our Barnsley cult award. Ronnie Glavin was 28 when he headed south from Celtic in 1979. He proved an inspired signing and the Oakwell fans loved his midfield grace and goalscoring panache. Barnsley was the capital of the south Yorkshire coal fields. The locals prided themselves on their commitment to their club, but to this day Glavin is acclaimed as the club's greatest import. And that's some acclaim to gain from the Barnsley sporting public.

THE FAN'S VIEW

Steve Yates: *"Ronnie was in a strong Barnsley team but he was the top entertainer, the best we've had at Oakwell in recent times."*

BIRMINGHAM CITY

 Trevor Francis    Robert Hopkins

There were no more than a handful of people at St Andrew's on the day that changed the course of Birmingham City's history. After all, it was just an English Schools Cup game, watched by a few proud parents and a couple of fans with nothing better to do.

But when a skinny 14-year-old kid from Plymouth scored a hat-trick, Birmingham's manager, Stan Cullis, suggested to his youth coaches that they invite the lad back for a trial. And after talking to his parents, Trevor Francis decided to give it a go.

So began a romance between player and club that remains as deep as it ever was. At a club where passion and commitment is never in short supply from the supporters, Francis was the boy who gave the same level of love in return.

Within months of starting with the club as a 15-year-old apprentice the word was going round that the Blues had discovered a special talent. Freddie Goodwin, who had taken over as manager with the brief to build a side that could gain promotion to the old First Division, took note, and on 5th September 1970 decided he would wait no longer to test young Trevor's potential.

Francis was named as substitute for a game in Cardiff, and an injury to John Vincent saw him make his debut aged just 16 years and 138 days. The youngest player ever to appear in a Birmingham shirt, it was just the first of many records he would break during his nine years as a player with the club.

A week later he started against Oxford and scored; Blues fans, who love to see home-grown talent, had a new hero. By December he was a fixture in the team alongside centre-forward Bob Latchford, and as the New Year began went on an astonishing run scoring 12 goals in eight games. That included all four in a win over Bolton, a game Francis still recalls as the best memory of his time at Birmingham.

Goodwin was building a swashbuckling side with Francis feeding off the work of Latchford and Bob Hatton and they went unbeaten from early January to the end of the season to achieve a place in the top flight. What followed was probably the club's most exciting era, and Francis their most glamorous player.

By 1977 he won, somewhat belatedly many said, the first of his 52 England caps, and in that season he scored 27 goals, 25 of them in the First Division. Twice they reached the FA Cup semi-finals, losing one of them to a Leeds side that Francis still considers was the greatest club team he ever played against. It started in historic fashion, and ended that way too, with Brian Clough doubling the transfer record of the time by paying £1million to take him to Nottingham Forest. Coventry were also willing to meet that fee, and offered bigger wages, but Francis wanted medals and got his wish by scoring the winner in a European Cup final.

He played for more big clubs in England, Italy, Scotland and Australia, but Birmingham, his first football love, never left him. "I had such a special relationship with the fans if you weren't there you couldn't understand it," he says now. "I worried about going back as manager later for the fear of that relationship ending. Maybe I shouldn't have, because even though that period ended in disappointment I still get a great reception whenever I'm at Blues."

When it comes to a cult hero, Birmingham have had plenty. Frank Worthington, Steve Claridge and Christophe Dugarry are a few that spring to mind. But the one who stands out has to be Robert Hopkins, not so much for his ability but for his devotion to the club.

"Hoppy", who played more than 200 games in two spells at the club, was a born and bred Blues fan. Rejected by the club when he went for trials as a teenager he signed for Aston Villa, and caused uproar by wearing a Birmingham City shirt underneath his Villa top when he played his one and only first-team game for them.

He got his move to the Blues in a swap deal for Alan Curbishley, and became the driving force of the Ron Saunders side of the 1980s that were notorious for their hard approach both to football and life in general. Players like Noel Blake, Tony Coton, Pat Van Den Hauwe, Marcus Gayle and Mick Harford made Wimbledon's "Crazy Gang" look like a Sunday School team. They drank and scrapped together out on the town, and brought the same fire to the football pitch. Most of all they gave Birmingham an identity that their long-suffering fans could relate to.

THE FAN'S VIEW
Alex Smith: *"No Blues fan will look beyond TF as our icon. He was the epitome of class."*

BLACKBURN ROVERS

 **Jack Walker**

 **Tony Parkes**

Although founding members of the Football League and wearers of those distinctive blue and white halved shirts, not all Blackburn's landmarks are historic. Yet nobody should overlook the fact that in 1995 Rovers were the last provincial club to be crowned champions of England. It could be a while before it happens again.

It's a true measure of Jack Walker's standing in his home town that he is the only football club owner to be awarded iconic status in this book. Nobody connected with the friendly Ewood Park club will ever underestimate the impact the steel magnate, born and bred in the Lancashire mill town, had on their lives. The man affectionately known by Rovers fans as Uncle Jack did not enjoy fanfares and shunned any hint of a high-profile lifestyle. Everybody knew he was the club's owner and benefactor, but he never wanted to be chairman. He left the day-to-day running of the club to others. But Walker was a colossus to the people of Blackburn, and he would be happy that engraved on his statue outside Ewood Park are the words "Rovers greatest supporter."

Walker, who died in 2000, had left school at 13. With one of his brothers he transformed their scrap metal business into one of the country's biggest steel stockholders, which they eventually sold for a reported £360million. Walker became a vice-president of the club, and in the mid-Eighties agreed to step up his sponsorship.

But it was in January 1991 that he took full control and the revolution truly commenced. His commitment was beyond doubt. He funded a series of transfers, including the British record signings of Alan Shearer and Chris Sutton. Roy Keane had agreed to join the Blackburn bandwagon from Nottingham Forest, and even shook hands on the deal with Rovers manager Kenny Dalglish, only to change his mind after Manchester United matched the asking price.

It wasn't just players and manager Dalglish in which the benefactor invested big money. He spent £20million in transforming Ewood Park into an impressive modern stadium. He also built a new training ground at Brockhall Village, on the secluded slopes of the Pennines, north of Blackburn.

During 2012 the Premier League celebrated its 20th anniversary, and I was asked to be on a panel of judges deciding some of the awards. One of them was the best season of the past 20 years. The obvious contenders included Arsenal's Invincibles and Manchester United's Treble winners, but during the discussions there was a collective agreement that the achievement of Blackburn in 1994–95 could not be overlooked. That was the year that the team that Jack built won the League title as England's finest club side. The significance of that landmark grows with every passing year. The prospect of a provincial club being crowned English champions is surely a thing of the past.

Blackburn benefited from the funding of a multi-millionaire benefactor. But he was their home-grown benefactor: he hadn't purchased the club as an expensive plaything for his own amusement. Blackburn Rovers was in his blood.

Blackburn Rovers was one of the founding clubs of the Football League back in 1888, 13 years after their formation. Jack believed that with shrewd investment he could help his club become a power in the English game.

He was happy to have Robert Coar as chairman and Dalglish as his high-profile manager. I was covering Rovers at this time, and remember asking him for a contact phone number. Jack quickly jotted down his number at his Jersey home, but tellingly added: "You can call to check stories but I don't want to be doing interviews. Do you understand?" He was an emotional man, and cried tears of joys when he saw his beloved Rovers crowned champions of England at Anfield in 1995.

He also had a style of business negotiations that could on occasion go wrong. Ray Harford, the outstanding coach who failed when asked to succeed Dalglish as manager, had a wonderful insight into Jack's ways. Ray explained: "Before a meeting over contracts Jack would write out three different offers on pieces of paper and place them in different pockets. The highest in his breast pocket, the lowest in his trousers.

"When he'd listened to the demands of a player or club he'd explain that before he'd come into the meeting he'd written down the highest figure he could go to. Jack would then deliver with a magician's flourish the paper revealing his supposed top offer, which obviously would be below what the player wanted and invariably worked as the clincher in a make-or-break situation.

"Unfortunately I did see him go for the wrong pocket. So when he was trying to nail a lower price he produced the paper that suggested we would go even higher. I had to smile when I saw him fluff his lines but that was a rarity."

Walker's willingness to splash the cash saw some sensational transfers. Probably the best, and shrewdest, investment was Alan Shearer's recruitment from Southampton for £3.2million in the summer of 1992. Understandably fans value loyalty. A case can undoubtedly be made that the status of Rovers cult hero should be the man who led their attack when they won the title in 1995. In fact, it was during his Blackburn days that Shearer became the first man since Jimmy Greaves in the early Sixties to score 30 League goals in three consecutive seasons.

Indeed, Shearer's career stats highlight the fact that his time at Ewood Park was the most prolific of his career. He may have become a Tyneside legend after moving to his native Newcastle in 1996 for a world record fee of £15million, but he never matched, never mind eclipsed, his Rovers heroics when he was representing Toon. Rovers fans were dismayed by the treachery of his exit. Undoubtedly the loss of Shearer was a key reason behind Rovers' gradual slide from the highest level of the Premier League. But Walker could also see that his original investment had sparked almost a five-fold return. The key was to find a suitable replacement for Shearer. That challenge was never met – and understandably Rovers fans have never fully forgiven Shearer for his defection.

Nobody can doubt the loyalty of the men who are battling to be acclaimed as Blackburn's cult heroes. Two of them rank as Blackburn's finest England internationals from the Fifties and Sixties. Bryan Douglas was a wonderfully skilful right-winger who played for Blackburn between 1954 and 1969. He made 438 League appearances and scored 100 goals, an impressive return for a wide player. He also won 36 England caps, and during the World Cup finals of 1958 and 1962 was an ever-present in the national team. Ronnie Clayton, a powerful wing-half, was also an England regular, and captained the national side five times during his 35 international outings. Clayton made 581 League appearances for Rovers, his only senior club.

Clayton's career, amid the days of the maximum wages for players, highlights the difference with today's top flight and international stars. Back in the late Fifties, when Clayton was an England regular, he could be seen walking the streets of Blackburn delivering newspapers. He was trying to ensure the success of the newsagent's shop that he ran with his wife in order to supplement his wages and provide some security for the days when his football career was over. Douglas had a stall at Morecambe market at which he worked on his days off in the early Sixties. It really was a different world.

The great thing about the friendliness of Rovers, especially during the Jack Walker era, was that Clayton and Douglas were regular attendees at matches. The owner never wanted people to think that the club had moved into a modern era and forgotten their old heroes. Clayton passed away in October 2010, and as a mark of respect Rovers announced that their home end at Ewood Park would be renamed the Ronnie Clayton End, in permanent memory of a fine, loyal servant and ambassador.

As we've seen, Ray Harford was a fine man, an excellent coach who accepted that management was not his greatest forte. Ray passed away in 2003 aged 58. And Harford's departure from Ewood Park leads us to Blackburn's cult hero. This man spent 12 years on the club's playing staff and was part of the squad that won the old Third Division title in 1975. He would never claim to have enjoyed the same status as a player as Clayton and Douglas. Tony Parkes' greatest claim to fame was in being there whenever Blackburn needed him. That's how he was Blackburn's caretaker manager on no fewer than six occasions. He was the man the Rovers board knew they could turn to during any crisis. And he never let them down. His status as their cult hero reflects a career that saw him spend 34 years at Ewood Park. The sad part is that when Mark Hughes arrived as manager in 2004, and decided to bring in his own backroom staff, Parkes discovered news of his dismissal from his daughter. She'd heard the news on the radio. In truth, Parkes, of all people, deserved a better Ewood Park farewell.

The modern history of Blackburn will always be dominated by the impact Jack Walker had on the club. Jack Straw, the Blackburn MP and former Home Secretary, said at the time of Walker's passing: "Jack Walker did more than any individual in the last century to enhance the self-confidence and prosperity of his home town. Rovers were in many ways the love of his life. I salute a great local hero."

THE FAN'S VIEW

Simon Lee: *"I hate recognizing what Shearer did for us before departing but nobody can doubt what Jack Walker did for his beloved club. We miss him now."*

BLACKPOOL

 Sir Stanley Matthews  Jimmy Armfield

Blackpool has prided itself on being the entertainment capital of England. And alongside the attractions of The Tower, the Illuminations, the Pleasure Beach and the Golden Mile, there has been Blackpool FC. Down the years the Tangerines of Bloomfield Road have provided pleasure as well as pain for their fans. The critics who now dismiss Pool as just a small club on the Lancashire coast should remember that in the Fifties mighty Blackpool were one of the most successful clubs in the country.

There can be little dispute about Blackpool's football icon. After all, Stanley Matthews was the first international superstar of the world game and spent the best years of his career at Bloomfield Road.

It was in 1956, when Matthews was a member of an entertaining Blackpool team that finished runners-up to Manchester United in the League title race, that the brilliant English winger, then 41 years old, was acclaimed as the inaugural European Footballer of the Year. He beat Real Madrid legend Alfredo di Stefano into second place.

The sheer longevity of Matthews' career is astonishing in itself. Born in 1915, signed by his home-town team Stoke City as a 15-year-old, he only moved to Blackpool when he was 32, with some critics wondering whether, given his age, even the great right-winger could justify the £11,500 fee. Yet he was the biggest box office drawer in British football for the 14 years he spent at Blackpool before heading back to the Potteries and a four-year farewell that included playing a major part in helping Stoke win promotion to the top flight.

Matthews could mesmerize opponents with his dribbling skills, but he wasn't just a show pony on the flanks performing tricks and flicks. His crossing of the ball was deadly and an array of strikers who played alongside him for Blackpool, Stoke and England have saluted the pinpoint accuracy and weight of his crosses. Nat Lofthouse, the Bolton legend who played alongside Matthews for England, wasn't entirely joking when he revealed that, before their first international together, Matthews assured him: "Don't worry about heading the ball. I'll make sure I cross it with the lace away so it doesn't hurt."

Maybe Nat was exaggerating a little, but he steadfastly maintained that he was blessed to be the England centre-forward who had Matthews on the right flank and another legend, Tom Finney, on the left. Matthews had an FA Cup final named after him following his part in Blackpool's fight-back to beat Bolton 4-3 in 1953. Bolton were leading 3-1 with 35 minutes remaining. This triumph made up for being in Blackpool's losing Cup final teams of 1948 and 1951. The fact that the nation desperately wanted to salute Stan the Man actually undermined the hat-trick heroics of Stan Mortensen. Mortensen, a barnstorming striker of his day, could lay claim to being close to Matthews in the all-time ranks of Blackpool heroes.

With Matthews our icon we now need to find our cult hero. There were many fine players alongside him in that Blackpool team of the Fifties. As well as the goalscoring prowess of Mortensen there were the impeccable leadership skills of Harry Johnston, the skipper who spent his entire 21-year career at Bloomfield Road. And in the more modern era there was a Geordie midfielder called Alan Suddick. Suddick bent free-kicks around defensive walls like a Brazilian. Even David Beckham could not have eclipsed Suddy's skill at set-pieces. He was astonishing.

But, really, the Seasiders' cult hero has to be the man affectionately known as Mr Blackpool – Jimmy Armfield. Jimmy is acknowledged as the first overlapping full-back seen in the English game. He spent his entire 17-year career at Blackpool, until his retirement in 1971. Jim became captain of club and country and he led England at the 1962 World Cup finals in Chile. Injury in the countdown to the tournament prevented him appearing in England's triumphant 1966 World Cup team, but he did remain in the 22-man squad.

From his days in football management and later as a journalist with the *Daily Express* Jimmy became a trusted friend. It spoke volumes that he never moved away from Blackpool, preferring to commute when he had some challenging jobs like being manager of Leeds United after Brian Clough. Jimmy was a pillar of his local community, always trying to get to choir practice at the church where he was organist. One story of his daily commute across the Pennines to Elland Road remains my favourite insight into Jimmy. Having recently signed Paul Hart from Blackpool, he used to give his new signing a lift over for training in his company Ford Granada Ghia, a top-of-the-range vehicle with a natty vinyl roof. A confirmed pipe smoker, Jim would open the car's sunroof and tap out the ash from his pipe as he sped across the M62. One morning new signing Hart noticed other vehicles flashing their headlights and waving at them. He didn't know why. Then manager and player confirmed it was getting warm onboard and the light flashing became a cacophony of noise as other drivers hammered on their horns and pointed to the roof of Jim's car. The intrepid Leeds duo realized their problem. Jim's discarded pipe ash had set the vinyl on fire and flames were licking from the roof as they sped along.

The duo survived that scare and maybe it was an early warning for Jim to put the pipe away and give up smoking. In later life he was troubled by throat cancer. But he remained the totally trustworthy friend of an army of football men and journalists. Our Blackpool cult hero is Gentleman Jimmy Armfield.

THE FAN'S VIEW

Big Dave: *"Stanley Matthews was our greatest player. Jimmy Armfield our most loyal. We just wish Jimmy had had a go at managing the club. He might have achieved something special."*

BOLTON WANDERERS

 **Nat Lofthouse**

 **John McGinlay**

Bolton Wanderers, founding members of the Football League, are another of our famous old clubs whose roots lie within the church. Back in 1874 the boys from Christ Church Sunday School established a football club. However, when their president (the church vicar) started introducing rules about the use of church premises, the boys decided to break away – and in 1877 Bolton Wanderers was formed.

Of all the polls we conducted about club icons there was only one without any dispute – everyone agreed that the late, great Nat Lofthouse should win the Bolton Wanderers nomination.

The legendary centre-forward of Bolton and England died in 2011, aged 85. The old black-and-white footage of Nat in action only hints at the great man's raw physical power. His eye for goal was deadly – as his goal per game statistics for Bolton and England truly reflect. The nearest modern comparison to Nat is Alan Shearer. Shearer's status as a Geordie icon is assured even if he opted to play for other clubs as well as his beloved Newcastle. Lofthouse is revered by Boltonians because, despite all kinds of alternative opportunities, he stayed loyal to his local club. Up the road Preston North End had their own arch-loyalist in the great Tom Finney. But Bolton could boast the bravest, most lethal, explosive, tenacious and inspirational centre-forward of the 1950s.

When you see some of the bone-jarring collisions Nat had with opposing players – including goalies – you realize how the game has changed and become less physical. But Nat wasn't just a bully boy in a No. 9 shirt. He led the attack with skill and style. He was also on the receiving end of some shuddering challenges, boots and elbows. For instance, he was battered on England duty in Austria in 1952 as opponents tried to smash the attacking threat out of him. Even though he was carried off the field unconscious after one collision, Nat refused to buckle. These were the days before substitutes. He may have been groggy but he returned to inspire England to a brilliant 3-2 victory. Those deeds saw him earn a nickname that lived with him for the rest of his life: The Lion of Vienna.

It was a serious knee injury that cut short Nat's career in 1960. His career statistics only tell part of the story of his status within the national sport. But for Bolton he played 452 games and scored 265 goals. For England he scored 30 goals in just 33 appearances.

I never saw Nat play, but what struck me when I met Nat years after he'd left the game was his incredible physique. While some great athletes shrink with age and lose the muscular power of the sporting gods, Nat retained an incredible presence. Those broad shoulders, honed by working down the coal mine as a Bevin Boy during the Second World War, were still square and powerful. He stood straight and tall, looked you in the eye and delivered his views in a rich Lancastrian accent he never tried to disguise.

Once we discussed how goalkeeping had changed. Nat, who in his prime was every goalie's worst nightmare, told me: "They're a protected species now and what gets me is that if anybody goes near them they start yelping to the referee for protection."

Roughing up goalies was an accepted part of Nat's trade. And, with a wicked grin, he admitted that there had been a few superstar keepers he would have loved to have tested in the years since his retirement. If 1950s rules had applied there could only have been one winner! Alongside Lofty in the Bolton team of the Fifties were two other home-grown players who achieved cult status, full-backs Roy Hartle and Tommy Banks. For many years they were the most feared defensive duo in the English game. Hartle was brutal. Banks was teak tough but also had the skills to win six England caps at left-back.

In his autobiography, *Farewell but not Goodbye*, Sir Bobby Robson revealed how back in the Fifties no team fancied a trip to Burnden Park, Bolton's old home. Robson said: "Burnden Park was the worst place in the world to go. The pitch was built up on a plateau and Tommy Banks, their enforcer in chief, would hit you over the slope and into the ditch below. Nat Lofthouse owned up to it. Nat said: 'In the Fifties there were plenty of fellas who would kick your bollocks off. The difference between then and now is that they would shake you by the hand at the end and help you look for them.'"

Sir Bobby added: "I remember playing with Tommy Banks for England and our coach Walter Winterbottom saying to him: 'I want such and such a player put out of the game.' Tommy thought for a moment then said: 'Do you mean today or for life?' 'No, no,' was Walter's reply, his face contorting with horror."

But if Lofthouse is Bolton's undisputed icon even Tommy Banks has been eclipsed by three strikers in our pursuit of Wanderers' cult hero. Our final three are from different eras; from the Sixties John Byrom, from the Seventies Frank Worthington and from the Nineties John McGinlay. Byrom was unique. He was portly, not unlike Gerd Muller in build, and had the eye for goal of the German striker. He also had a dead-pan humour and absolutely no interest in exploiting his fame or popularity. Worthington was the self-styled Elvis Presley let loose on a football field. He scored the goals that won Bolton promotion to the old First Division and he was the top flight's leading goalscorer in 1978–79. A player of supreme skills and technique, he has been nominated as a cult hero by more clubs than other players. And given he played for 11 League clubs that's no mean feat.

McGinlay arrived at Bolton in 1992 as a Millwall cast-off, following his old boss Bruce Rioch north. The Inverness-born centre-forward delivered goals, creative assists, raw passion and a determination that rattled opponents and delighted the Bolton fans. If a ruck erupted involving rival players you could be sure McGinlay would be at the heart of it, if not the instigator. He fought the perceived injustices that afflicted his team, and when Bolton needed an emergency goalkeeper there was one man who you knew would volunteer. So our Bolton cult hero is John McGinlay.

THE FAN'S VIEW

Eileen F. Rigby: "As a Bolton Wanderers supporter there can only be one club icon – Nat Lofthouse. Not only was he a great footballer, but, more importantly, he was a great man. He always had time to talk to supporters. He had no airs and graces and treated everybody as equally important to the club. He was one of the true greats of the game."

Chris Carley: "Nat has to be our icon and as an older fan I remember the way JB (John Byrom) entertained us and Frank Worthington could be breathtaking. But John McGinlay produced some heroic performances. As well as his goals he was our talisman. I remember him being our emergency goalie in one game and starting a punch-up against Wolves in another. He's a fitting cult hero."

BOURNEMOUTH

Steve Fletcher  Ted MacDougall

They've always had a high regard for centre-forwards around Bournemouth. After all, Baven Penton was the first professional player employed by the original club in 1912. He cost the outrageous sum of £10 and enjoyed a spectacular start. He scored nine of his club's first 12 goals in the FA Cup. And he dispatched all of them in away ties because their home ground was deemed unfit to stage FA Cup ties in those days.

Dean Court is a pleasant stroll in Kings Park. And it's good to know that the fans of the Dorset club revere a modern striker who has never been as lethal as his predecessor Penton but gave his all for the Cherries during his lengthy career with the club.

Our Bournemouth icon is Steve Fletcher. The big target man holds the club appearance record accumulated during his two spells at Dean Court. He began his career at his home-town club Hartlepool United. In 1992, after two years with United, he headed all the way south to Bournemouth in a £30,000 deal. Little did he know the love affair he was starting.

The fact is that, throughout his career, Fletcher has never been prolific, elegant or a star name. But he has offered qualities such as commitment and honesty that have been saluted by the Bournemouth fans.

During his first 15 seasons at Bournemouth Steve scored 88 League goals in 493 appearances. There were brief interludes at Chesterfield and Crawley before the big man returned to Bournemouth in 2009. He became the club's assistant manager in 2011, although he stepped down from that role 11 months later, while remaining on the playing staff.

Big Steve is seen by Bournemouth fans as Mr Dependable. They know they can rely on him. He may have struggled with knee injuries down the years, but he has still got out on the field and given his all. Often his best work has been distracting opposing defences, so his attacking sidekicks can exploit the Fletcher-inspired openings.

There are plenty of jokes about old folk heading to Bournemouth for a quiet retirement and to pass away. Most football clubs wait for their legends to die before naming stands in their honour. So it was great that in April 2010 Bournemouth named their north stand in Fletcher's honour. That put the Bournemouth striker in exalted company – a living legend being honoured by a club, just like Sir Alex

Ferguson at Old Trafford.

There is a link between Bournemouth and Old Trafford in saluting our Dean Court cult hero. Ted MacDougall made that journey when he was transferred to United for £200,000 in September 1972. It was a record fee for a Third Division player.

MacDougall remains Bournemouth's highest League scorer in a season. He claimed 42 goals in the 1970–71 campaign. That was the form that attracted interest from a posse of top flight clubs, although there was still some surprise when United's beleaguered boss Frank O'Farrell decided MacDougall was one of the men to build a new team around as he prepared for the end of the Bobby Charlton, Denis Law and George Best era. It was a task beyond even the Dean Court goal machine.

At Bournemouth, MacDougall was unstoppable after John Bond became the Cherries manager in 1970. He scored six past Oxford City in an FA Cup replay that eventually finished 8-1. He topped that by dispatching nine goals in Bournemouth's 11-0 victory over Margate in the first round of the FA Cup. This is still the largest-ever individual haul of goals by any player in an FA Cup match.

MacDougall's goal stats with Bournemouth remain remarkable. He scored 126 goals in just 165 appearances.

BRADFORD CITY

 Stuart McCall

 Bobby Campbell

It's remarkable to discover that a man who spent only six years as a professional footballer, and left the club in 1988, is widely acknowledged as Mr Bradford City. But that fact reflects the esteem in which Stuart McCall is held in at Valley Parade.

McCall was born and brought up in Leeds, but City offered him his big break in League football. He made his debut in 1982 and quickly earned a burgeoning reputation as a talented central midfielder. By the 1984–85 season McCall was an established part of the City team that won promotion as Third Division champions. The title was clinched in the penultimate game when City beat Bolton 2-0; McCall scored from the penalty spot that day.

The final game of the season was set to mark Bradford's coronation as champions. Tragically, 11th May 1985 will forever be remembered for the Bradford fire disaster in which 56 people died when the main stand at Valley Parade caught fire after 40 minutes of play. Stuart McCall's father, Andy, was attending the game with other members of his family. In the immediate aftermath Stuart spent hours searching the hospitals looking for his father who had suffered severe burns and required skin grafts to his hands and head.

The link between the McCall clan, Bradford City and the terrible events of that day in May have never been broken. In fact, in April 2002, towards the end of a playing career that had taken Stuart to Everton, Rangers and back to Bradford, a testimonial game was staged in his honour at Valley Parade against the Glasgow giants. Over 21,000 fans were in attendance and Stuart gave part of the proceeds from the game to the Bradford burns unit which had been set up in the wake of the fire tragedy.

But it would be wrong to link McCall's status as the City icon purely to the events and ramifications of one of football's most tragic events. There was much for Bradford fans to admire in the way McCall played the game.

Although he was born and bred in Yorkshire he qualified for Scotland through his father and revelled in becoming a Scotland international in 1990 when he was at Everton. But the other aspect of McCall's career that delighted Bantams fans was that he didn't make a move to a top-flight club his sole priority in life. McCall actually turned down potential transfers in the hope that he could play his part in guiding City into the big time.

McCall was just 21 when he was made club captain in November 1986. Terry

Dolan, the astute Bradford manager at the time, realized he was close to putting a team together that could make a historic breakthrough and take the club into the old First Division. His two key players were McCall and Scottish striker John Hendrie. Both were constantly trailed by clubs ready to sign them. I recall a certain Alex Ferguson heading south from Aberdeen with his assistant Archie Knox to run the rule over McCall in a pre-season game at Halifax. McCall's fame was spreading.

Understandably, the Bradford stars had lofty ambitions, but they agreed in 1987 to shelve any ideas of parting to promote themselves to being part of the City collective. Covering Bradford matches in the wake of the fire, and for the 19 months during which they were tenants at Odsal while Valley Parade was renovated, was an uplifting experience. Even sour old hacks realized that out of the fire tragedy a unique bond had developed between club and community and that players like McCall and Hendrie were key elements in that synergy. The challenge was to harness all the goodwill and make another promotion push.

The 1987–88 season was critical. For much of it Bradford's form was impressive, but they began to lose their composure in the New Year. In heart-breaking fashion they missed out on automatic promotion on the last day of the League season following their 3-2 defeat at Ipswich Town. They still had a chance in the promotion play-offs, but lost to Middlesbrough. The season finished in a bitter anti-climax. McCall was sold to Everton for £850,000.

A decade of success later and McCall was back at his beloved Bradford. This time Paul Jewell was manager and the club stunned many neutrals by putting together a promotion challenge. The previous seasons had been spent averting relegation, so Jewell's impact was remarkable. While Sunderland were the runaway leaders at the top of the table Bradford were in a three-horse race for second with Ipswich and Birmingham. The contest went to the last game of the season. A 3-2 win over Wolves at Molineux clinched promotion to the Premier League for the first time in Bradford's history. They were back at the top level of English football for the first time in 77 years and McCall was also voted the supporters' Player of the Year.

McCall stayed and played his part in keeping City up at the top, but in their second season financial problems began to engulf the club. McCall moved to Sheffield United and at the age of 38 operated as player-coach.

But he always said he wanted the chance to be Bradford manager, and that chance came in June 2007. Sadly, there was no happy ending. City had slipped back into the lowest division of the Football League. Despite their loyal fan base and belief in their manager, McCall could not guide them out of League Two.

But it speaks volumes for his status as Bradford's icon that even though he could not create a sporting miracle McCall is still acknowledged as City's favourite son.

Our Bradford City cult hero, on the other hand, can be summed up in one word – loud. Bobby Campbell was a Northern Irishman who spoke in torrents and very, very loudly. He had a piercing, high-pitched voice. You didn't have a conversation with Bobby. He overwhelmed you with his machine-gun attack of opinions and ideas.

He did a brilliant job as a striker for Bradford. He became their leading marksman with a total of 143 goals in two spells at the club. He was in the side that won promotion from the old Fourth Division in 1982 and won Division Three some three years later – the day of celebration that was wrecked by the fire.

Feisty, aggressive, explosive in the penalty area, and very loud – Campbell is our Bradford City cult hero.

THE FAN'S VIEW
Jim Ferris: *"Stuart McCall brought dignity and decency to our club and remains one of our greatest ambassadors."*

BRENTFORD

 Terry Evans  Terry Hurlock

Two famous managers were savouring a late drink in a London hotel after attending the Football Writers' dinner in the mid-Eighties.

Howard Wilkinson, then in charge at Sheffield Wednesday, was picking Harry Redknapp's brain on players. Howard ventured: "I really need Graeme Souness but we can't afford him. You got any brainwave, H?" Redknapp, at that time in charge of Bournemouth in the old Third Division, made an immediate recommendation. "Howard, you need to go and get the boy Terry Hurlock from Brentford. He's going to be a blinding player."

Well Wilkinson didn't get his man. Hurlock spent six memorable years at Griffin Park. He really was the Souness of the lower divisions. People tried to sort him out and thought they could out-play him. They rarely, if ever, did.

The Hackney-born player was released by West Ham as a kid and drifted into non-League football. In many respects rebuilding his career and proving his true worth was a permanent calling for Hurlock. He never rested on his laurels. He also didn't suffer fools. On occasions, when opposition fans were taunting him as he left the field, Terry turned to confront his abuser. The menacing Hurlock glare and shouting: "What did you say?" invariably prompted the fan to sprint to the exit.

With one Terry as our cult hero another is our Brentford icon. Terry Evans was a giant of a centre-back, standing around 6ft 5ins tall. His physical power and presence was immense. He was also a natural leader, so emerged as a great Brentford skipper. He led the Bees to the Division Three Championship in 1992. And one of our Brentford correspondents, who nominated Evans as his iconic player, insisted: "I saw Terry make a clearance on the edge of our penalty area that flew to the opposition area. And I saw him do that more than once."

Evans joined Brentford from non-League Hillingdon Borough for £5,000. By the time he was signed by Wycombe in 1993 his value had risen to £40,000. Although he'd left Brentford the fans at Griffin Park continued to have a soft spot for Terry. Even after he'd scored for Wycombe against them, Bees fans still sang "There's only one Terry Evans." Now that's a real icon.

THE FAN'S VIEW

Phil Jacobs: "We've had more skilful players than Terry Evans but you always knew he'd given everything for our team. He never let us down when it came to sweat and determination."

BRIGHTON AND HOVE ALBION

 Peter Ward

 Bobby Zamora

Mark Lawrenson must rank as one of Brighton's finest ever players. He spent some of his formative days there before becoming a serial winner at home and abroad with Liverpool. He was asked once to sum up the talent of the man we're nominating as our Brighton icon, Peter Ward:

"There were times when you'd play a ball forward into the strikers and expect them to hold it up then bring team-mates into play, maybe knock the ball back to a supporting midfielder. With Peter you realized something else was likely to happen.

"You'd play the ball into him and he'd do the unpredictable. He'd keep the ball, turn past the opposition defence and the next thing you knew the ball was in the net."

That wonderful gift of doing the totally unpredictable was a vital part of Peter's repertoire and it's why, to this day, Albion fans chant: "He shot, he scored, it must be Peter Ward."

The striker with the bubble perm arrived at the old Goldstone Ground in 1975. A part-time footballer (he'd taken up an apprenticeship as an engine fitter with Rolls-Royce in Derby), he cost just £4,000 from then non-League Burton Albion. But from his debut Ward displayed a precious gift for scoring goals. In the 1976–77 season he scored 36 goals – a remarkable return for a virtual rookie. It should be remembered that he wasn't in a one-man team. The likes of Lawrenson, skipper Brian Horton and centre-back Steve Foster were fine players. Horton, the skipper and midfield hard man, was particularly underrated in some quarters. He was the competitive heart-beat of the team.

But Ward delivered the goals and the glamour. He could poach goals by anticipating openings in the 6-yard box, but what Brighton fans remember him for the most were those mazy runs when he tricked his way past back-pedalling defenders, spotted a goalie rushing out at him and duly dispatched a clinical finish into the net. He scored that precise goal so often there was nothing flukey about it. When Ward was put through on goal Brighton fans were confident he'd score.

After finishing second in the old Second Division in 1979 Brighton were promoted to the top flight. Former Brighton boss Brian Clough, by then at Nottingham Forest, made a move to sign Ward but backed down, though a year later Ward's move to Forest did go through. While Ward had never played for Clough at Brighton there was the Peter Taylor connection linking the two. Taylor was the manager who'd signed Ward for Brighton. He was Clough's assistant at the City Ground when the striker headed north.

Ward did return to Brighton on loan a couple of years later. He scored a few goals, including the winner in a 1-0 victory over Manchester United.

When we were assessing cult heroes for the club one suggestion was Dick Knight. I have immense regard for Dick, having met him at various Football League forums. Most wise Brighton fans will accept that Dick is the man who saved their club. Following the sale of the Goldstone Ground and the slide towards oblivion, it was Knight who picked up the reins, held the club together and tenaciously fought for a permanent new home for his beloved football club. And rest assured Brighton fans: if you think the Withdean years were hard for you there weren't too many visiting teams who relished playing at the little stadium.

Knight conducted himself impeccably as he fought to keep Brighton alive. He has now passed on the challenge of leading the club forward to Tony Bloom, but he should be proud of the legacy he handed over. Knowing Dick's self-effacing demeanour he won't be annoyed that we've selected another goalscoring star as our Brighton cult hero.

Bobby Zamora was a lifelong West Ham fan who'd endured the ignominy of being released by the club he loved after spending time in their academy. Most youngsters in these circumstances fall by the wayside. Yet Zamora moved to unfashionable Bristol Rovers to try to build a career there. Even that switch wasn't a success. But his arrival on loan at Brighton was a turning-point in his career and his life.

He arrived in February 2000 on a three-month loan and dispatched six goals in six games. His confidence rocketed. Brighton recognized his talent as a skilful leader of the line with a wonderful left foot. They managed to seal a permanent £100,000 transfer that summer and an exciting run of fine form and great goals was about to commence.

Brighton won consecutive championships to storm from Division Three to the Championship. Zamora was an integral figure in that astonishing run. Bobby scored 83 goals for Brighton in 136 appearances.

Just like Peter Ward two decades earlier, the big boys started trailing Brighton's matches, assessing the talent, and Zamora became a wanted man. In July 2003 he joined Tottenham for £1.5million. It wasn't the happiest union, but Brighton fans to this day remain deeply appreciative of what Bobby brought to the club and the style, as well as the success, they enjoyed along the way.

THE FAN'S VIEW

Alastair Ryan: *"The Brighton icon must be Peter Ward."*

BRISTOL CITY

 John Atyeo  Dariusz "Jacki" Dziekanowski

As part of their original names, Bristol had a South End just as Preston were North End. But whereas Preston stayed with their title, Bristol South End switched to Bristol City in 1897 when the club turned professional. By 1904 the club were based at Ashton Gate, their home to this day.

In the modern era all top players have agents. But in John Atyeo's day fathers could shape their sons' careers – and Bristol City will always be indebted to the calm guidance of Walter Atyeo, a railway signalman who sent his boy in their direction.

John, born in 1932 in the village of Dilton Marsh just outside Westbury in Wiltshire, was a great all-round sportsman as a boy. Outstanding at cricket and rugby, it was as a goalscoring centre-forward that he really excelled, and so Portsmouth, then the English champions, wanted him to join them – twice getting him to appear as an amateur.

Instead it was Bristol City's chairman, Harry Dolman, who walked down the railway line to meet Walter in his signal box and came away with a signed contract after agreeing to some unique clauses. John, then aged just 19, would always be on top wages, would always be allowed to live at home and continue training to be a quantity surveyor, would go to training only twice a week, and should never be put on the transfer list without his father's consent.

So the legend of Atyeo was born, the part-timer who became the club's greatest player. At 6ft tall he was a strapping, powerful man, known and loved by everybody as "Big John". Powerful in the air, he was also comfortable with the ball on either foot, scoring 351 goals in 645 games over a 15-year career. Selected by England, he scored five times in six internationals, including the goal that took Walter Winterbottom's team to the 1958 World Cup finals. Atyeo never finished on a losing England side.

But what was different about Atyeo was that he never wanted fame, or fortune, from the game. When he chose a different career path to quantity surveying he selected not full-time football but to retrain as a maths teacher, and until his untimely death, aged 61, there were thousands of children who learned from his patience and care. He held revision sessions from 7am on the day of exams.

He had offers at different times to join Chelsea, Liverpool, Tottenham and AC Milan for fees that would have been the equivalent of millions in today's money. But he always preferred to stay in the classroom and remain loyal to his beloved

Bristol City. Maybe it was the tradition of Atyeo, the bull at a gate centre-forward, which made Joe Jordan so popular at Ashton Gate three decades later. Persuaded by his old Leeds team-mate Terry Cooper to sign in the twilight of a fabulous career in England and Italy, City fans loved the Scot whose smile was toothless but whose strength and aggression could still terrorize any defence. And beyond the tough guy approach there was a skilful striker who justified a move to Italy where he spent two years at AC Milan and one with Verona. There was so much more to Joe's game than brute force and menace. In fact, throughout his career he would turn up at a rival club's mid-week matches to study the opposition. In his Leeds days, Gordon McQueen was his regular match companion. Perhaps this was big Joe preparing for his long-term future as a coach.

Yet Jordan, who managed the club twice, misses out as our Ashton Gate cult hero to a figure who was the polar opposite of gentleman John Atyeo both on and off the field. Dariusz "Jacki" Dziekanowski was City's record signing at £250,000 from Celtic in 1992, and his quicksilver skills left defences dazzled. John Motson's famous commentary clip from an FA Cup win at Leicester summed him up: "He may come from a different country, today he's been from a different planet."

Jacki had been sold by Celtic because of his love of the Glasgow night life where he was known as "The Disco King". In Bristol his penchant for vodka and women – in no particular order – actually made him an even bigger star with fans who enjoyed meeting him and sharing his nights on the town. It couldn't last – he went home to Poland – but it was fun while it did and 20 years later he remains a City superstar.

THE FAN'S VIEW

Paul Binning: *"John Atyeo is the ultimate City icon, top goalscorer and appearance maker and those 5 goals in 6 games for England. From the more recent past I'd have to mention Scott Murray. Again, legendary on the pitch and so popular around club he became our kit man just so he can help out!"*

BRISTOL ROVERS

 Jackie Pitt

 Ian Holloway

Always proud to be recognized as older than their neighbours City, Bristol Rovers originally went under the name of the Black Arabs and wore black shirts. They changed their name to Eastville Rovers in their second season and later to Bristol Rovers. Their blue and white quartered kit ranks as one of the most distinctive in the Football League.

The 1950s was a unique era for Bristol Rovers. While the rest of the professional game prepared to wheel and deal in the modern transfer market merry-go-round, their manager, Bert Tann, chose a different route.

"No buy – no sell," was his policy. And his belief that he could form a team from young local players and then enjoy their loyalty produced arguably the greatest decade of the club's history. Not surprisingly, it also meant that Tann's team still holds most of the long-service records. *Nine* of the players he picked in his first year in charge fill places in the top 17 of long-serving stars.

So how do you choose between them for an icon? How do you separate legendary strikers Geoff Bradford (245 goals in 461 League games) from flamboyant playboy striker Alfie Biggs (174 in 414)?

The answer is to ignore them both and choose the favourite player of "Mr Bristol Rovers" himself, kit man and odd job person at the club for half a century, Ray Kendall. Ray would always plump for right-half Jackie Pitt, a man who didn't turn pro until he was 26, but then played 467 League games and went on to become the club's coach and groundsman.

Pitt embodied the passion of the supporters from Rovers, traditionally the city's more working-class club. He brought neat touches and tidy passing to feed little winger George Petherbridge in front of him, as well as taking the free kicks that brought so many of Bradford's headed goals. But what made him really special was his fiery character.

A fairly small man, Pitt never ducked a tackle and brought fierce commitment to the cause, which played a huge part in the promotion season of 1953 and then the record years of 1956 and 1959 with two sixth-placed finishes in what is now the Championship.

He was just as committed to his jobs as first coach then groundsman and relished tending the old Eastville pitch despite lack of resources, rising just as bravely to a bigger challenge, helping when the club moved to share home at Bath City. He was fiercely loyal, and remained a regular visitor to games right up to his death, aged 84, in 2004.

Perhaps Alfie Biggs should be the cult hero – but for a club without a stellar history there have been some unique players to give him competition: think of Paul Randall and Archie Stephens who had been stocking supermarket shelves and working as a painter and decorator respectively before they got their big break in the early 1980s.

But ultimately nobody has ever been more passionate about the club than Ian Holloway – as player in three spells with Rovers, then cutting his teeth for his management career. Born in a Cadbury Heath council house, when he was 12 he turned down the chance to sign for Bristol City because they offered him free boots and a long contract. He preferred Rovers, who offered only the chance to work hard and make a career.

Hard work remained his watchword through 397 League appearances, including a starring role in the side that won promotion from the old Division Three as champions in 1990 thanks to an emotional last game of the season victory over arch-rivals Bristol City.

As manager he oversaw the club's move back to Bristol into the Memorial Stadium, discovered the talents of £5million worth of strikers who were sold to fund the club's development, and was hugely unlucky not to win promotion when his side got 80 points but in a freak year finished just a place outside the play-off zone. He has been certain of a warm welcome on any visit to Bristol since those emotional days.

BURNLEY

 Jimmy McIlroy

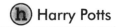 Harry Potts

F ounding members of the Football League, Burnley were proud of the fact that, until the maximum wage limit was withdrawn in the early Sixties, they were one of the most efficiently run, successful clubs in football. Their scouting system was the envy of all. They were the ultimate little club who could be relied upon to punch above their weight.

Burnley can be a forbidding place. Head into the east Lancashire mill town via Manchester Road, climb through the wonderfully named villages of Crawshawbooth and Cliviger, and suddenly your destination lies at the bottom of a valley. On a wet day I swear the clouds that envelop the place create Burnley's unique microclimate – and it's not very welcoming.

And yet within this town, with a population of around 73,500, stands a football club that has been at the cutting edge of developments within the English game. It's easy to forget that in the Fifties, amid the final days of the maximum wage limits for players, Burnley were right up there with Manchester United, Wolves and Tottenham as the superpowers of the English game.

Triumphs, such as winning the League title in 1960 and finishing runners-up in the League and FA Cup final two years later, were just part of the inspired, intelligent management style present at Turf Moor. The club were among the forerunners in having their own youth development programme. They were one of the first to purchase and develop a training ground at Gawthorpe Hall where young players could be developed and then, usually amid much acrimony, sold to predatory rivals.

Bob Lord was the dictatorial chairman prepared to trade any popularity in town with his belief that the club had to sell to survive. The trend was relentless.

It's totally accepted that the Clarets' greatest player was a Northern Irishman called Jimmy McIlroy. McIlroy was signed from Glentoran and played for the club through their glory years from 1950 to 1962. But when chairman Bob decided it was time to balance the books he didn't bothered to tell McIlroy. Burnley's greatest player discovered the news of his move to Stoke City via the local media.

In modern terms McIlroy would be seen as a brilliant midfield player, adept at creating an opening for others and scoring goals himself. How good was he? Well, Tom Finney, probably the best English player of their generation, was unequivocal: "Jimmy McIlroy was the greatest player I ever played against."

When you consider that Finney's career, including World Cup appearances and competing for Preston in England's top flight, his tribute to McIlroy is both sincere and immense. McIlroy still holds the Burnley club record for most international appearances. He made 51 appearances for Northern Ireland during his days at Turf Moor and was a kingpin of the 1958 Irish team that reached the World Cup quarter-finals in Sweden.

If Jimmy Mac is unquestionably our Burnley icon, the search for their cult hero is a much tougher challenge.

Through the Sixties and Seventies there was a virtual conveyor belt of talent – often recruited from the north east or South Wales – that was the envy of top-flight rivals. But just as the finest Claret had been sold to balance the books, the Turf Moor sales became regular and increasingly frustrating. Winger Willie Morgan headed to Manchester United while Ralph Coates went south to Tottenham. Wing-half Brian O'Neil had become a firm crowd favourite with his never-say-die approach. He was sold to Southampton. Wingers Dave Thomas and Leighton James went to QPR and Derby County respectively, and then there was the sale of skipper Martin Dobson to Everton in 1974. Balancing the books was again cited as the reason for the deal. The fact that the unpopular chairman had built the opulent Bob Lord stand ensured that irate fans branded the edifice the Martin Dobson stand. After all, in their opinion the elegant midfielder's departure had paid for it, and he continued to enjoy cult status at the club. He is also the answer to Alistair Campbell's favourite sports quiz question, "Who was the last Burnley player to be capped by England?"

James, a supremely talented games player, had been a Wales rugby union schoolboy star and 12th man for Lancashire at county cricket level. He wasn't the shy, retiring type either, as the author can confirm from playing in the Bacup Sports Club's badminton team alongside Taff and another of his Burnley and Wales team-mates, Brian Flynn. Oh, they sold Flynny as well. He joined Leeds, the path that was also trodden by burly striker Ray Hankin. James was genuinely two-footed, had a wonderful turn of pace and without his contact lenses was as blind as a bat! He had a fine career, but with his gifts perhaps he could and should have been even better.

Alongside him in the Burnley team of the early Seventies was a rare incoming transfer – Peter Noble. Nobby developed hero status at Turf Moor because he was so selfless and committed to the cause. Whenever there was a selection crisis from right-back to centre-forward Noble could be relied upon to answer any call-to-arms. In Burnley's small first-team squad Nobby, and his younger sidekick, the late Billy Ingham, were absolutely priceless. Ingham, nicknamed the Ginger Pelé, was one of the nicest, most modest men you could meet. After his career ended he became a bus driver in Burnley. He died in 2009, aged 57.

But the winner of our Burnley cult award is the man who probably did more than anybody else to inspire the club to the upper reaches of English football and managed to keep them there throughout his tenure as manager. Harry Potts came from Hetton-le-Hole, the same County Durham pit village as Liverpool's legendary manager Bob Paisley. Paisley was the older by just nine months.

Potts prided himself and his backroom staff on improving players through coaching and training drills. He masterminded a coaching team that were ahead of their time and was based around Burnley old boys, including Jimmy Adamson, Brian Miller and Joe Brown, just as his friend Paisley was part of the Anfield boot room team. It's an incredible statistic and insight into Potts' impact as manager that, after taking over at Turf Moor in 1958, his first cash transfer saw Alex Elder recruited for £5,000 from Glentoran in 1959. It was eight years later before Potts spent another penny in the transfer market.

In retirement, and after the club had endured years of mediocrity, the awareness of what Harry Potts had given Burnley became abundantly clear. For his efforts at Turf Moor he deserved to be rated alongside the legends of his time – Shankly, Busby, Cullis and Nicholson. Harry died in 1996, aged 75. In his honour the local council renamed the road outside Turf Moor as Harry Potts Way: a fitting tribute to a football visionary.

THE FAN'S VIEW

Richard Newman: *"It took Burnley long enough to recognize what Harry Potts had achieved here and for our town. Now we all know he was a blinding manager."*

BURTON ALBION

 **Darren Stride**    **John McGrath**

Darren Stride, Burton born and bred, was a colossus during his 17 outstanding years with his home-town club.

Stride achieved his ambition of playing in the Football League after helping Albion to the Blue Square Premier title in 2009. Injury restricted him to nine Football League appearances before he left for Alfreton Town in 2010 at the age of 34.

He made his Albion debut in 1993 and began as a combative midfielder. A leader on the pitch, Stride switched to central defence towards the end of his career with the Brewers. As skipper for more than 11 years, he made a club record 654 appearances, scoring 124 goals. He was captain of the 2002 Northern Premier League title-winning side.

His proudest possession is a signed photo of himself, presented by Burton, from the Brewers' famous 0-0 FA Cup third-round draw with Manchester United when he shut out Cristiano Ronaldo and Wayne Rooney.

Our Burton cult hero is John McGrath. The amiable Irishman has endeared himself to the Pirelli Stadium fans with his commitment to the club.

"Macca", as he is known in Burton, has been an instrumental part of the Albion since arriving from Staffordshire rivals Tamworth in 2007. A combative and talented midfielder, McGrath has been a key figure in Albion's midfield as the club proudly marched from the Conference to the Football League. He began with Aston Villa, for whom he played in Europe, and was well travelled before being signed by then Albion boss Nigel Clough.

He helped propel the Brewers to the Conference play-offs in 2008, then collected a League winners' medal 12 months later. McGrath's consistency was rewarded when he was made skipper, and he has been a huge influence on Burton's ability to flourish in the Football League.

BURY

 Craig Madden

 Alec Lindsay

Which club holds the record for the widest victory margin in the FA Cup final? Bury would not be the name that would spring to many people's lips, but the Lancastrians, nicknamed The Shakers, can proudly boast about their 6-0 victory over Derby County in the 1903 final.

And fancy being nicknamed The Shakers! As a boy I always wondered if it was to do with having their Gigg Lane ground right next to a cemetery. In fact, one goalstand at Gigg Lane is called the Cemetery End. It's obviously the place to bury visiting supporters, with the home support at the Manchester Road End.

It's claimed the real reason for their being known as The Shakers dates back to 1892. The name was used originally by the club's manager/chairman J T Ingham as his club prepared for a Lancashire senior Cup tie. Bury, who then played in the Lancashire League, were on a Cup run and due to face mighty Everton, the reigning champions. It's believed Ingham told reporters: "We shall shake 'em. In fact, we are The Shakers." A nickname was spawned.

Gigg Lane was famed for having one of the best pitches in the country and Bury were rightly proud during the Sixties and Seventies of the players they developed. Colin Bell was their greatest young star and export, but there were others, such as the duo who left to become England internationals – Terry McDermott and Alec Lindsay.

Bury were known as a friendly club that exuded warmth and hospitality. For many years Canon Reg Smith, the vicar of Bury parish church, was on the board of directors. So the club's spiritual fellowship was taken care of as well as their sporting prowess. Canon Reg was a witty, jocular man who in his youth had been a handy cricketer in the Manchester Diocesan cricket team.

Bury offered a home to a man of notoriety as well. Peter Swan, originally banned *sine die* for his part in the Sheffield Wednesday match-fixing scandal of the early Sixties, turned up at Gigg Lane after his ban had been lifted and skippered the side for the 1973–74 season. Swan was a veteran but still produced some imperious performances as he led his team to the Fourth Division title. He retired at the end of his single season at Gigg Lane – he was offered only a monthly contract – but during that time there were glimpses of a magnificent, powerful centre-back. It made you realize how he had squandered his career.

Our Bury icon, though, is a Mancunian who turned up as a youngster and spent nine years at the club. Craig Madden was a thrilling goalscorer. In fact, in one memorable campaign he scored 35 goals, which is still a club record. In lower division football he was dynamite. His goalscoring return with Bury was 129 goals in 297 appearances. And he wasn't playing in teams that were expected to be in the upper reaches of their divisions every year.

Madden's loyalty delighted the Bury fans. Scouts from higher division clubs kept checking his form. They had to, because his goalscoring record was so good. He was 28 when he moved to West Bromwich Albion for a brief spell before heading back to Lancashire and rediscovering his goalscoring form with Blackpool. But for Bury fans there was a simple football equation: Madden equals goals.

As for Bury's cult hero, we'll opt for a player who left the club in 1969 to join Liverpool in a £60,000 transfer. Alec Lindsay was a Bury lad who had joined his home-town club. His greatest virtue was his exquisite left foot. His passing was inch perfect and he could strike a ball so sweetly. His biggest weakness was easy to spot. Let's just say the ginger-haired defender was not the quickest player in the land.

But he still established himself in the last team Bill Shankly built at Anfield, the line-up that thrashed Newcastle in the 1974 FA Cup final.

Lindsay's Anfield career went into decline once Shankly retired and Bob Paisley took over. There is, though, one wonderful tale about his early days at Liverpool. Perhaps it's a legend now but it's worth retelling.

It's claimed that on his Liverpool debut Shankly told his new recruit: "When you get the ball I want you to beat opponents and smash the ball into the net, just the way you used to at Bury." A stunned Lindsay replied: "Boss that wasn't me, that was Jimmy Kerr." This prompted Shankly to turn to his assistant Paisley and say: "Christ Bob, we've signed the wrong player."

Nice story, but you can't really see Shankly and Paisley getting something like that so wrong. Mind you, it has happened before in the wonderful world of football transfers.

CARDIFF CITY

 **Fred Keenor**    **Phil Dwyer**

They like their heroes to be hard men at Cardiff City. And nobody was tougher than their most celebrated figure of all, Fred Keenor.

Keenor was the man who captained Cardiff to the greatest day in Welsh football history, when they defeated Arsenal 1-0 at Wembley to win the FA Cup in 1927. It remains the only time the trophy has been taken out of England.

And the celebration pictures of Keenor, the cup by his side, a cigarette in one hand and a beer in the other, tell their own story. "He always liked a pint and a fag. The first thing he'd do after training was light up," recalled former team-mate Ernie Curtis, Cardiff's youngest player at Wembley that fabled day.

"He had no airs or graces. He was a Cardiff boy (one of 11 children born to a brickie dad) and he never forgot his roots. He was hard, though. I used to wince when I watched him tackling. A lot of people said he was dirty. I don't think he was. But nobody took liberties with him!"

Keenor needed all that steely resolve just to make it as a footballer. Born in 1894, he played for Wales schoolboys before joining Cardiff in 1912. His fledgling career had to be put on hold, though, when the First World War erupted two years later and he joined the army. Of all the horrific battles in that conflict, the Somme has its own place as the most hellish of all. And it was in the trenches there that Keenor's life, let alone his career, almost ended. His left leg was shattered and his shoulder badly injured when he was struck by shrapnel. He spent months in hospital, fearing he would never play again, that he might need a stick just to walk. "It made me realize just how much football meant to me. I was desperate," he later admitted.

The skill of the surgeons and his own mental resolve helped him through. And he was ready to lead Cardiff to their glory years in the roaring Twenties when they were a real force in the land. He captained Wales to three British Championships as well, before moving on in 1931 to a three-year stint at Crewe. He spent 20 years at Cardiff. Typically, Keenor's last goal for them ensured a 1-0 win at Southampton.

It took the club a further 81 years to finally recognize their most fabled son, when a bronze statue of Keenor was unveiled at their new stadium in 2012. But his name has never been forgotten by generations of Bluebird fans.

From Keenor's time, centre-halves have always held a special esteem in the eyes of those supporters. And three men who dominated that role through 30 years from the mid-Fifties to the mid-Eighties have carved their names into club legend.

Danny Malloy and Don Murray were two rough, tough Scots who could brawl with and trample over any striker who ever showed the courage (or madness) to take them on. Malloy has his own special status as the captain who took them up to the old First Division in 1960, but the pair of them were pure Scottish granite.

Phil Dwyer, who followed, was born little more than a goal kick away from Cardiff's old Ninian Park stadium, but when it came to the hard-man stakes he could claim to be anybody's equal. "I just used to give everything I had when it came to tackling. I was brought up watching Don Murray, so I knew what hardness was!" he said. And Dwyer went on to outlast Murray and Malloy, playing 471 games – a record that still stands.

Perhaps the only time Dwyer was nervous was when his one-time team-mate Robin Friday was around! Friday lasted just a year and played only 21 games for Cardiff. But his wild ways will never be forgotten. Having signed from Reading for £28,000 in December 1976, Friday's arrival was delayed when he was arrested by transport police on the train to Cardiff – for travelling without a ticket and hiding in the toilets! That story made the first headlines of a crazy year. Friday, who had started dabbling with drugs when he was 15, had served time in Borstal in his teens. By the time he came to Cardiff he was also heavily into drink. He would regularly miss training, sometimes disappearing for days on end.

When he did play, he could be a complete striker. "He had so much skill and strength, he could have played for England – if he'd had the right attitude," said Dwyer.

The fans loved him for his excesses, though. Friday was the ultimate anti-hero. His professional career lasted just three years – two of those at Reading – and his life thereafter spiralled out of control, with a prison spell before he was found dead from a suspected drug overdose at the age of just 38.

A tragic ending. But the fact that supporters of both clubs named him among their all-time cult heroes illustrates the incredible impact he made on those around him.

THE FAN'S VIEW

Amarpreet Poonia: *"I'd nominate Scott Young. A local lad, one-club man, model professional and THAT goal against what was then a formidable Leeds United side in the 2002 FA Cup win.*

"He wore his heart on his sleeve, and was a no-nonsense centre-half and stuck his head in where it hurts. A man who was everything a Valleys boy grows up to be. Tough, resolute and spirited, and a fantastic servant to Cardiff City."

Keith Lewis: *"Phil Dwyer was the best full-back of his era and a Cardiff City icon."*

CARLISLE UNITED

 **Ivor Broadis**

 **Hugh McIlmoyle**

Carlisle United stand unique as the northwest outpost of English football. They have some of the most loyal travelling supporters, considering the distances they cover to follow their heroes. Carlisle has the smallest population of any town or city in England to host a top-flight football club – they were in the old First Division for the 1973–74 season.

Many Brunton Park followers rate England international Ivor Broadis as the finest player to have represented Carlisle. An intelligent and quick-thinking inside-forward, Broadis represented England at the 1954 World Cup finals while a Newcastle player. He won 14 England caps and became the first England player to score two goals during a World Cup match at the 1954 finals. He scored twice in England's 4-4 draw with Belgium and was followed into the record books by centre-forward Nat Lofthouse.

Broadis had first played for the Cumbrians as a guest player during the Second World War, before becoming Carlisle player-manager in 1946 at the age of just 23. He remains the Football League's youngest ever player-manager.

Broadis sold himself to Sunderland in 1949 for £18,000 but has always insisted since those days that the actual deal was sanctioned by the Carlisle board: "Imagine a 23-year-old among a 12-man board of directors whose average age was 70," Broadis said. "It was doomed."

"All I did was exercise the right to be transferred. Blackburn, Man City and Preston were all in for me as well, but I chose Sunderland.

"They paid big transfer fees, and treated players the best. It was a great move for Carlisle too because they got £18,000 for me. It was an incredible amount in those days."

Coincidentally, by leaving Brunton Park in 1949 he paved the way for the appointment of his successor – a certain Bill Shankly. It was Shankly's first managerial position.

After spells with Sunderland, Manchester City and Newcastle, Broadis returned to Carlisle in 1955 as player-coach. He made more than 250 appearances for the Cumbrians. He later became a highly-respected sports journalist.

One of the amazing things about Broadis remains his London accent. Born and brought up in East London he may be a naturalized Cumbrian these days, but he's never lost his original accent. Given his celebrated status as one of English football's all-time greats it's also astonishing to discover that Broadis' real name is not Ivor. Although christened Ivan, when he played for Tottenham as a guest amateur player after the Second World War an official misheard his name and Ivor Broadis, our Carlisle icon, was created.

A number of truly fine players could claim the status of Carlisle's cult hero. After being released by Newcastle, Peter Beardsley made his name as a budding young striker at Brunton Park. His all-action, skilful style made him a popular player. He showed a toughness and resilience that silenced the doubters who claimed he was too small to succeed. He went on to enjoy an outstanding career, particularly with Liverpool, Newcastle and England. But his debut was very definitely made at Brunton Park.

Chris Balderstone is another contender. The Huddersfield-born inside-forward was one of the last sportsmen to combine a prolonged career in both first-class cricket and football. Balderstone won several cricketing trophies representing the successful Leicestershire team of the 1970s, played in two Tests for England and later became an umpire, officiating at two one-day internationals.

He wrote his name into the Brunton Park history book by scoring on his debut in a 4-1 home win over Norwich City, a goal which gave him the distinction of scoring the club's first-ever goal in the second level of English football.

And it was a Balderstone penalty against Spurs keeper Pat Jennings that briefly had the Cumbrians topping the First Division after just three games in 1973–74.

His 11 years at Carlisle coincided with the club's most successful spell. He made 376 appearances, but admitted it took him some time to win over the fans: "They gave me a bit of stick at first because I wasn't the quickest player or the hardest tackler. I always had confidence in my ability and I knew there'd be somebody in the crowd who appreciated a bit of skill. I won them over and they were very good to me after that."

He died in 2000, aged 59.

But our Carlisle cult hero has to be Hugh McIlmoyle. Born in Port Glasgow in 1940, McIlmoyle was one of 11 children. He was a nomadic striker of the Sixties who turned up at a host of clubs, bounced opposing centre-backs around and, invariably, chalked up goals wherever he went. While Broadis had two spells at Carlisle, McIlmoyle managed three. And he never disappointed the Brunton Park faithful with his committed displays, brave heading and fierce shooting power. There's a statue in his honour outside Brunton Park. He thoroughly deserves it.

THE FAN'S VIEW

Kathleen Rowley: *"I nominate Ivor Broadis who sold himself as a player to save our club from going under."*

Beccy Potts: *"I would nominate Peter Murphy. He has given Carlisle United over 10 years great service, scored some memorable goals and is an amazing man."*

CHARLTON ATHLETIC

 **Sam Bartram**

 **Derek Hales**

Unfortunately, it's one of football's most brutal, basic truths: there are two types of managers, those who've been sacked already and those who will be sacked in the future. Even winning the World Cup for England and earning a knighthood couldn't shield Sir Alf Ramsey from that fundamental law of football logic. Management and the termination of contracts appear indivisible. And that's why it almost pains us to discuss Chris Powell as a potential Charlton Athletic icon.

As everyone who's played alongside him, interviewed him, met up with him as a fan and now worked alongside him as Charlton boss, will confirm, we don't want the fairytale to end.

Of course, Powell is not the only good guy in football. And he must have a tough, decisive, ruthless streak. He couldn't have led Charlton to promotion as League One champions in 2012 if he hadn't. But even though he's in his early forties there's still a boyish charm and openness to Powell's demeanour. He proved to be an excellent chairman of the PFA at a time when racism in life – as well as football – has become a massive issue. Never one for the outrageous sound bite, Powell understood the issues, as well as the history of the problem, and had some lucid ideas regarding the way forward. He spoke his mind and had real gravitas when he addressed the problems facing football.

He's revered at most of the clubs he played for but especially by Addicks fans. They appreciate the way he committed himself to their cause during his three spells as a player. There's a vivid memory that has entered folklore at The Valley of Powell's final playing appearance for the club on 4th May 2008. He came on as a substitute for the final five minutes. Everyone knew it was the chance to share an emotional farewell. Chris duly scored only his third goal for the club on his 270th appearance as the home side beat Coventry 4-1. What happened next was especially poignant in reflecting Powell's status in the game and the esteem in which he was held by his colleagues. The Charlton players spontaneously lifted him onto their shoulders as a mini lap of honour took place, and the home fans saluted their departing hero.

Not all our club icons are home-grown stars, long-service award-winners or, quite simply, the biggest name to ever play for that club. Powell was two months short of his 29th birthday when he joined Charlton in a £825,000 transfer from Derby County in June 1998. His talent and outgoing nature had seen him enjoy his time in the Midlands. In fact, he had been voted Player of the Year by Derby's fans for the 1996–97 season.

But his career – and reputation – really took off in his time at The Valley. In 2001 he became the oldest England debutant since Luton Town's Syd Owen 47 years earlier. Powell, 31, was a shock selection for Sven Goran Eriksson's first game in charge. England played Spain in a friendly. Powell held onto the left-back berth for a World Cup qualifier against Finland, but the emergence of Ashley Cole, then at Arsenal, undermined his international career.

Powell, impeccably genial, was grateful for his opportunity. He commented: "It was good because a manager came in with fresh eyes and said, 'I like this player, regardless of who he plays for and his age.' Regardless of the Beckhams, the Scholes and the Campbells, there are places for people from clubs that aren't associated with international success. It's 36 years since Charlton had an England international. My name's on the honours board in reception. I'm very proud of that."

Clearly, as a manager, Powell cannot afford to live in the past. But, given his time as players' union chairman and an eloquent spokesman for the game, we have to hope that nothing will ever unhinge the relationship between Powell, Charlton Athletic and their supporters. It's surely too priceless a bond to be broken.

Older Charlton fans will point out that the man who must be recognized as their club icon is goalkeeping legend Sam Bartram. When he died, aged 67, in 1981, most tributes included the phrase "the finest goalie never to win an England cap". But the absence of international recognition never undermined Bartram's status at Charlton. A goalie blessed with incredible athleticism, bravery and talent, he was also a showman who loved bantering with the crowd and producing crowd-pleasing moments. These could include him dribbling the ball downfield, not just past one opponent, and then passing to a team-mate. Sam would keep going on his mazy, solo slalom, and had been known to reach the opposing penalty area before releasing possession.

He was flamboyant. He stood out on the field with his shock of thick red hair and his powerful build, but he made sure every fan spotted the performance of the Charlton goalie. After heading south from South Shields, where in his youth he'd played as a striker, Bartram broke into the Charlton team and in his first three years played his part in the club winning consecutive promotions from the old Third Division and then finishing runners-up in 1936–37 to Manchester City in the First Division title race. This was Charlton's first season in the top flight. In 22 years with Charlton, spanning the Thirties, Forties and Fifties, Bartram was never dropped.

Bartram's legend spread even after his retirement in 1956. I recall as a boy being told by my father the story of Bartram keeping goal on a foggy day against Chelsea at Stamford Bridge on Christmas Day, 1937. To be blunt, I didn't believe the tale and feared it was one of those apocryphal stories that had gained lustre with the passage of time. I was wrong. In his autobiography Bartram recalled: "Soon after kick-off fog began to thicken rapidly at the far end. The referee stopped the game and then, as visibility became clearer, restarted it. We were on top at this time and I saw fewer and fewer figures as we attacked steadily.

"I paced up and down my goal-line, happy in the knowledge that Chelsea were being pinned in their own half. Time passed and I made several advances to the edge of my penalty area, peering through the murk, which was getting thicker by the minute. Still I could see nothing. The Chelsea defence was clearly being run off its feet.

"After a long time a figure loomed out of the curtain of fog in front of me. It was a policeman and he gaped at me incredulously. 'What on earth are you doing here,' he gasped. 'The game was stopped a quarter of an hour ago. The field's completely empty.' I groped my way to the dressing room and the Charlton team, already out of the bath and in their civvies, convulsed with laughter."

Bartram contrived to get married on the morning of a game, chasing from the reception to play in goal. He used to joke that Wembley was his second home. This thought was supported by the Addicks appearing in four consecutive FA Cup finals either side of the Second World War. He was 40 in 1954 when he came runner-up to the legendary Tom Finney in the Footballer of the Year poll. Two years later he decided to retire and move into management at York City.

After six years in management Bartram moved into sports journalism as a reporter with the *Sunday People*. To his death he remained one of the country's most popular sporting heroes. Statistics don't do Bartram justice, but in those 22 years with the club he made a record 583 League appearances. In his honour there is a 9ft-high statue outside The Valley – an oversized salute to a colossal football figure. Bartram is our Addicks icon.

Our Charlton cult hero, though, is from a very different school from that of Sam Bartram. This man was a striker who could not be described as smart or elegant either in his on-field displays or his off-field persona. I remember seeing Derek Hales and his attacking sidekick Mike Flanagan climbing off the team coach one evening at Preston North End and thinking that they must be on their way to the Isle of Wight rock festival. They had a way of making club issue blazers and tracksuits appear incredibly scruffy.

The duo came to international fame in 1979 with their punch-up in an FA Cup tie at Maidstone United. Flanagan delayed a pass, fearing his team-mate was off-side. Hales erupted with fury, threw the first punch and a shocking punch-up between team-mates ensued. Both were sent off. Hales was initially sacked by Charlton but after legal advice was allowed back to the club.

He may have had an unkempt appearance but there was nothing dubious about Hales' eye for goal. At times his finishing was clinical, and that's why he remains Charlton's most lethal marksman. During two spells with the club he scored 168 goals in 368 games. His nickname was "Killer". That was partly down to his lethal touch in front of goal and also the fact that his family owned a butchers shop with a slaughterhouse attached to it where Hales had worked before becoming a professional footballer.

Hales' roots were in non-League football. He played for Faversham Town and Dartford before joining Luton Town for £2,000 in 1972. A year later he moved to Charlton for the princely sum of £4,000. There was always a hint of the non-League maverick about Hales. But there was also inevitably a shock in store for the football people who wanted to ignore his talent and write him off as a scruffy lay-about. As Charlton fans grew to appreciate, Hales was one of the finest goalscorers of his generation. But a few people beyond The Valley just didn't want to know it.

THE FAN'S VIEW

Alec Evans: *"Curbs did a great job as our manager but our cult hero has to be from that tag team of Flanagan and Hales."*

CHELSEA

ⓘ Gianfranco Zola   **ⓗ Peter Osgood**

The modern Chelsea is perceived as a soulless football club, driven relentlessly forward by a ruthless Russian oligarch who revels in the remorseless pursuit of glory. Of course this is a brutally simplified view of Roman Abramovich and his decade or so in charge of the Blues. But it hides a rich irony. Chelsea, now viewed as serial trophy hoarders, were once dismissed as the great entertainers who promised so much but delivered so little in terms of silverware. Oh how perceptions can change within the space of a decade.

The late, great Dave Sexton was the manager when Chelsea came closest to fulfilling their potential in the late Sixties and early Seventies. A shy, private man, it remained one his frustrations that he had not been able to oversee a longer period of trophy-winning at the Bridge. This was all the more galling in that, during his seven years there, they managed to make the big breakthrough by beating Leeds in an epic replay to lift the 1970 FA Cup and followed up by winning the European Cup Winners' Cup. But Dave was challenged to harness the undisputed skills of some breathtaking talents within a functioning team framework. Despite the apparent mood of self-destruction coursing through Chelsea veins at the time, the outcome in terms of under-achievement was perhaps predictable.

But part of the joy of following Chelsea in those days was to deal with the capricious nature of Peter Osgood, Charlie Cooke and Alan Hudson. On their good days they weren't just good, they were football gods. On their bad days it seemed as if they didn't really care. That was a source of pain to Sexton, a fine student of the game and willing mentor. It's interesting to hear from long-time Chelsea fans about their considered view about Stamford Bridge's icons and cult heroes.

Alec Stewart, the most capped England cricketer, is a lifelong Blue. He remains a season ticket holder at the Bridge. He reveals a particular support for his personal hero from childhood as well as acknowledging the bigger picture. Stewart said: "John Hollins was my all-time Chelsea hero and the reason why I wore the number 4 shirt when playing one day international cricket for England. However, the best player I've ever seen in the blue shirt has to be Gianfranco Zola."

It's perhaps of little surprise that one of the players Sexton took with him from Chelsea to QPR, where he performed an outstanding job, was Stewie's hero Hollins. The England international midfielder was quiet in his demeanour but that did not totally camouflage his steely commitment. Stewart went on: "My cult hero has to be the King of Stamford Bridge himself, the late, great Peter Osgood. The No. 9 is an iconic shirt at many clubs and Ossie wore it with great pride and passion for the Blues. He epitomized everything that Chelsea stood for. He was a big-time player at a big-time club. He fitted in perfectly in and around the Kings Road scene. His 150 goals from 380 appearances, along with his style of play, meant that he endeared himself to the Chelsea faithful and even now his name is sung at every home game 'Osgood – Born is the King of Stamford Bridge'.

"The statue that has been erected by the West Stand entrance in his honour is a mark of the great man."

A trip through the *Mirror's* photo library highlights the japes Ossie and mates got up to in the late Sixties. If a boutique or hairdressers was opening, the Chelsea boys were the men to invite to add glamour and publicity to any proceedings. They were top of the guest list at most showbiz-style events and they revelled in their infamy. Ossie really could play at a level that made him the most feared centre-forward in the country. He had burst on the scene as a precociously gifted 17-year-old in 1964. The only real set-back in his rise to superstardom came when he broke his leg in a clash with Emlyn Hughes, then a Blackpool player, in a League Cup tie in October 1966. He missed Chelsea's 1967 FA Cup final defeat to Tottenham and the injury took its toll on Ossie. He never quite regained the scintillating turn of speed that once saw him sprint away from defenders. He later admitted "I put on two stones from that injury and never really lost it again."

And there, among the old photos, is a shot of Raquel Welch, back in 1972 recognized as one of the world's most beautiful women, watching Chelsea in a game at Stamford Bridge. Legend has it she attended a photo shoot sporting a T-shirt with the message: "I scored with Ossie".

Understandably, the gregarious Osgood, who married three times, remembered meeting the Hollywood legend. Ossie said: "She was over promoting a film and Sir Richard Attenborough brought her along and she said she wanted to meet Peter Osgood. Terry O'Neill, who was her photographer, was also my photographer at the time. She was gorgeous, lovely, stunning."

It was as a centre-forward that memories are most vivid, but Sexton also utilized Osgood to good effect in midfield for most of the 1969–70 season. However, he was back in his favoured role the following season for Chelsea's memorable FA Cup replay win over Leeds at Old Trafford. He also joined an elite group to score in every round of an FA Cup campaign. Yet Osgood's career at Chelsea ended with rows. Sexton believed Osgood and young midfielder Alan Hudson were not showing enough self-control and professionalism. Both were sold. Ossie made 380 appearances for Chelsea and scored 150 goals. He died on 1st March 2006, aged 59.

So, if Ossie is our Chelsea cult hero, who is their greatest player, the ultimate Chelsea icon? By winning the European Cup in such dramatic fashion in Munich the class of 2012 transformed their status as true blue Chelsea heroes. The backbone of the Chelsea team that won three Premier League titles, four FA Cup finals and two League Cup finals was consistent. The likes of goalie Petr Cech, centre-back John Terry, Frank Lampard in midfield and Didier Drogba in attack were the well-paid and reliable assets who invariably produced on the big occasion. The shoot-out triumph over Bayern Munich in the German club's own arena marked striker Drogba's last appearance for the club.

Within weeks a poll of Chelsea fans hailed Drogba as their greatest ever player. Their support for the Ivory Coast centre-forward was understandable. Drogba was stunned by the news. He said: "This makes me honoured and proud because so many big players have been at the club before me – and at the same time as me.

"It is unbelievable. When I joined Chelsea I came to play my part and I'm so happy to have been part of the club's history. My ambition was to win all the major trophies in England and I think awards like this and success go together."

I recall speaking to a Premier League goalie a few weeks earlier who was analysing the merits of various top-flight strikers. He confirmed: "When he puts his mind to it Drogba is the toughest opponent in the Premier League. Sometimes he's not up for it and, if you catch him on one of those days, you're happy. But when he's fierce and focused, he's virtually unplayable."

Better than Zola, the brilliant Italian who joined Chelsea from Parma in 1996 and spent seven years at the club? Many seasoned Chelsea fans – including the likes of Alec Stewart – salute Drogba but insist Zola was the finest footballer to sport a blue shirt. The diminutive Sardinian was a creative genius. He possessed an imagination that allowed him to unlock the most impregnable defence with a shimmy, a turn, a deft flick or a turn of pace that saw him drift past opponents at ease. And, given his Italian pedigree, he was never shaken by intimidation or crude fouls or challenges. He played his football with a smile – no, a cheeky, impish grin, because to Gianfranco football was competitive but it was fun, too. He became the first Chelsea player to be elected Footballer of the Year when the FWA saluted him in 1997.

Zola fitted into that heritage of Chelsea entertainers. Unlike some of his predecessors, his manager didn't have to worry where he'd be the night before a game. Perhaps with the passage of time the Chelsea fans who hail Drogba because of that Saturday night of Munich glory might just review their assessment and support our belief that the Chelsea icon remains Gianfranco Zola.

CHELTENHAM TOWN

 Steve Cotterill    Neil Grayson

Born in Cheltenham, Steve Cotterill played semi-professionally as a striker for his home-town club in their non-League days.

But his influence at Cheltenham was more profoundly felt after returning as manager in 1997, guiding his former club from the fifth tier in the League pyramid to the third in five exciting years.

Cotterill joined Cheltenham as boss when they were still non-League and he built up a successful side which won promotion from the Southern League Premier Division to the Conference in 1999, his first full season at the club. He had guided Cheltenham to an FA Trophy final win over Southport in 1998.

A run to the FA Cup fifth round in 2001–02, the club's best achievement in that competition, came just before he oversaw a play-off victory over Rushden and Diamonds which took Cheltenham to League Two.

But his success – which had earned him the nickname of "The Messiah of Whaddon Road" – quickly saw him enticed to short-lived jobs as Stoke City boss and Sunderland assistant manager. From his Cheltenham days Cotterill was pinpointed as one of the bright young things of football management. Currently working for Harry Redknapp at QPR, perhaps he still has the chance to fulfil all that early promise.

Our Cheltenham cult hero is Neil Grayson. The £25,000 bargain buy from Hereford United became a huge Cheltenham hero during his five seasons at Whaddon Road.

York-born Grayson was with the Robins between 1998 and 2002 and was hugely influential in Cheltenham's promotion to the Football League in 1999. He scored a memorable goal against Morecambe and then the winner against Rushden and Diamonds in a Conference Championship showdown. He was then voted Conference Player of the Year.

His final appearances for Cheltenham were in the successful 2001–02 play-off campaign where he scored a vital 88th-minute equalizer in the semi-finals first leg at Hartlepool, while he converted his penalty in the shoot-out in the second leg after an aggregate 2-2 draw.

And in his last game for the Robins in the Millennium Stadium final – a 3-1 win over Rushden and Diamonds – he came on as a substitute and smashed a drive against the woodwork that allowed John Finnigan to net the rebound. A true Cotswolds legend!

CHESTERFIELD

 Ernie Moss

 Jack Lester

Given the town's impressive pedigree for producing goalies you'd expect our icon or cult hero for the Derbyshire club to be a No. 1.

Gordon Banks, acclaimed as England's greatest goalie and a member of the 1966 World Cup-winning team, started his career with the Spireites. Arsenal's serial trophy winners Bob Wilson and John Lukic were both born in Chesterfield. But in any debate about Chesterfield's iconic player it's hard to look beyond Ernie Moss.

Ernie had three spells at the club and remains their leading League marksman with 162 goals – not one of them a penalty. He was actually working as a clerk in the Derby County Council offices in Matlock when he initially joined the Spireites as an amateur in 1968. A few days after his 19th birthday he made his debut and signed professional forms soon afterwards.

Ernie was never sleek of movement or delicate in his play. He was a 6ft 2ins centre-forward with a great eye for goal and bundles of determination to make sure he stuck that ball in the opposition net. His attitude was one of the things that endeared him to the fans. He was a never-say-die player, so that when things were going wrong he would still chase lost causes and challenge for every header.

Jimmy McGuigan, the shrewd Scottish manager who developed Ernie's raw talent, once described him as "a big, willing bloke, a charming fellow who had raw potential. His balance was nil, therefore his ball control was nil. He knew where the goal lay but he couldn't often hit it. So I had to work like hell on his balance and ball control because without it, you can't play professional football."

From that raw material McGuigan helped a player become one of the most respected players in the lower divisions. With Chesterfield he won the Fourth Division title in 1970 and 1985. He also won titles or promotion with Port Vale, Doncaster Rovers and Mansfield Town. He scored with headers, left and right foot shots and even dispatched some impeccable volleys.

The other great thing about Ernie was his friendliness to fans and media. He was always willing to give his time. He went into partnership with the Derbyshire and England cricketer Geoff Miller in 1979, opening sports shops in Chesterfield and Matlock. Fans regularly called in to see him just for a chat and he was so open and friendly they saw him as one of their own. Moss left Chesterfield for the last time in 1986, yet he remains a huge hero in town.

As for a Chesterfield cult hero, we could look at Jamie Hewitt who performed so brilliantly in Chesterfield's shock run to the FA Cup semi-finals in 1997. On the managerial front there was also Arthur Cox, who was at Saltergate from 1976 to 1980. But we're opting for another fine attacking player as our cult hero – Jack Lester.

Lester joined the club in 2007 on a Bosman free transfer from Nottingham Forest. In his first campaign he was the club's top scorer with 27 goals. The fans took to Jack and he clearly relished his new surroundings. In the 2010–11 season the goals continued to flow. This time it was 17 in 29 games and Chesterfield won the League Two title.

One of the managers who worked with him at Forest was Paul Hart, who also had a couple of seasons at Chesterfield. Hart's assessment of Lester is glowing: "Jack's a hugely intelligent footballer. He's very strong-minded in a positive way. He doesn't suffer fools. He has a great picture of how the game should be played and his role and he's proved his worth at Chesterfield.

"You can play Jack right up-front as a striker or just behind the front man in a more withdrawn role. He's so smart he handles that deeper role so well. He looks after himself off the field, too. That's obvious given the length of his career. He's never a shirker. He loves hard work and wants to play. In many ways he's understated but he's a smashing pro."

THE FAN'S VIEW

Steve Magnall: *"Ernie Moss remains our hero. You just knew he'd score. What a legend."*

COLCHESTER UNITED

 **Micky Cook**

 **Lomana LuaLua**

Sometimes you find a man so committed to his club's cause that you have to check the statistics are factually correct. Micky Cook, the man who has made most appearances for Colchester United, is one of those people.

Cooky spent his entire playing career at Layer Road, from 1969 to 1984. There were some highs and plenty of lows along the way, but nobody could dispute right-back Micky's commitment to the club's cause. In the end he had clocked up 614 appearances but the longevity of his playing days only tells half the story of Cook's importance to the Essex club.

After his playing career was over Cook switched to a youth development role. And what a job he did. He was pragmatic enough to accept that at Colchester's level the club may not be able to hang on to a group of outstanding youngsters. The game is to work with them until they're ready for the first team, help them make their names in League football and then, hopefully, attract bids from the predatory big boys paying the kind of fees that help Colchester survive.

Cook was instrumental in the youth set-up that found Lomana LuaLua. Following Cook's blueprint for glory helped the U's rake in £2.25million from Newcastle when the winger was sold in 2000. He also worked with the likes of Greg Halford, who also made a £2million exit from the club. Halford joined Reading in 2007.

And it's Cook's pupil, LuaLua, who wins our cult hero award. There were a number of contenders for this one, including Ray Crawford, the legendary centre-forward who was 34 when he led the Colchester attack in their FA Cup victory over mighty Leeds in 1971.

Don Revie's team were one of the most powerful in the land at that point, but Dick Graham organized a U's line-up that pulled off one of the greatest Cup shocks of all time.

But LuaLua was a very different kind of player. He was a spectacular, tricky, exciting winger. Some days he destroyed opponents. On others he looked as if his boot laces had been tied together. But U's fans grew to love him. A hat-trick he scored in a League Cup tie against QPR is remembered with special affection. That was to prove his final appearance for the club.

The lasting memory of Lomana at Colchester remains that he played his football with a smile on his face. He was a natural, untroubled enthusiast. There was no cynicism in his approach to the game. He had just two seasons with the U's, but he was a joy to watch.

COVENTRY CITY

 George Curtis

 **Steve Ogrizovic**

They called him the Ironman. And in an age that bred hard, uncompromising defenders there were few as tough as George Curtis.

Born in Dover in 1939, he came from a mining community, and his first football was played for Snowdown Colliery Welfare. He was barely 15 when he took his place in the first team, yet quickly gained a reputation as the hardest defender in the side – an accolade that attracted scouts from Coventry who persuaded him to leave home and sign professional terms in October 1955.

He may have been young but he was pure granite, and played his part in manager Billy Frith's team that won promotion from the Fourth Division in 1959. When Jimmy Hill became boss at Highfield Road in 1961 he saw the leadership skills that Curtis would bring to the team, appointed him captain, and so began a romantic climb all the way to the First Division.

Curtis wasn't the tallest man – but he was built like a bull. In fact, in later years when people met Curtis they often commented on his short stature. Off the field they could not have understood his combative qualities, but in the game he was ferocious in the tackle, powerful in the air, fearless if he had to block a shot and also able to hit a telling pass that could turn defence to attack. He was seriously injured two games into the club's opening season in the First Division in 1967, and legend has it that somebody rang his home to break the bad news to his wife. "George has gone to hospital. He has broken a leg," they said. "Oh, whose was it?" asked Mrs Curtis.

When he left in December 1969 for a brief spell with Aston Villa he had played 487 League games, which was then a club record. But the story of George Curtis and Coventry City was still to have its final flourish. After hanging up his boots he returned as commercial manager, and was then made managing director in September 1983. When Don Mackay left the club three years later and there was no obvious candidate to take over team affairs, Curtis took on the responsibility together with John Sillett.

This proved an inspired move. Curtis and Sillett were a dream double act and could never be described as a pair of shrinking violets. Sillett was the man who got the players to relax and chose the tactics, Curtis was the hard man who imposed discipline and standards. Between them they led the club to its finest hour – the FA Cup final triumph in 1987.

So Curtis covered all bases. He had been an inspiration as player and as manager, and his work behind the scenes helped to build the structure of the club. The Cup was the icing on the cake. Nobody connected with the Sky Blues will quibble at George being our Coventry icon.

As for the cult hero, that FA Cup-winning team had plenty of candidates. Keith Houchen came from York and scored a diving header that remains one of Wembley's best goals; skipper Brian "Killer" Kilcline was a ferocious warrior at centre-half, even if he didn't quite – thankfully – live up to his nickname. But our choice is the man who took Curtis' appearance record from him, goalkeeper Steve Ogrizovic.

Ogrizovic gave up a career as a policeman to sign full-time for Chesterfield, and won European Cup winners' medals as an unused substitute with Liverpool during a spell as the understudy to Ray Clemence, before arriving at Highfield Road via a spell at Shrewsbury. In 13 years he played 502 times in the League, and established another club record of 241 consecutive appearances.

But there was so much more to Oggy. His nose, which seems to be bent in about 20 directions, bears testament to his bravery, diving in where the boots were flying to get the ball in a crowded 6-yard box. He also has the distinction of having scored in open play – a spectacular, wind-assisted clearance at Sheffield Wednesday. He gave total commitment to the club, and carried on with the same approach when he worked on the coaching staff, inspiring the right attitudes in City's younger players.

THE FAN'S VIEW

James Alderton: *"We've had a torrid time in recent years so the memory of Oggy's commitment becomes even sweeter. Great man."*

CRAWLEY TOWN

ⓘ Dave Haining   **ⓗ Sergio Torres**

They may be new boys in the Football League circus but Crawley Town have a history dating back to their formation in 1896.

And our icon and cult hero were both at the club before Town finally stormed their way into League Two in 2011. They finished their Conference-winning season with a record 105 points and on the back of a 30-match unbeaten run.

Dave Haining was known throughout football as Mr Crawley Town, serving the club as a player, manager, club secretary and vice-president. The Londoner made 500 first-team appearances plus 44 as a substitute, and scored 80 goals. He was part of the squad that won promotion to the Southern League. Haining had five separate spells managing Crawley. He died aged 68 in 2012, and Crawley chief executive Alan Williams recalled: "He was part of the fabric of this football club for four decades and without people like Dave Haining we would not be in the position we are now." Crawley launched a Dave Haining Supporters Player of the Year award to honour their legend.

Our Crawley cult hero is Sergio Torres. The Argentinian with an Italian passport mirrors Crawley Town's unflinching desire to succeed in football.

Midfielder Torres funded his own trip to England in 2004 determined to succeed in professional football and, like Crawley, he succeeded in a rags-to-riches dream. He knew failure meant returning to Argentina to work in his father's brick factory.

Torres worked as a shelf-stacker at Boots and cycled to work at 5.30 am before his path to Crawley in 2010 made life more comfortable. Then, a last-minute FA Cup third-round winner against Championship Derby County in 2011 brought Crawley national recognition and made Torres a cult hero. Torres was mobbed by jubilant Crawley fans and his place in Sussex soccer history was assured.

He was part of the Crawley team that was crowned as Conference National champions in 2011, taking their place in the Football League, and a year later Crawley won promotion to Division One.

THE FAN'S VIEW

Tim Banks: *"It's been an incredible time to follow the real Red Devils and Sergio Torres has been a hero to us."*

CREWE ALEXANDRA

ⓘ Dario Gradi    **Geoff Thomas**

There was once a time when Crewe Alexandra was a music hall joke of a club. The team from the famous railway interchange seemed rooted in the old Fourth Division; it was hard to attract players, and managers came and went with alarming frequency. The evidence comes with the bald statistic that in the 12 years before Dario Gradi arrived in 1983 the club had gone through eight different managers. Some of those men, such as Tony Waddington, Peter Morris and Arfon Griffiths, had done well elsewhere. But there was a mood of doom and gloom around the place that seemed to prevent any long-term strategy. In those days keeping League football alive in Crewe seemed to be the name of the game.

I'm sure when Dario walked into Gresty Road for the first time he never thought he'd one day be looking back at a 25-year career as Alex boss. In the modern era only Sir Alex Ferguson could top his longevity. And Fergie has been one of Gradi's most outspoken supporters – he admired what the gifted coach has done to change the mentality surrounding his club; Gradi has gradually made Crewe one of the best development clubs for young players in the country.

One of Gradi's greatest achievements at his club is to establish a coaching mentality. Youngsters go there to be taught and encouraged in the right way to play. I recall attending an FA Cup replay between Crewe and Southampton at Gresty Road in 1985. It was a cold February night. Crewe have all-weather, floodlit training pitches next to the main stadium. An hour and a half before kick-off in the first-team match Gradi was out coaching the Under-14 team. It was a sight you might never see at any other club but it spoke volumes for what was happening at Crewe.

While Gradi offered wise leadership in football matters he was backed by a sound chairman in John Bowler. Gradi won three promotions and Crewe didn't get carried away and hock the silverware. When they endured the pains of relegation they didn't sack the manager. They backed Gradi to re-group and battle back for more glory.

The volume of players tutored at the club, or offered sanctuary in the wake of being rejected by illustrious neighbours, is remarkable. Gradi has the ability to spot raw talent and burnish it into the finished football article, as can be seen from the list of players he has helped become top-flight regulars and international stars. Crewe fans know them all, and it's from the list of future England internationals that we chose our Crewe cult hero.

In a sense Geoff Thomas gets the gong not simply because of what he achieved in his three years with the Railwaymen. Plucked from Rochdale after Gradi had spotted the potential of the athletic and abrasive midfielder, Thomas blossomed and became a firm favourite with the crowd before being bought by Crystal Palace in 1987. He captained Palace in the 1990 FA Cup final, and four years after leaving Crewe he was playing for England.

Thomas never forgot his football roots. He was a rounded young man who had to display immense bravery when he was diagnosed as suffering from chronic myeloid leukaemia in June 2003. He battled through his time of personal crisis and inspired many others who were suffering illness. In 2005 he won the BBC Sports Personality of the Year Helen Rollason Award after he raised £150,000 for Leukaemia Research by cycling 2,200 miles in 21 days. He completed 21 stages of the 2005 Tour de France.

It was more tour de force than Tour de France, but the bravery required epitomized our Crewe cult hero.

CRYSTAL PALACE

 Ian Wright

 Peter Taylor

Beyond Selhurst Park some fans love him and some fans hate him; but to the Crystal Palace faithful Ian Wright remains an iconic figure.

Maybe it was the cavalier spirit he showed in his six years with the club, arriving as an unknown on trial from Dulwich Hamlets, that led to his leaving as the club's record marksman in the post-war years. Yet statistics alone don't reflect the impact Wright had at Palace, the way the team played and the success the club enjoyed while he was with them. Wright brought a will-to-win that every supporter connected with. He also stunned opponents. I remember a top-flight player telling me he'd never played against anybody who nattered as much as Wrighty. He would chase around the field in his hyper-active way audibly announcing "I've got to score. I'm going to score" – often uttering the words to himself. On such single-mindedness legends are built, and there is no doubt that Wright became a Palace legend.

In assessing the emergence of Wright you also have to salute the intuitive nature of Palace's then manager, Steve Coppell. In any assessment of Palace icons and cult heroes Coppell merits mention. He had three separate stints as the Eagles' manager. His first was the best, and between 1984 and 1993 he displayed one of the sharpest minds in top-flight football. Coppell took on board the then relatively modern virtues of organization at set-pieces, pressure play on opponents, raising fitness levels to new heights and being able to negate opponents' star players. Steve wasn't a genius in these areas. Others were at it too. He just had the wit and intelligence to put the whole thing together so that his Palace team could spoil games as well as win them.

The attacking verve and panache was provided by one of the best attacking duos in the modern English game. Ian Wright arrived at the club first. When he was joined by Mark Bright an attacking tandem was created that many teams just could not live with. Bright was no mean finisher in his own right but he tended to be the focal point for Wright to play off. And with those scintillating bursts of speed – with and without the ball – Wright burst onto the big-time stage in such spectacular fashion.

People often forget that Wright was no callow youngster when he joined Palace in August 1985. He was just three months short of his 22nd birthday, the age when a lot of clubs believe a young player will have been signed up or left to drift around non-League football. In that first season he showed he was not out of his depth but it was the following season that Bright arrived from Leicester City for £75,000. Like Wright, Bright had been forced to show some tenacity in making the grade as a player. He had worked in a factory and turned out for non-League Leek Town before getting a chance with Port Vale. Those humble origins often seemed to work in favour of the Palace strikers. They were hungry for success.

Wright and Bright were unleashed by Coppell in the old Second Division during the 1986–87 season. They aimed for promotion but finished just outside the play-off zone. The following season Bright was the division's leading marksman with 24 goals, but, yet again, the play-offs proved agonizingly beyond Coppell's predominantly young team. However, there was an impetus around the club and it has to be said that when Selhurst Park is really rocking there are few more inspirational theatres in football. The old ground may not be of classical design, the pitch may be traditionally lumpy and bumpy, but the Palace fans can make a racket backing their boys and when the home side are hitting peak form few visiting sides relish a trip to SE25.

Palace finished third in the 1988–89 season to secure a play-off place. They beat Blackburn 4-3 in the final to secure promotion to the top flight.

By now Wright had emerged as the most lethal predator. En route to promotion he dispatched 24 goals in the Second Division with nine more in other competitions. A broken leg disrupted Wright's debut season in the top flight but he had already established himself as a match-winner with the Palace fans. That's why there was fervour around his potential appearance for the Eagles when they reached the 1990 FA Cup final against Manchester United at Wembley. Modern football is full of supersub heroes – Manchester United can claim more than most – but on this occasion it was Wright who, to the delight of the Eagles supporters, delivered the goals. His first goal forced extra-time, his second put Palace ahead and the game eventually ended 3-3. It's easy to forget that Alex Ferguson had been manager of United for less than four years and was still to break his trophy-winning duck. The stakes for the Thursday night replay were massive. Fergie responded by making one of the biggest selection calls of his career by dropping his long-term ally and first-choice keeper Jim Leighton. Instead he called up Les Sealey.

After the six-goal thriller in the first game the replay was a tighter affair and the Mancunians ran out 1-0 winners. Fergie, and United's, remorseless pursuit of cups and championships had begun. Palace left Wembley defeated but firm in the belief that they were building a team on solid foundations. In a sense that was proved the following season when Wright earned his first England cap and Palace returned to Wembley to beat Everton in the Zenith Data Systems Cup. The tournament didn't have the glitz or status of the FA Cup, but Palace were winners.

Wright scored 117 goals in 277 appearances for Palace. In 2005 he was named their Player of the Century and yet bold facts and stats don't do him justice. His genius for goalscoring just about eclipsed his ability to wind opponents up, which ensured Wright had fans on the edge of their seats wondering what was going to happen next. That irresistible attraction creates football icons.

Our Palace cult hero is another forward who could dispatch the most spectacular goals and run defences ragged on his solo attacking sorties. Peter Taylor only spent three years with Palace but his impact was immense. And a reflection of his impact on the game was that he was selected for England senior honours while playing for Palace in the Third Division.

A personal, special memory of Peter and that Palace team that Malcolm Allison was in charge of was their FA Cup fourth-round trip to Leeds in January 1976. The home team were hot favourites to get through. They were playing well and were third in the top flight at that time. The team still boasted stalwarts like Billy Bremner, Allan Clarke and Paul Madeley, and a few months earlier had appeared in the European Cup final, a game they were unfortunate to lose to Bayern Munich.

Big Mal arrived sporting the fedora that was his fashion statement for Palace's Cup run and an XXXL-sized sheepskin coat to insulate him against the bitterly cold Yorkshire day. Jimmy Armfield, the affable Leeds boss, bumped into Allison as the Palace team arrived, spotted Allison's coat and quipped: "When it has pups I'll have one!" Malcolm had the last laugh that day and Taylor's role in one of the biggest Cup shocks of the decade was mesmerizing. He delivered a pinpoint free-kick from the left that Dave Swindlehurst headed home to seize the 1-0 victory. Taylor did much more too. He repeatedly collected possession on the right flank and tormented the Leeds defence. At one point he nut-megged Frank Gray with a deft flick that left the Scotland international staring at Taylor's slipstream in disbelief. Taylor delivered a masterclass in counter-attacking at pace.

Palace then knocked out Chelsea and Sunderland to reach the semi-final. The prospect of a Third Division team reaching Wembley seemed very real but Palace lost 2-0 to Southampton, the eventual Cup winners. "That was a brilliant time," Taylor recalled. "We travelled to some great clubs and beat them on their own patch. We missed out on promotion that year, which we shouldn't have done. But I still have very fond memories of that year."

Allison had given Palace a new profile. Taylor became the cult hero of that team. And as defender Jim Cannon recalled: "Malcolm had all sorts of ideas about how to boost our image. There was the infamous photo shoot with Fiona Richmond in the bath, and whether you agreed with it or not it certainly seemed to work. I remember a game with Millwall on a Tuesday night in Division Three and we still got a gate of 37,000."

DAGENHAM AND REDBRIDGE

 Tony Roberts

 Paul Benson

It was Frank Sinatra who was famed for comebacks. In Dagenham and Redbridge's history they'll be glad that Tony Roberts was persuaded to keep on playing.

The popular Welshman made a club record of 507 appearances for the club despite not joining them until after his 30th birthday – and announcing his first retirement.

Holyhead-born Roberts had originally retired in 1998 after a finger problem had dogged him at QPR and Millwall. Joining the Daggers in 2000 after a spell with St Albans, he had to repay part of a £150,000 compensation pay-off as the price of resuming his career. But injuries rarely bothered him at Victoria Road and he became a fixture between the Daggers posts for more than a decade, helping the Essex side to make history by winning promotion to the Football League in 2007 and being granted a testimonial match against West Ham United. The highlight of his Daggers career was being part of the side that beat Rotherham 3-2 at Wembley in 2010 to win promotion to the third tier of English football.

Roberts won two full Welsh caps and was understudy to Neville Southall 30 times. He was also understudy to England star David Seaman in their days together at QPR. After his second, and final, playing retirement he worked as a goalkeeping coach at QPR before joining Arsenal in a similar capacity.

If Roberts is our Daggers icon, our cult hero is Paul Benson, who became the darling of the Victoria Road faithful when his goals fired the club into the Football League for the first time in 2007, just 15 years after the merged club's foundation.

Benson's rapid elevation to prominence was almost as spectacular as that of the burgeoning Essex club he joined in 2005. He rose from playing parks football in the Essex Intermediate League with White Ensign to become the Conference's leading goalscorer in the space of two years as the Daggers won promotion to the Football League.

He scored 28 goals to secure that coveted place in Division Two – the most ever in a season by a Daggers player – and Benson achieved his cult status with the opening goal at Wembley when Rotherham were beaten 3-2 to secure League One football.

That goal was the 22nd of a memorable campaign and all told he hit 74 goals in 178 games for Dagenham and Redbridge before moving to Charlton shortly after the Wembley triumph. Benson's considerable efforts for the Daggers earned him an

England non-League cap and typically he celebrated his debut with a goal against Northern Ireland. Benson may not have been as big a name as other Daggers strikers, such as Mark Stein or Craig Mackell-Smith, but there was no doubting how important his goals were to the little Essex outfit.

THE FAN'S VIEW

Bill Phillips: *"Tony Roberts brought top flight class to the club. You could see he'd played at the highest level. Great goalie and great club man."*

DERBY COUNTY

(i) Dave Mackay  **(h) Igor Stimac**

Dave Mackay was a truly great player. Brian Clough didn't have to be a football genius to know that. The evidence was blatantly obvious during the tough Scotsman's career with Tottenham and before that with Hearts in his native Edinburgh.

The act of genius on Clough's part was persuading Mackay, then 33 and preparing for his retirement, to postpone his move back to Hearts and a backroom role to play on with unfashionable Second Division Derby.

Peter Taylor, Clough's assistant, had sparked the pursuit of Mackay. He had nominated the tough wing-half as the final part of the team they were building at the Baseball Ground. Nominating Mackay was the easy bit. Getting him to move to Derby was the first massive challenge. The second was to persuade him to switch from being an all-action midfield inspiration to playing as a sweeper in defence and guiding the youngsters around him. Clough and Taylor convinced him he was up to a tactical task he'd never considered. Mackay became a defensive master.

Ask any opposing player from the Sixties, from Bobby Charlton to Johnny Giles, and they will talk with reverence about Dave Mackay. The barrel-chested, high energy wing-half transformed midfield play. He refused to stay in the set position favoured by his contemporaries, and created a template that the likes of Bryan Robson and Roy Keane would follow in later years. Mackay was everywhere. He tackled harder than anyone. He ran harder as he covered every blade of grass. Then, when he had possession, he could pass the ball like an angel. His vision was inspired. He read the game to perfection. And he had skill, too.

Tottenham manager Bill Nicholson didn't think Clough had a chance of persuading Mackay to join Derby. But after two hours of Clough detailing his vision for the Midlands club the famous Scotland international was hooked. He was willing to postpone his retirement, accept Clough's offer of £14,000 over three years and move to the Baseball Ground.

Mackay was made for Derby, and the club was made for its new superstar skipper. Taylor's vision was to ask Mackay to tutor a brilliant young centre-back called Roy McFarland and full-backs John Robson and Ronnie Webster. As Clough pointed out: "I'd never seen anything that was perfect – Dave Mackay playing in that defence was as near to perfection as makes no difference."

In his book *Cloughie: Walking on Water* (Headline) Old Big 'Ead added: "I can't overstate the impact and influence Mackay had at the Baseball Ground. Our self belief – mine, Peter Taylor's and the entire team's – stemmed from the confidence of Mackay himself. It won him the Footballer of the Year award and it won us the Second Division title (in 1969)."

Mackay played brilliantly for Derby for three years until he moved to Swindon Town as player-manager in 1971. Within two years, and after a brief spell as Nottingham Forest boss, he was back at Derby as manager. With the club in turmoil following the departure of Clough, and an ensuing civil war, Mackay may well have been the only man capable of winning over the furious County players who were loyal to their departed boss. Proof of the calming job he did came when Derby finished third in his first season in charge. The following campaign saw them crowned as League champions in 1975.

Mackay was a great football man. An inspirational player. A respected manager. A worthy icon of Derby County. And as Roy McFarland, a player who must be considered as a cult hero, remarked: "Dave Mackay was the best player I ever played with at Derby."

McFarland had been recruited from Tranmere Rovers. Taylor had spotted the raw material again. Clough was to harness him into becoming one of the best ball-playing centre-backs we've seen in the modern English game. Firstly, alongside Mackay and later with Colin Todd as his sidekick, McFarland stood out as a defender who could dominate opponents in the air and deal with battling, bruising strikers while retaining the calm and poise to get the ball down and play. McFarland insists that much of the credit for his self-belief came from Mackay's tutelage.

McFarland spent 14 years at Derby and later returned as manager. But it was in his role as cornerstone of their defence that Roy Mac deserves consideration as a cult hero. Another contender as cult and member of the long service crew must also be mentioned. Kevin Hector's 486 League appearances, during two spells at the club, remain a Derby record. It was his clinical instincts as a goalscorer that made Hector so popular. He was signed from Bradford Park Avenue by Tim Ward, inherited by Clough and was a key player in the Derby teams that won the Second Division title, the League Championship twice and reached the European Cup semi-finals in 1976.

A small, nippy player, his goal-poaching became legendary. First with John O'Hare and later with Roger Davies, he formed classic little and large attacking partnerships.

But our Derby cult hero comes from a more modern era, and arrived at the club from Hajduk Split in 1995 in a £1.5million deal. Igor Stimac was a Croatia international, played centre-back and didn't mess about. His larger-than-life personality proved a critical force in turning around a County team that was languishing in the lower reaches of the First Division. He effectively kick-started a promotion campaign. He was a transforming presence at the club, and the Derby fans spotted a man who had made the kind of impact Mackay had generated almost 30 years earlier. Stimac spent four years at Derby. He was hugely influential and was adored by the fans, and is a worthy winner of our cult award.

THE FAN'S VIEW

Leslie Harper: *"I'm old enough to remember Dave Mackay. He was inspirational. What a player and what a man."*

DONCASTER ROVERS

 Alick Jeffrey

 Ian Snodin

The legend of Alick Jeffrey lives on. Our Doncaster Rovers icon passed away in 2000. He was 61. But his story – from being a teenage prodigy who saw his dream move to Manchester United wrecked by a badly broken leg and then, when people had written him off, proving he could still play League football – remains totally compelling.

He made his debut for Rovers when he was just 15 years old. Every First Division club knew of his talent. Most tried to sign him. Yet he opted to join his home-town club, Doncaster Rovers. That loyalty, allied to his astonishing talent, helped establish him as our Doncaster icon.

Two clubs dominated the development of young players in those days – Wolverhampton Wanderers and Manchester United. And it was United boss Matt Busby, building one of the greatest home-grown teams seen in English football, who decided to prise the wonder boy away from Rovers.

He was a regular visitor to south Yorkshire in these days. Tommy Taylor had moved to Old Trafford from Barnsley in 1953 and been a resounding success. While Taylor was a traditional English centre-forward, Jeffrey was a different type of attacking weapon – a more rounded player who could link play, beat opponents but also had the power to unleash ferocious shots. The verdict on Jeffrey was unanimous. Peter Doherty, his Donny manager, said: "Alick would have been even better than George Best. There's no doubt in my mind that he would have been the greatest scorer of goals England has ever seen."

The mention of Best's name is intriguing because Alick was a handsome guy. He was also blessed with talent beyond football and in the Seventies could be seen at the Black Cat club in Doncaster playing guitar and singing.

Jeffrey was playing for the England Under-23 team when he was just 17. It was on international duty that he sustained the broken leg that wrecked his career in October 1956. At the time he was being tipped for selection for the senior England team. That promotion would have seen him eclipse the legendary Duncan Edwards as the youngest ever England international.

Jeffrey appeared in 13 games during the 1956–57 season before that fateful Under-23 outing. He scored 15 goals in those games. He suffered his first leg break on international duty. When he attempted his comeback from injury he broke his other leg. Jeffrey emigrated to Australia to rebuild his life but returned to Belle Vue in

1963 to launch another attempt at a comeback. He had been out of the game seven years. Yet in his first season back became the Football League's leading marksman.

As a boy he made his spectacular start by scoring 34 goals in 71 games. As a man, fighting to prove a point, he scored 95 goals in 191 games. People who worked with him on a daily basis insist to this day that Jeffrey was a football genius, a really warm-hearted man and great fun to be with. We can only guess what he might have achieved in his career. What we know is that in the face of massive adversity he became a club icon.

Our Donny cult hero comes from a more modern era. It's a man who played for, skippered and managed the club. Ian Snodin was an exciting central midfielder. His competitive streak was immediately spotted by Donny boss Billy Bremner, who knew a thing or two about being combative. Ian's older brother Glyn was also at Doncaster in these days and top-flight scouts regularly visited Belle Vue to check on both Snodin brothers.

Running free in midfield Ian had a turn of pace that would take him away from virtually every opponent. He also had some dig in his tackling and a competitive streak that Bremner appreciated. It came as no surprise when young Snod was signed by Leeds in 1985 in a £200,000 deal. Manager Eddie Gray made him the Leeds captain when the new boy was just 22.

Snodin impressed at Elland Road and eventually moved to Everton, where he won a League title. But injuries began to hamper him. He enjoyed a longer career than Alick Jeffrey, but those of us who saw the young Snodin rampaging through midfield realized his lengthy stints at right-back for Everton were just a cameo of the real thing.

THE FAN'S VIEW

Syd Jackson: *"Alick Jeffrey deserves recognition as the greatest talent who saw his career wrecked by injury."*

EVERTON

 Dixie Dean

 Peter Reid

There's a wonderful moment in a modern play where a little lad, who's an Everton fan, keeps pestering his family with questions about "Dizzy" Dean.

The long-suffering relatives keep putting him right, explaining that the great man's name was Dixie, not Dizzy. Well, as every Evertonian really knows, the greatest goalscorer English football has ever seen was actually called William Ralph Dean. Apparently he wanted to be known as Bill but the football world called him Dixie.

He was at Everton from 1924 to 1938 and achieved a level of fame that made him the David Beckham of his day. He was a true superstar of English football.

Down the years Everton have prided themselves on having some wonderful, creative players who have helped them win trophies in style. The midfield axis of Kendall, Ball and Harvey springs to mind from the team that won the League title by a massive nine points in 1970. Those were the days when teams collected two points for a win so they were more than four victories clear of second-placed Leeds at the summit of the English game.

The likes of Alex Young, known as "The Golden Vision", played his part in Everton's early Sixties glory days, but nobody can match the feats of Dixie Dean. And that's not just a challenge that a succession of fine Evertonians have found daunting.

Dixie's achievement in scoring 60 goals in the 1927–28 season remains an all-time League record – an achievement that surely will never be surpassed. Predictably, with a goalscorer like that in their ranks, Everton were champions that season. Although Everton did endure relegation in 1930 they kept Dean and bounced back in spectacular style. They won the Second Division in 1931, followed by the League title again in 1932 and the FA Cup in 1933.

The other issue that modern fans don't appreciate is that in Dixie's day the battle between centre-forwards and centre-halves was something akin to gang warfare. Their physical confrontations bordered on GBH. Challenges that would merit FA disciplinary inquiries today were deemed part and parcel of the game. When it came to being the king of the penalty area, there was only one Dixie Dean, and a record of 377 goals in 431 appearances for Everton reflects his lethal touch. Dixie undoubtedly deserves acclaim as Everton's icon.

So we turn to Everton's cult hero. Many contenders come to mind. One is centre-forward Duncan Ferguson. The lanky Scot was much more than a hard man with a reputation for aggression and abrasiveness who was tagged Duncan Disorderly by a media keen to exploit some of his disciplinary problems. Big Dunc could play. Indeed, when he was ready to leave his first club, Dundee United, a posse of English bosses sought advice from a famous manager with impeccable contacts north of the border. Alex Ferguson, already at Manchester United in 1993, decided he did not need Duncan's services but supported the belief that the player would have a major impact in the Premier League.

Duncan initially opted to join Rangers and endured disciplinary problems there that led to his imprisonment for an on-field assault. His critics will highlight a career in which he was sent off nine times. His supporters will point out that he scored more goals than any other Scottish player in the Premier League.

To some Evertonians Dunc is a perfect cult hero. But can we place him ahead of Heavy Nev? I was covering Everton in the 1984–85 season when they achieved a memorable Double by lifting the League title and the European Cup Winners' Cup. Southall was surely the best goalie in Europe at that time.

He'd joined Everton for £150,000 from Bury in 1981 and blossomed into his role as the antithesis of a superstar. The former bin man never forgot his roots and never got carried away by the glory days.

And that Everton team, so skilfully assembled by Howard Kendall, had some superb elements. Defender Kevin Ratcliffe had pace to burn and remains the most successful captain in the club's history. In attack, Graeme Sharp was a skilful striker, initially with Adrian Heath and Andy Gray as his sidekicks, later with Gary Lineker. Sharpy is Everton's most prolific marksman since the Second World War.

And then there was the all-round midfield endeavour Peter Reid. Back in 1985 Howard Wilkinson paid a glowing tribute to Reid and his team-mates when he said: "They are a fine team, a real team. They're the champions with dirty knees." During their pursuit of Euro glory in 1985 Reid was at his inspirational best. The image of his sock turning pink then red with blood after being the victim of a high tackle against Bayern Munich in the semi-final remains vivid. Lesser players might have been forced out of the fray such was the depth of the cut.

Reidy, at his inspirational best, raced to the touchline, rammed the trainer's sponge down his bloodied shin, pulled up his sock and got back into the game with a snarl. He was majestic as Everton battered the Germans 3-1 in an epic second-leg triumph.

The events at the Heysel Stadium, and the subsequent five-year ban that prevented English clubs competing in Europe, destroyed Everton's hopes of building on the momentum they had displayed at home and abroad over the previous couple of seasons. Surely Kendall, Reid, Southall plus new boy Gary Lineker would have gone on to become champions of Europe?

And for the way he snapped, snarled and inspired the Blues to glory Peter Reid is our Everton cult hero.

THE FAN'S VIEW

David McMordie: *"The Howard Kendall team of 1985 didn't get the credit they deserved and my favourite cult hero was in that side. Peter Reid was my Everton hero for the way he played. He wasn't the most gifted player but he never stopped trying."*

EXETER CITY

(i) **Tony Kellow**   (h) **Adam Stansfield**

Tony Kellow began his working life as an electrician in Falmouth Docks. He turned out to be the man who put a 2,000 volt charge into Exeter City. Kellow, born in the Cornish village of Budock Water, might never have been a pro at all if he hadn't been spotted by Penzance AFC playing for the Docks team. They made him part of the side that won the Cornwall Senior Cup in 1973, but it was still another three years before Exeter offered him the chance to turn pro. From his first game – when he scored both goals in a 2-2 draw at Hartlepool – he was destined to be the club's great hero.

In all he scored 150 goals in 377 games, but there was so much more to why Kellow is so fondly remembered than just the statistics of his goals – even if they do put him top of the club's all-time scoring charts. He was a hugely colourful character who loved life and loved football, playing the game with a smile on his face that made the supporters beam back.

Steve Perryman, the Tottenham legend who became Exeter City's managing director, recalls: "He was a traditional No. 9, big and strong with a ferocious shot in his right foot. I only played against him once – for Spurs when he had helped Exeter into the sixth round of the FA Cup in 1981. We were told he was just a goalscorer, but I thought he was a terrific target man, with great movement and the ability to bring others into play. That was a great Spurs team, we went on to win the Cup, but he caused us all sorts of problems at White Hart Lane that day."

When we launched this book and asked fans to send in their nominations for their icons and cult heroes we discovered that every Exeter fan who contacted us shared the same name as their club icon – Kellow. Exeter's cult hero is a sad story. When the club was on its knees, bust and relegated back to the Conference, they signed a striker by the name of Adam Stansfield. He wasn't the greatest technically, but no player has ever run harder or tried more, and his effort won him instant recognition.

Born in nearby Tiverton, Stansfield had worked in a factory and played local football before getting the chance to join Yeovil then Hereford before signing for Exeter in 2006. His first season saw the club lose the promotion play-off final, but a year later they were back at Wembley to beat Cambridge and return to the Football League – following that up by scoring 10 goals as the club won automatic promotion next season. He scored seven more to help maintain League One status, but his campaign was tragically cut short by a mystery stomach illness that was later diagnosed as bowel cancer. He underwent surgery and even returned for pre-season training, but his condition deteriorated and he passed away on 10th August 2010.

The club retired his No. 9 shirt, but his name is still chanted at every game. As Perryman says: "He had a special affinity with the supporters, because they could recognize his effort. As a player he would run his legs off, and then run a bit more – it's what the fans themselves would do if they were ever lucky enough to wear the shirt of the club they love."

THE FAN'S VIEW
Ian Grove: *"It's got to be Tony Kellow."*
Richard Sturman: *"Our cult hero is Tony Kellow."*

FLEETWOOD TOWN

ⓘ Nathan Pond **ⓗ Jamie Vardy**

There was once a time when the nearest Fleetwood got to big time football was being at the end of the tramline to Blackpool.

But chairman Andy Pilley's dream, and investment, has come to spectacular fruition. Along the way Nathan Pond has emerged as an icon of the club. He played a sterling role in helping the club to make the big breakthrough in reaching the Football League in 2012.

Preston-born Pond has served Fleetwood with distinction for a decade, making more than 300 appearances and scoring 48 goals – an excellent return for a defender-cum-defensive midfielder.

Before the win over Mansfield in March 2012, chairman Pilley made a presentation to Pond in recognition of his 300th game. The deafening applause from his many followers in the Cod Army showed how highly the fans rated his efforts.

And that tribute was eclipsed at the end of the memorable 2011–12 campaign when Pond and his colleagues took a bow after winning promotion to the Football League.

Our Fleetwood cult hero is a man who enjoyed a brief but spectacular stay with the club.

Jamie Vardy may have enjoyed only one season at Fleetwood, but his precious goals have forever ensured him a place in the affections of the Cod Army. The former Halifax striker hit 31 Conference National goals in just 34 games to inspire Fleetwood to promotion to the Football League.

Vardy also scored three FA Cup goals in four outings, and one of those in a defeat at neighbours Blackpool. This helped to prompt the Seasiders to make a £700,000 January bid for the prolific striker.

Both Fleetwood's then manager Micky Mellon and chairman Pilley insisted Vardy must stay for at least the remainder of the season to aid the club's promotion bid. When promotion was won Fleetwood actually accepted a £1million deal for Vardy – a record for a non-League player. Vardy moved to Championship club Leicester City.

It's fair to say that Vardy proved an extremely profitable player for the Lancashire club in his sensational, but brief stay.

THE FAN'S VIEW

Chris Waistle: *"I nominate Jamie Vardy."*

FULHAM

(i) **Johnny Haynes**　　　　　　　　　(h) **Gordon Davies**

There are many clubs whose roots can be traced to the church. Fulham fit this identikit to perfection, having been formed originally as Fulham St Andrew's Church Sunday School FC in 1879. They won the West London League in its inaugural season of 1892–93 and became known as Fulham in 1888.

There have been times when Fulham have recruited some of the biggest names in football. They don't come much bigger than Bobby Moore, George Best, Rodney Marsh and Kevin Keegan. But that quartet performed mere cameo roles in the roller-coaster history of the West London club.

Just as Preston have Tom Finney and Bolton salute Nat Lofthouse, the late, great Johnny Haynes stands out as the Craven Cottage club's indisputable icon.

The statistic that became a millstone around his neck was that after the abolition of the maximum wage limit in 1962 Haynes became the first £100-a-week footballer, earning five times more than a player could earn before the restriction was lifted. Haynes was much more than a footnote in history to Fulham, England and the development of English football.

He wasn't an inside-forward in the old-fashioned style of fetcher and gatherer with creative touches and a few goals added into the mix. He was the archetypal midfield general. Nobody had mastered the art as well as the London-born player before he strutted his stuff and actually made his full international debut when aged just 19.

Haynes was a perfectionist who could deliver pinpoint passes to unlock the most ruthless, organized defence. Jimmy Greaves, the greatest marksman of the era and the beneficiary of Haynes' creative genius, explained: "John was a brilliant footballer. He completely dominated midfield. To this day I've never seen a better passer. I loved playing with him. He set up so many chances for me with through balls I could run onto.

"Haynes trusted his ability. He trusted his judgement. There was no one in his class as the passer of a ball."

That level of praise was echoed by the late Sir Bobby Robson who had the pleasure, and privilege, of playing alongside Haynes for club and country.

Sir Bobby said: "John was a truly great player. He was a master of passing – both long and short. He could keep possession but he had real penetration in his passing. He could play the ace in the whole pass. His selection of a pass was spot on and that's why he was a star."

Haynes made 594 League appearances for Fulham and scored 145 goals. Even his greatest admirers would admit he was a perfectionist and would tear a strip off team-mates who failed to meet his high standards. He could be seen hands on hips, delivering a sharp verbal telling off or shaking his head in dismay. It has to be stressed, though, he was even more critical of himself if he dropped a clanger.

Haynes explained: "I always voiced my opinions. I had responsibility thrust on me. But even when I wasn't captain I'd still say what I thought. I was involved in the game, very intense and got carried away in the playing of a game."

Jimmy Hill, a Fulham team-mate, explained: "Johnny could be a miserable so and so on the field. He didn't suffer fools. If one of his comrades was responsible for losing the ball he'd let them know he wasn't pleased. Even worse, if he was responsible he was twice as vile. He set higher standards for himself than anyone else."

The word genius is often used to describe Haynes. It is not misplaced. Greaves said: "He was the captain of England and he was the best. He expected the best from himself and everybody with him. If you did anything wrong he'd have his hands on his hips, he'd moan like hell. He wouldn't stop whingeing. But people who thought he was dour were wrong. He was good fun. He had everything going for him. He was one of the true greats."

Haynes epitomizes the ethos of Fulham. There has always been something off-beat and entertaining about the character of the old club. He explained: "In the Fifties we had a great forward line but dodgy defence. It was not unknown for us to score 100 goals in a season but let 100 in as well. You can't win promotion doing that but we did attract big crowds to Craven Cottage. The attendance figures were high."

Haynes died in October 2005, aged 71. After retiring from English football he had played in South Africa with old mates like Budgie Byrne and Bobby Keetch. On his return he surprised many of his friends by choosing to turn his back on his native London and moved to Scotland. He stayed north of the border until his passing.

If Haynes is our undisputed Fulham icon, the search for a cult hero is broader. Nobody can dispute the impact Alan Mullery had with the club at the beginning and end of his career. The duo are inextricably linked.

On the day of Haynes' death, Mullery paid tribute. "He was the only reason I went to Fulham as a young boy of 15 leaving school. He was my hero. The word great rolls off the tongue quite easily these days but he really was. He was the best passer of a ball I have ever seen – I don't know anyone who could pass a ball as accurately. Anyone who saw him will know what a great player he was."

Mullery had returned to Craven Cottage for a golden farewell alongside the likes of Bobby Moore. The former England team-mates were in the Fulham team that from the Second Division reached the 1975 FA Cup final only to lose to West Ham.

But our Fulham icon is a striker, and a prolific one at that. Gordon Davies came from Merthyr Tydfil and in two spells at Craven Cottage – of six years and five years respectively – established himself as the club's record marksman. He scored 159 League goals in 394 appearances.

Davies was lethal in the penalty area. He was sharp of thought and movement and while not the biggest, this power-packed player would pinch a yard on defenders and display his predatory skills.

THE FAN'S VIEW

Elsie Bodin: *"Johnny Haynes was not just a Fulham icon. He was one of the golden boys of English football. Sadly some people now forget that."*

GILLINGHAM

(i) **Bob Taylor**   (h) **Adrian Pennock**

Priestfield fans were hugely unimpressed by Bob Taylor when he arrived from Brentford in 1998. He was as reviled as much as pin-up boy Adrian Pennock was loved. His Gills critics branded him "Fat" Bob Taylor and questioned his commitment and attitude.

But, incredibly, within just a matter of months, Priestfield saw a dramatic change of fortune – and the much-travelled striker became "Super" Bob Taylor.

His five-goal blast at Burnley guaranteed Taylor iconic status and his haul of 33 League goals in 61 games totally won over the Gillingham faithful. His admirers still drool over his hat-tricks against Wrexham and Bristol City. But Gills fans were devastated when the best form of his career was ended by a £1.5million move to Manchester City.

It is worth noting that in that purple patch at Priestfield, Taylor plundered 39 goals from only 67 starts. But Gillingham probably did some astute business because when Taylor returned later to Priestfield on loan the old magic was gone. He failed to find the net in any of his 11 games in his second spell.

We had several nominations for Gills' cult hero, including that pocket warrior Andy Hessenthaler who offered distinguished service as a player and manager. He might have been an obvious choice but we've opted instead for Adrian Pennock.

Pennock was hugely popular with Gills fans during his stay with the Kent club between 1996 and 2003, skippering them to Wembley glory over Wigan in 2000. The centre-back's rapport with supporters was as much down to his cheeky sense of humour and penchant for practical jokes as much as his skill as a footballer: nicknamed the "Football Genius' by admirers with a shared sense of humour, Pennock was such an idol that he even had his own fan club.

Signed for Gillingham by his former Bournemouth boss Tony Pulis for £30,000, he began by scoring on his home League debut and went on to make more than 200 appearances.

But only one more of his total of four goals came in the League. And after later sticking one in his own net, the Gills terrace chant became "Own goals! You only score own goals!" But the banter was always met with a smile.

Not so, however, when his Gills career was finished by injury and he angrily claimed that controversial owner Paul Scally had reneged on the promise of a testimonial.

HARTLEPOOL UNITED

(i) Ritchie Humphreys   **(h) Ken Johnson**

Given that Brian Clough launched his managerial career at Hartlepool in 1965 it's some achievement for Ritchie Humphreys to be named as the club's greatest iconic figure.

But while Clough and his managerial sidekick Peter Taylor moved to Derby County after less than three years at Victoria Park, Humphreys clocked up 11 years with the club.

Ritchie, a burly, blond striker in his youth, began his professional life at Premier League Sheffield Wednesday before dropping back to a midfield role and was signed by Chris Turner for Hartlepool in 2001. The key to his elevated status among the Hartlepool faithful has been his consistency and durability.

In 2008, Humphreys was not only voted club Player of the Year, but also became Hartlepool United's Player of the Century. It was in 1908 that the club had become a professional outfit and joined the North Eastern League.

In February 2011, Humphreys played his 473rd game to break the club appearance record previously held for over half a century by Watty Moore. But his proudest moment came in 2011 when he walked on to Victoria Park for a richly deserved testimonial against Sunderland with daughter Eliza in his arms. He was saluted by fans who have seen their club struggle down the years and got used to the nomadic nature of virtually every player at this level.

In 2012 Ritchie made his 500th appearance in a 2-0 win over Rochdale – a tremendous achievement given the regular comings and goings during his time at the club. Still playing for Hartlepool in 2013, utility man Ritchie is a member of the PFA management committee and working towards his UEFA coaching badges. When it comes to honouring contracts and loyalty few players can set a better example, so Ritchie is our Hartlepool United icon.

As for cult hero, we're still going to ignore Old Big 'Ead and nominate Ken Johnson.

In the Fifties and early Sixties Johnson was Mr Hartlepools (that's the correct spelling before the name of the club was changed). Born in the town, Johnson joined United from Seaton Holy Trinity in 1949, spending his entire professional career with his local club.

He made his Pools debut on New Year's Eve 1949 against Bradford City and went on to play 413 matches for the club – his final appearance coming against

Newport County on 6th April 1964.

Only three players have made more appearances than Johnson, and the accomplished inside-forward is the club's all-time top scorer with 106 goals in all competitions. He was a key player when Pools went on a long, unbeaten run during the 1954–55 season. They were unbeaten for 20 games in League and Cup. This run included playing local rivals Darlington five times in three weeks. United won three of those games and drew the other two.

Johnson is fondly remembered for scoring against Manchester United's Busby Babes side in 1957 when Pools lost a thriller 4-3 in front of their record crowd of 17,426. It was a game that Old Trafford boss Matt Busby described as "the most exciting match I've ever watched."

In 1956 Johnson played for the Football League Third Division North select team for the match against Division Three South, along with his team-mates George Luke and Watty Moore. He later ran a local fish and chip shop; he died in December 2011, aged 80.

HUDDERSFIELD TOWN

 Denis Law

 Frank Worthington

Huddersfield Town have a proud claim to football history. In 1926 they became the first club to win three consecutive League titles. This was a remarkable achievement for a club that was established just 18 years earlier.

Perhaps the Twenties, under Herbert Chapman's astute management, were the headiest days so far in Town's history. But there have been plenty of moments along the way to create an abundance of icons and cult heroes.

It's astonishing to think that the West Yorkshire town of Huddersfield, famed through the Victorian era for its woollen mills, was the first superpower in English football. That fact was largely down to one man – Herbert Chapman. Chapman had overturned a life ban linked to financial irregularities at the defunct Leeds City and hoped to rebuild his career at Leeds Road. He did so in some style, and some of the ideas he came up with and persuaded the powers-that-be to introduce were truly imaginative. Many of them are now fundamental parts of the English game.

After joining the Town coaching staff in February 1921 he initiated changes that involved tactics, scouting the way opponents played and setting up a scouting network to aid the recruitment of new players. Within a month he was in charge as manager-secretary, and the revolution that would make Huddersfield the most powerful force in the English game was instigated.

He led Huddersfield to two League titles and an FA Cup triumph before accepting an offer to transform a club that had been struggling in the lower reaches of the old First Division – Arsenal. He was to inspire them to become champions of England and FA Cup winners, too.

His status as a football visionary is justified by a quick review of his ideas – some of which came into fruition after his days at Huddersfield but reflect the mettle of the man who made Town great. In no particular order he was one of the first managers to take control of football affairs rather than allowing the directors to select the team. He introduced physiotherapists and masseurs to improve players' fitness levels and recovery. He travelled abroad and, unlike his contemporaries, became a student of foreign football. In fact, 20 years before the launch of the European Cup he predicted a European competition involving the best club sides.

Chapman was one of the first managers to sign black players and he also attempted to recruit continental players to England. After attending a night game in Belgium in 1930 he strongly advocated the introduction of floodlights to England.

You can add to this list the recommendation that white balls be introduced plus numbers on players' shirts and that, from 1930, when Huddersfield met Arsenal in the FA Cup final, the players involved marched out together.

Chapman's status in those early days cannot be underestimated, even though he is widely acknowledged to have produced even more sterling work with Arsenal right up to his death from pneumonia in 1934 when he was just 55. Three decades later another managerial great arrived at Leeds Road. Again, this man's finest work was delivered at his next job, but there can be no doubting the impact Bill Shankly had at Leeds Road.

Shanks had seven years' managerial experience at Carlisle and Workington before pitching up as his old friend Andy Beattie's reserve team coach at Huddersfield. After a relegation and failure to rebuild the club, Beattie resigned and Shanks was appointed in November 1956. He'd already worked with a crop of outstanding young players and immediately started promoting them into the first team. None of them was more precociously gifted than our Huddersfield Town icon, Denis Law. The 16-year-old from Aberdeen was handed his first-team debut on Christmas Eve 1956. Thus began the career of a player who just eight years later would be acclaimed as European Footballer of the Year. And he's a man still acknowledged by Manchester United manager Sir Alex Ferguson as his favourite player of all time.

Law played football like a whirling dervish. He was irrepressible. Athletic, balletic and brave, he could dispatch the most spectacular headers and volleys. And for such a frail, weedy looking lad he would take on all-comers. No opponent was too big for the Lawman.

That's why he was a firm fans' favourite wherever he played. Supporters knew they had at least one player out on the field who would give his all fighting for the cause and fighting opponents who got out of hand. In more recent times Denis has explained: "If somebody kicks you and you don't do anything then they'll kick you again. No matter how big or dirty they were I'd kick them back. But I was always a retaliator. I was not an instigator."

Many Town fans thought young Law would follow Shanks to Anfield after the manager had tired of Huddersfield, selling their most promising youngsters. The transfer was discussed but never came to fruition for a very basic, commercial reason. Law explained: "Shanks was like a father to me at Huddersfield after I'd come down from Aberdeen as a boy. When he left for Liverpool everyone felt I'd follow Shanks. The problem was that Liverpool were then in the Second Division and didn't have the money to pay the fee. Instead I was eventually sold to Manchester City."

When he contributed the foreword to Denis Law's book *My Life in Football* (published by Simon and Schuster) Sir Alex Ferguson wrote: "Anyone who has the slightest doubt about his (Law's) stature in the game might care to heed the words of no less eminent a judge than Pelé, who once said that the only British player who could possibly get into the Brazil team was Denis Law."

To this day it's rare to hear any Huddersfield fans dispute the Lawman's nomination as their club's football icon. Several players can lay claim to the status of Town's cult hero, but we'll turn the clock forward a decade from Law's days at Leeds Road and salute another eyecatching, crowd-pleasing striker. Our Huddersfield cult hero is the Elvis impersonator and crowd pleaser extraordinaire, Frank Worthington.

Frank, who played for 11 English League clubs in his nomadic career, thrilled fans wherever he journeyed. In fact, during the research for this book he received more nominations than any other player to be acknowledged as a cult hero. He wins the Huddersfield nomination but supporters from Birmingham, Leicester City and Bolton also hailed him as their cult hero.

Worthy might even have joined Shankly at Liverpool. Unfortunately his off-field lifestyle ensured he failed the Liverpool medical. It was pointed out that if he cleaned up his act the Anfield club, on the brink of true European greatness, might return to sign him. Frank decided to enjoy life to the full. He became an England international, enjoyed his fame and took to the road with an apparent view that every two years he'd move on.

But the Yorkshireman was found and developed by Huddersfield and he remains a cult hero to this day.

THE FAN'S VIEW

Tom Dolan: *"We've had some half decent players and wonderful characters down the years but Frank Worthy stands out as the biggest character. For a Yorkshireman dead flash but he delivered too."*

HULL CITY

 **Raich Carter**    **Ken Wagstaff**

There is little dispute about the most gifted player to ever represent Hull City. That man was Raich Carter, who cost just £6,000 and turned out for the Tigers in his dotage. He was 34 years old when he arrived from Derby County. Within a month the Hull manager had left and Carter took on the task of being City's player-manager. He guided the club to the Third Division North title and displayed a great knowledge of the game and organizing his team.

In that sense Carter was ahead of his time. He had a ferocious shot and a clear vision of players and setting up systems of play. He was the manager who recruited Don Revie for City and later had a masterplan when he was the manager of Leeds to utilize the unique talent of John Charles.

Horatio Stratton Carter's football talent was as unique as his name. He was an inside-forward – now he'd be seen as an attacking midfielder – who was blessed with an uncanny awareness of openings and team-mates on the field. Little wonder that his England colleagues, such as Stan Mortensen and Tommy Lawton, raved about his ability on the ball and vision to spot openings.

Carter captained Sunderland to the Football League title in 1936, at that time the youngest man ever to have captained a First Division title-winning side. He followed that up with victory in the FA Cup final a year later, scoring the second Sunderland goal in a 3-1 win over Preston North End.

The Second World War interrupted his career, but afterwards he won another Cup winners' medal with Derby in 1946, joining an exclusive band of players to win Cup winners' medals both before and after the war.

Tommy Lawton, England's legendary centre-forward of the era, recalled: "Raich was the master of the pass which sneaks its way through the seemingly impregnable defence, but Raich was also an opportunist of the highest order. Yes, I know everyone knew all about his tremendous shot, but Raich had something else. He could size up a chance in a flash, and he would be on it before anyone could move. For instance, the centre-forward has only to leap for a ball and nod it downwards and backwards, and Raich would be tearing in to ram the ball into the net."

Stan Mortensen, another England attacking star, agreed: "Raich was a double-purpose inside-forward. He was clever and brainy enough to make openings for other players, and would be worth his place in any side for that alone. He also had the knack of cutting through for goals himself, and from the edge of the penalty area could hit a ball as hard as most.

"If you observed him closely on the field, you'd see that he was blessed with a pair of strong legs. Trainers usually say first: 'Let's look at the thighs'. Carter had it there, and his deep knowledge of the game enabled him to skip clear of a lot of trouble.

"Raich was a double-purpose inside-forward. He is clever and brainy enough to make openings for other players, and would be worth his place in any side for that alone. He also had the knack of cutting through for goals himself, and from the edge of the penalty area can hit a ball as hard as most."

Those who saw him, played with him or against him, insist Raich Carter must be acknowledged as one of the true greats of English football. He thoroughly deserves the honour of being our Hull City icon.

From the modern era a number of players can lay claim to being Hull's cult hero. Three words that don't sum up Dean Windass are shy, quiet and retiring. He was loud, proud and brash. And what a job he did by scoring the only goal of the promotion play-off triumph that took City into the Premier League for the first time in their history in 2008! Windass also scored his last Premier League goal at the age of 39, Hull's oldest-ever scorer.

There were few rougher, tougher centre-forwards in Hull colours than Billy Whitehurst. He was a bricklayer-turned-footballer and he sweated buckets as a player. He wasn't the most skilful target man and a centre-half who opposed Big Billy, John Fashanu and Mick Hardord claimed that when it came to hard opponents nobody beat Whitehurst.

I remember being invited to interview Billy at his home and wondered what I might walk into. Let's say Billy had a reputation for not suffering fools gladly and his tough-guy status was legendary. But he was charm personified, brewing pots of tea and chatting away in relaxed fashion.

But we're looking beyond Windass, Whitehurst and Nicky Barmby – a truly class act so savagely treated by Hull when they terminated his contract – to name our cult hero. That title falls to goalscoring legend of the Sixties, Ken Wagstaff.

Coincidentally, Raich Carter played a major part in Wagstaff's career. After leaving Hull, Carter discovered Wagstaff, spotted his genius for scoring goals, and later recommended him to the City board as a worthy recruit. In November 1964 Hull paid a then club record £40,000 for Wagstaff. Wagstaff explained: "Raich looked after me all my life and it was him that set it all up. I wasn't sure where Hull was. Raich made a huge impression on me. I will always remember something he did with me when I was 17. He said I wasn't training one day and told me to come with him. He took me to a special school and there were kids in wheelchairs with one leg or missing an arm. He said 'Take a good look at them because to be born healthy is the greatest gift you'll ever have. To have the gift you've got, never waste it.' That's stayed with me all my life."

Wagstaff played for Hull City between 1964 and 1975, scoring 197 goals.

THE FAN'S VIEW

Andy Bond: *"I loved watching Billy Whitehurst hammering opponents. They were scared of him."*

IPSWICH TOWN

 Sir Bobby Robson

 **Kevin Beattie**

Down the years there have been some outstanding players in fine Ipswich Town teams. Alf Ramsey had not been knighted when he led the Suffolk club to the League title in 1962, but it was another footballing knight, Bobby Robson, who inspired success for the Portman Road club that saw them win the affections of football fans across Europe.

Robson was Ipswich manager from 1969 to 1982. During that period the Tractor Boys won the FA Cup, UEFA Cup and finished runners-up in the First Division, then the top flight of the English game, before Robson became England manager.

Under Robson's inspired tutelage Ipswich won regularly and won with style. They also celebrated in style with parties around the club to mark successes at home and abroad, becoming the subject of legend.

Ipswich had a host of outstanding players during this spell. There was Mick Mills, the epitome of loyalty and football intelligence as Town skipper. Down the years they had a posse of powerful, reliable centre-backs, including tough Irishman Allan Hunter. He spent 11 years at Portman Road and won 53 Northern Ireland caps.

Later, Russell Osman and Terry Butcher formed a partnership that was the foundation of the real glory years. And Butcher, who is hailed as a legend by many Ipswich fans, has no hesitation in supporting the clear nomination of Ipswich's cult hero.

Butcher said: "When I was a schoolboy, I always wanted to watch a young rising star called Thomas Kevin Beattie, who played in my position of centre-half at Ipswich Town. Kevin made his debut for the Blues four years before I joined the club, but he became my hero because of his power, pace and passion for the game. He was just an incredible powerhouse of a player – he could out-jump, out-fight and out-muscle any opponent, and his pace was frightening for such a strongly built defender. When Bobby Robson eventually signed me, I couldn't believe I would actually have the 'Beat' as my team-mate. He was everything I expected my hero to be – courteous, caring, modest and real fun to be with. It is a travesty that he only won nine caps for England, as he was simply the best player I have ever seen."

LEEDS UNITED

 Billy Bremner

 **Gordon Strachan**

Leeds United were born out of a financial scandal at Leeds City in 1919. City had been accused of making illegal payments to players and closed down. There was then a proposal for the new club to amalgamate with neighbours Huddersfield Town, but that plan didn't come to fruition.

In the Sixties, if one player could epitomize a team and all they stood for it was Leeds United skipper Billy Bremner. The tenacious, flame-haired midfielder was manager Don Revie's right-hand man out on the field. Opposition fans hated him for his belligerence. Opposing players accepted he was fierce but truly gifted. His Leeds colleagues adored him and recognized his inspirational qualities. He was once succinctly described as "ten stones of barbed wire". But that was for Bremner the battling footballer. There was another side to King Billy that fans never saw. He was a witty, funny guy who loved cracking a joke and playing a practical joke. On one infamous Leeds sortie into Europe an old colleague and friend of mine was the victim of a typical Bremner prank.

The senior journo had false teeth, which he always removed for safety's sake when sleeping. So as he prepared to sleep en route to Germany he removed his dentures. Like a street urchin from Oliver Twist, little Billy struck. The dentures were stealthily removed, the sports reporter woke to eat his breakfast but couldn't find his teeth. To the mirth of the Leeds party – players and press – the victim was watched trying to gum his meal, bewildered by the identity of the thief. Bremner and the journalist were great mates, and Billy accepted that revenge would be exacted. But there was a fun side to him beyond what fans saw on the pitch.

Eddie Gray, a fellow Scot and Leeds team-mate, explained: "Billy was fiercely competitive but he was also a funny man. He would make you laugh with his wit and banter. He also let you know if you were letting the side down."

Mick Bates, another colleague, said: "Billy firmly believed he was the best midfielder in the world. It turned out he probably was."

In some respects it's easy for Leeds personnel to hail their hero. But Sir Alex Ferguson, manager of Manchester United, can deliver a totally objective view. Fergie said: "Billy had a temper but he also had immense ability. Billy had a great heart, great enthusiasm and great fighting spirit. He also had great feet, great perception of passing and an ability to score match-winning goals. What a player."

Bremner just beats John Charles, their superstar of the Fifties, to be our Leeds icon.

The Welshman, who was known as the Gentle Giant, was an astonishing all-round talent. As Jack Charlton, his team-mate at Elland Road, observed: "If I picked the best team in the world John Charles would be in at centre-half and centre-forward. He was that good. I can remember days at Leeds in the Fifties when he was 90 per cent of our side."

During their roller-coaster history two signings stand out as the playing inspirations behind Leeds United's revival. Both were diminutive Scottish midfielders. Both had a point to prove having been written off at their previous clubs. Both delivered sustained periods of excellence that saw Leeds win promotion and establish itself as a major football power.

The duo were Bobby Collins, who was a critical part of the team Revie built at Elland Road in the early Sixties, and Gordon Strachan, king of the team Howard Wilkinson put together that won promotion and two years later were League champions.

Both players were midget gems, great team players who skippered Leeds to glory. Both were acclaimed as Footballers of the Year – Collins in 1965 and Strachan in 1991.

Wilkinson, who signed Strachan for £300,000 from Manchester United, said: "I've worked with some truly influential players but never one to match the part Gordon played in my career and the development of Leeds United. After being cast off by Manchester United there were times when he carried our team on his shoulders and made sure we fulfilled our ambitions."

Players like David Batty, Gary Speed, Johnny Giles and Vinnie Jones all earned nominations as United's cult hero. But for his overall impact and role in making Leeds the last champions of a 92-club Football League, Gordon Strachan is our Leeds cult hero.

THE FAN'S VIEW

Colin Patterson: "There were a few heroes in our well-drilled, hard team of the Sixties and Seventies. Jones, Hunter, Madeley and we also had one little beast in Billy Bremner."

LEICESTER CITY

 Steve Walsh    **Alan Birchenall**

You could describe Steve Walsh in one word: "Warrior". Actually, maybe that should be "Gladiator", because when it came to courage and commitment to the cause nobody has ever offered more to Leicester City.

There have been plenty more skilful players to wear the Leicester shirt down the years and some, like Gordon Banks, could lay claim to stellar achievements to put them top of the list of the club's greatest players. But poll the fans and it is Walsh who is the unquestioned choice to be their icon.

He spent 14 years in all at Filbert Street, first as a centre-half of rugged determination, and later as a centre-forward with the knack of scoring or making crucial goals. He's returned since as assistant manager to Nigel Pearson, and nobody could be better qualified to set standards of hard work and total determination to succeed.

Born in Preston, he started out his career at Wigan and played a crucial role in the club's first steps after winning a place in the Football League. And when Latics manager Brian Hamilton was offered the chance to become manager at Leicester in 1986 it was hardly surprising that he immediately paid £100,000 to bring with him the man he felt could be a cornerstone of his new team.

It proved sound judgement. While Walsh's disciplinary record was a nightmare – he shares, at 13, the record number of red cards in the Football League – his problems with refs came only from his fierce desire and full-blooded tackling. As Leicester fans always remember, when a perceived injustice had been done by an opponent or a battle had to be won, Walsh was their hero. That's a vital ingredient of why he's such an iconic figure to them.

While off the field he was mild-mannered and unfailingly polite, on it he underwent a Jekyll and Hyde transformation that inspired his own team and struck fear into opponents in equal measure.

Made club captain by Brian Little in 1992, he scored 15 goals that season, including one in the Division One play-off final against Swindon. A year later, after fighting back from a knee ligament operation, he led the way at Wembley again, this time getting two against Derby as the Foxes won promotion to the Premier League.

Because of injury he shared little of that campaign, as the club failed to survive in the top flight – but when Martin O'Neill took over, Walsh was the man whom he identified as his leader. Restored to the captaincy, he was the rock on which the club's most successful era was then based.

A play-off victory in 1996 was followed by the crowning glory of lifting a major trophy, as Leicester won the League Cup in 1997, beginning a UEFA Cup adventure including a memorable tie against Atletico Madrid. There was another trip to Wembley to follow for the 1999 League Cup final. In all, Walsh played more than 400 competitive games for Leicester, 369 in the League. He's our Foxes icon.

Leicester are one of many clubs where the mercurial Frank Worthington gets votes to be considered as their cult hero. Frank strutted his stuff at Filbert Street in a team of style – on and off the field. Remarkably, he was nominated by fans from four of his 11 clubs as their cult hero.

We've already mentioned the great Gordon Banks at Chesterfield, and Leicester fans will appreciate that it was at their club that the man acknowledged as the best goalie in the world during the Sixties honed his skills. Banks was, of course, a vital part of the England squad that won the World Cup in 1966. Many observers, including England players of the time, believe the squad that went to Mexico four years later was even better. Banks was still England's number one. But it was the impact of his absence – he was stricken by a stomach bug – that saw Peter Bonetti named for the quarter-final tie against West Germany, a game England were to lose 3-2. The England defence was not at its best that day. Perhaps having England's undisputed top goalie might have transformed that?

The pedigree of Leicester goalies saw Banks make way for Peter Shilton, who also went on to become a record-breaking England international. But the celebrated duo do not win the status of being Leicester's cult hero.

The man who does played in the same team as Worthington and was a crowd pleaser, too. Alan Birchenall arrived from Crystal Palace for £80,000 in 1971, as one of three players bought by manager Jimmy Bloomfield to bring new dash and adventure to his team. Jon Sammels and Keith Weller were the others, and they set the adventurous tone that helped attract Worthington to be the biggest star of the strolling band soon after.

Birch, a centre-forward with a left-foot shot that could be ferocious, was popular for his personality and sheer vivacity. He loved playing the game, he loved scoring goals – but most of all he loved the club he'd joined – so much so that more than 40 years later he is still the match day announcer and figurehead for the club's community efforts. In fact he played less than a third of the 499 League games in his career for City, and yet feels as deeply for the club as the supporters do for him.

Birch *is* Leicester City.

THE FAN'S VIEW

Liam Finn: *"The Leicester City icon has to be Steve Walsh."*

Roger Jay: *"I'm a Leicester fan and my nomination for cult hero is Frank Worthington."*

LEYTON ORIENT

(i) Peter Kitchen **(h) John Chiedozie**

Peter Kitchen remains a legendary figure among Orient fans and it's easy to understand why. He was 25 when he arrived at Brisbane Road in a £40,000 transfer from Doncaster Rovers in the summer of 1977. His talent had already been spotted by Bobby Robson, who invited him for a trial at Ipswich but did not complete a deal. Kitchen was a Yorkshireman born and bred, so heading to the East End of London was something of a challenge. But he got off to a flier and never looked back.

Kitchen had been discovered by a certain Lawrie McMenemy, who was learning his managerial trade at Doncaster Rovers, and he scored after just two minutes of his professional debut with Doncaster. He scored on his debut for Orient, too.

Kitchen was a small, sharp player who revelled in playing off a conventional target man. At Doncaster he'd played off the giant Brendan O'Callaghan, who went on to play in the top flight for Stoke City, and the hard-working Mike Elwiss. Give Kitchen a sniff of goal and he would pounce, and he was never overawed by taking on more famous opponents.

He earned iconic status in London E10 by his exploits in Orient's charge to the FA Cup semi-finals in his first season with the club. These were pre-Premier League days and the O's were playing in the old Second Division, the second level of League football. They were managed by Jimmy Bloomfield, who had proved such a shrewd manager of attacking talent throughout his career. His work at Leicester in assembling the likes of Frank Worthington, Len Glover and Keith Weller was particularly accomplished. Just as at Filbert Street he had encouraged some maverick players to express themselves, so at Orient he spotted Kitchen's goalscoring instincts and harnessed them within a high-tempo team.

On their way to the FA Cup semis Kitchen scored seven goals – finding the net in the third, fourth, fifth and sixth rounds before Arsenal beat them 3-0 in the semi-final.

In that spectacular Cup run Orient beat Norwich, Blackburn, Chelsea and Middlesbrough. And it is with particular joy that Orient fans remember Kitchen's two individual goals in a fifth-round replay at Stamford Bridge as Orient won 2-1. He tormented Chelsea's giant defender Micky Droy in that game. Kitchen ended the season with 21 goals before he left for Fulham for £150,000. His move to Craven Cottage never really worked out though, and Kitchen returned to Orient via Fulham, Cardiff and Happy Valley, Hong Kong, for another couple of seasons.

After his return in 1982 Peter scored 21 times in 49 games. This was impressive form but, in truth, it was those Cup heroics that made him an icon. One of his team-mates from that Cup run merits consideration as our Orient cult hero. Tutored by manager Bloomfield to display his calm, cultured authority, Glenn Roeder was a wonderful talent. Roeder made 115 appearances for Orient, his first club, between 1973 and 1978, and achieved cult status. His rangy build defied a player of outstanding skill and when he broke forward from his position of central defender he did it so well and with such elegance. He was a key member of the Orient team that reached that FA Cup semi-final in 1978 before moving to QPR where he was captain in the 1982 FA Cup final at Wembley against Spurs, missing the replay only because he had been suspended.

But Roeder is eclipsed as our cult hero by a man whose £600,000 transfer caused massive, divisive issues within the club. John Chiedozie was born in Owerri, Nigeria, but grew up in London and joined Orient as an apprentice in 1977. He was a flying winger with pace to burn and he made 145 appearances for the club and scored 20 goals. On his good days he was unplayable and in those early days of his career Chiedozie wasn't troubled by the injury problems that effectively halted his progress.

But manager Bloomfield realized Chiedozie possessed a special talent and he wanted to harness it within his side. Unfortunately, the board saw things differently and sanctioned his sale. That transfer forced Bloomfield out of Brisbane Road.

Chiedozie remains Orient's most capped player. He is our O's cult hero.

THE FAN'S VIEW

Steve Lewis: *"I've no hesitation in naming Peter Kitchen as our idol. He's our top man."*

LIVERPOOL

ⓘ Kenny Dalglish   ⓗ Bill Shankly and Bob Paisley

Liverpool's proud status of being five-time winners of the European Cup ensures they have so many great players to choose from when they assess their idols and cult figures. From the great Billy Liddell, a one-club man who played for the Reds from 1938 to 1961, to current skipper Steven Gerrard, there has been an awesome array of star names parading their skills for Liverpool.

When you assess Anfield icons it's also impossible to overlook the merits of managers like Bill Shankly and Bob Paisley. Both played critical roles in building Liverpool into the most successful club in English football. They may have been overtaken by Manchester United in terms of League titles, but their European Cup and Champions League triumphs still elevate them to a higher plane.

No Liverpool fan will underestimate the role Shankly played in building the modern Liverpool, just as a succession of Liverpool players will never underestimate the role Paisley played as Shankly's assistant and eventual successor. Indeed, it was under Paisley that the Liverpool winning machine cranked up a notch and hit the real heady heights.

Paisley was a canny fox. He couldn't match Shanks' eloquence or popularity as the people's champion, but he possessed different virtues that created a dynamic that inspired players and laid down a blueprint for greatness. As the judge of a footballer Paisley was incisive and invariably correct – as when he nominated Kenny Dalglish as the greatest player to wear the Liverpool shirt.

Of course you didn't need to be a football genius – which Paisley undoubtedly was – to hail Dalglish as Liverpool's best. In 2006 Liverpool fans responded to a poll asking for their all-time hero: Kenneth Mathieson Dalglish was the overwhelming winner.

Many critics who were not of Anfield red persuasion would have agreed that Dalglish was the finest player of his generation. Paisley was unequivocal. The wisest man I ever met in football opined: "Of all the players I have played alongside, managed and coached in more than four decades, he is the most talented."

There was a huge mutual admiration between Paisley, the manager who recruited Dalglish from Celtic for £440,000 in the summer of 1977, and the Glaswegian who went on to become Anfield manager. Indeed, one of King Kenny's first requests on agreeing to succeed Joe Fagan as manager in 1985 was to ensure that Paisley would return on a regular basis as the club's managerial advisor. Far from seeing the old boy as an unwelcome shadow on his personal horizon, Dalglish sought out the guidance and expertise of his previous boss. That initiative speaks volumes for the trust and understanding of both parties.

I was a young reporter when I was first deputed to go to Anfield in pursuit of Liverpool stories. I had been warned by a senior colleague. "Introduce yourself to Shanks but don't ask him for an interview. If you do he'll say he's too busy. But always go and say hello to him and jump at the chance of a cup of tea in his office." The advice was impeccable. At our first meeting, after my introduction, the great man growled: "You can't turn up and expect to see me, son. I'm a busy man." But the next time, or maybe the one after that, Shanks got off the coach returning the squad to Anfield from training and declared: "Come on, son, let's go and have a cup of tea in my office." I was elated.

Shanks is not the only manager who can be deemed to have built a modern football club. His great friend Sir Matt Busby did the same at Manchester United, while Don Revie created a European superpower at Leeds, at a club which had never seen any real success in their history. But when Shankly arrived at Liverpool he walked into a club in the Second Division doldrums. He didn't just inspire a revival and return to the big time, he was a visionary who identified what his football club could mean to the people of Liverpool. Shanks identified with the people who supported his club. They responded to him and bought into his vision.

Without Shankly, the foundations would not have been laid that made Liverpool in the late Seventies and early Eighties the most successful club in European football. Yet it was under Paisley that Liverpool refined their style and fulfilled Shankly's dreams about his Red Army conquering the world – Shankly produced moments of inspirational rhetoric and Paisley still got his message across in his own inimitable way. They worked together for 14 years from Shanks' arrival in 1960. They were a formidable partnership.

I was grateful that as a young reporter Bob decided to take me into his inner sanctum and offer his insight into football. In his office, on the wall behind his desk, he had a clock that went in an anti-clockwise direction with all the figures in reverse. So the 3 was where you'd expect to see the 9. I had to ask Bob why he had a clock that went backwards. "Because when a player comes in asking why he's not in the team any more I point out that there's one thing he can't do and that's turn back the clock." His ability to spot when a player was past his best was uncanny.

A simple lesson Paisley understood 40 years ago still proves to be beyond the likes of Roman Abramovich, Chelsea's billionaire owner. He recognized that while the clock couldn't be turned backwards you couldn't draw a line in the sand and write off everyone over 30 years old. Some players trained on in their thirties.

Others didn't. But there was no way he'd dismiss Ian Callaghan from Anfield simply because the midfield dynamo had turned 30. History proved him right.

At his funeral I explained to Bob's dear wife Jessie my gratitude for the lessons I'd learned at her husband's feet. Jessie immediately replied: "That's nice, David, but did you really understand what he was saying to you?" In December 2012 the League Managers Association staged a dinner in honour of the three most successful English managers – Sir Alf Ramsey, Brian Clough and Bob Paisley. They showed video footage of the trio and old interviews before inviting ex-players on stage to discuss their old gaffers. Graeme Souness and Phil Neal went up to debate the merits of their Anfield boss, but when Souness was asked whether Paisley was the greatest English manager he choked on his words. Souness, one of the finest and hardest players to wear the red shirt, had been moved to tears. He asked for a moment to compose himself, then explained: "I've not seen that footage for so many years and seeing it now really brings home to me what Bob meant to us all. We were so very different and yet got on so well. He made me captain of Liverpool and helped me achieve so much. I owe him so much."

So for all their glory years Liverpool are one of the clubs with an undisputed iconic player in the great Kenny Dalglish. But when it comes to naming their cult hero perhaps we should allow them two: Shankly and Paisley. They were different, and maybe Bob put his finger on one key difference when he said: "Bill was a softie at heart." The fact was that when it came to making the ruthless, big personnel calls Paisley was probably better than Shankly.

THE FAN'S VIEW

Faith Fulcher: *"Bill Shankly taught Liverpool what football was all about. He was a fantastic man-manager and could get any player to play for him. He was also great with us the supporters, and having met him several times I can certainly say that he took notice of what you had to say."*

MANCHESTER CITY

 Colin Bell    Mike Summerbee

No supporters have lived on an emotional roller-coaster to match Manchester City's. In fact, City fans know better than to expect a sea of tranquillity to engulf their club. After all, City remain the only club to be champions of England one season only to endure the embarrassment of relegation the next. That's life with the Blues.

When we launched this book we asked *Sunday Mirror* readers and members of the Football Supporters' Federation to send in their views on their club's icon and cult heroes. No group of fans responded more than Manchester City's.

It's impossible to escape the fact that two players dominate the nominations as their greatest ever player. Colin Bell, from the great team of the Sixties that won trophies at home and abroad, and Peter Doherty, who played for City in the Thirties when, with the club's penchant for the unpredictable, they went from being League champions to being relegated in successive seasons. The passage of time isn't kind to pre-war stars like Doherty. The lack of television footage handicaps any real analysis of their prowess. However, the personal testimony of their contemporaries – both players and fans – underlines the impact Doherty had on the game.

Danny Blanchflower, a fellow Northern Ireland international and one of the most eloquent players of his generation, said: "They called him Peter the Great. It should have been Peter the Greatest." Joe Mercer, who was to be the architect of the City revival of the Sixties, recalled his playing days with Everton when he faced Doherty. Mercer recounted: "Of all the opponents I faced I particularly remember Doherty, who was unplayable on his day. He was built like a greyhound, very fast and elusive but with stamina, too. He had a Rolls-Royce engine in him."

Doherty was top scorer with 30 goals in the 1936–37 season when City, after a poor first half of the campaign, won the League title for the first time in their history. He had reluctantly moved to Maine Road from Blackpool in a £10,000 deal the previous February. He rounded off an attacking unit that possessed blistering firepower. Rounded off is actually an understatement. City were prolific goalscorers and Doherty delivered goals, guile and running power.

He was the complete inside-forward – he'd now be seen as an attacking midfielder. In those days players could still make their names as crowd pleasers rather than team players. Doherty achieved both those qualities. Ironically, one of the best insights into Doherty's prowess came from the legendary Len Shackleton who was known to be the greatest entertainer of the era but not totally committed to any collective cause.

That's why it's particularly pertinent that Shack said: "Peter Doherty was surely the genius among geniuses – possessor of the most baffling body swerve in football, able to perform all the tricks with the ball, owning a shot like the kick of a mule, and, with all this, having such tremendous enthusiasm for the game that he would work like a horse for ninety minutes."

City fans from a more modern era will read Shackleton's tribute and immediately make the connection between Doherty and the star of their Sixties team, Colin Bell. Bell was athletically supreme, blessed with both stamina and a change of pace that earned him the nickname of Nijinsky, the legendary thoroughbred racehorse that won the English triple crown in 1970. Bell, who had been recruited from Bury for £40,000 in 1966, became a key part of a side that won promotion to the top flight then in quick succession won the League title, FA Cup, European Cup Winners' Cup and League Cup.

The chemistry among the players was perfect, too. While the likes of Francis Lee, Mike Summerbee and Mike Doyle could be outspoken and opinionated, Bell preferred a lower profile. He was always well mannered and courteous but delivered a shy smile and a polite "no thanks" to most invitations for an interview. Malcolm Allison, the coach who worked with manager Mercer to create a team of champions, recognized that within his outstanding squad Bell really was the kingpin. In later years, when asked to analyse that great side, Big Mal acknowledged: "It was an excellent team but Colin Bell stood out. He was the best player I ever worked with. He was so gifted. He had so much talent. He could score goals from midfield. He had great pace and was good in the air. He had everything."

It was the advent of the Second World War that wrecked Doherty's career. Only 26 when war broke out, the war deprived him of the prime years of his career. We know how good he was in his formative days. By the time he could resume his career post-war he was approaching veteran status.

Bell, of course, was denied a full career too. He was 29 when he was tackled by Manchester United's Martin Buchan in a League Cup derby at Maine Road. He suffered massive damage to his right knee that prevented him from playing for over two years. He bravely attempted to return, but he never regained full fitness and was forced to retire.

In a rare interview in 2005 Bell told the *Manchester Evening News*: "His tackle smacked me just below the knee, on the right leg, which had my full weight on it. It felt like my leg had been screwed into the ground. My knee bent backwards, bursting blood vessels in the bottom of my thigh and in the top of my calf. All the ligaments in my knee were torn. Within seconds the knee was just a bag of blood. Very soon I was in an ambulance on my way to hospital. My knee had swollen up to the size of a football. My leg was black and blue from the hip joint right down to my ankle. And I was quite generally unwell, too, not just from the injury but because of the shock to my system. I was told by the doctors that the trauma was similar to that suffered by someone involved in a serious car smash. The knee was a complete mess. As well as the ligament and muscle damage, the cartilages had been destroyed and there had been massive internal bleeding. Perhaps with today's surgical techniques my treatment would have been different. But that kind of expertise simply didn't exist in those days.

"I don't blame Martin Buchan for the injury. There were players in the game who set out to kick and injure you, but I don't think Martin was that type.

"I was a little disappointed, though, that he didn't visit me during my time in hospital."

So Bell just beats Peter Doherty as our City icon; but what about the cult hero? As mentioned earlier, the range of nominations for this title was far-reaching and reflected the turbulent times the club has endured over the past 30 years. The roller-coaster City have experienced saw nominations come in for Shaun Goater and Paul Dickov. Two strikers who would hardly earn nominations for an all-time great City XI but whose selfless efforts won over fans who respected their total commitment.

City fan Joe Highton wrote: "I would nominate Paul Dickov. He always gave 100% in every game even during the worst period in our history. His work-rate was immense and for his obvious contribution in our promotion play-off final win by penalties against Gillingham affords him legendary status in my eyes! I'd also like to mention another side to his character that maybe isn't as well known. At the end of an era day at Maine Road against Southampton they had an ex-players parade. He took the time to stop for a picture with my eight-year-old son even though his family were on their way up the steps into the ground and he was plainly in a rush. It was more important to make a young boy's request for a pic come true. That's why he'll always be a superhero in our household."

City fans from the Fifties nominated Bert Trautmann, the German goalie who defied a broken neck to help his team win the 1956 FA Cup against Birmingham, and Roy Paul, the man who skippered City that day. City followers who revel in baiting neighbours promoted the cause of Mike Doyle, the United hater supreme and another key ingredient in the Mercer–Allison team.

But one name did finally emerge as our City cult hero. I'll let a City fan from the Sixties explain. Paul Hart, the former Nottingham Forest and Portsmouth manager, grew up in Manchester. His father John played, coached and managed City. Hart was a youngster looking on with awe at the City team of the Sixties. He insists: "Colin Bell has to be the greatest player but my choice of cult hero would be Mike Summerbee. A fine player, he played with a raw passion that the fans loved. He was like our representative out on the field. He gave his all."

THE FAN'S VIEW

Kevan Bowring: *"My Manchester City icon is the great Colin Bell. If it were not for the bad injury he received playing against Manchester United he would have been one of England's greatest. I remember his comeback game against Newcastle, it was 0-0 at half time and then Nijinsky came on as substitute. I remember the emotion as grown men were crying. I have never heard a roar at a football ground like it. Sadly he did not last many games after that, but thanks for the memories Colin, you were the greatest."*

MANCHESTER UNITED

 **George Best** 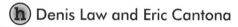 **Denis Law and Eric Cantona**

For many years United had been acknowledged as England's most fashionable and popular club, but they were never serial trophy winners – until Sir Alex Ferguson arrived to put that right over the past 20 odd years or so. Fergie has made United the most successful club side in English football. Their domination of the Premier League years has been single-minded and impressive.

It's a measure of Manchester United's array of superstars that the debate surrounding their icon can span players from five decades. Most of them dedicated the bulk of their playing careers to the United cause. The likes of Bobby Charlton, Denis Law, Bryan Robson, Ryan Giggs and Paul Scholes were, or in Giggs and Scholes' case remain, part of the Old Trafford fabric for a decade or more.

Other contenders to be their ultimate heroes didn't match that longevity. In fact, both Eric Cantona and Duncan Edwards enjoyed first-team careers of just five years at Old Trafford. Cantona is widely acknowledged as the catalyst to United's run of domestic glory dating from the critical 1992–93 campaign. He arrived in a bargain £1.2million deal and was to play a critical role in ensuring that United's wait to be crowned English champions was to finally end after 26 years.

Bobby Charlton, now knighted for services to football and a United director, is adamant that if Edwards's life had not been cut short by the Munich air disaster the powerfully-built young Englishman would have gone on to be hailed as the greatest footballer England has ever seen. Edwards was just 21 when he died. He had battled for 15 days to recover from the dreadful injuries he sustained in the air crash of 6th February 1958. Edwards had made his League debut aged just 16 years and 185 days. At the time he was the Football League's youngest ever top-flight player.

By the time of his death Edwards was a stalwart of two United Championship-winning teams. Sir Bobby is unequivocal in his judgment: "Duncan's death was the biggest single tragedy ever to happen to Manchester United and English football.

"He has always been in my mind the best player I ever played with or against. He was strong and had a fantastic football brain. His ability was complete – right foot, left foot, long passing, short passing. He did everything instinctively. Without question he would have played in the 1966 World Cup and been the England captain. In today's football he would be priceless. He was just sensational."

Bobby has always been an eloquent advocate of the merits of the Busby Babes team that was decimated on that snowbound Munich runway. He has also readily saluted the football principles laid down by United's first great manager, Sir Matt Busby. Busby was the man who had the vision to build a Championship-winning club from a thriving youth policy while inculcating the principle that his teams won with attacking style and brio.

It is often overlooked that in the wake of Munich Busby built another great United team – including Bobby Charlton – that won special merit. The team was built around United's Holy Trinity. In Best, Law and Charlton United had three different breathtaking stars who were all crowned European Footballers of the Year. They were on a two-year cycle, with Law starting the run in 1964 and Best completing it in 1968. 1966 was quite a good year for Bobby. As well as being acclaimed as Europe's best footballer he played a significant part in England winning the World Cup. Other clubs such as Real Madrid, Ajax and AC Milan may have seen their conquering heroes saluted with awards down the years, but only that United team of the Sixties had three stars playing in the same team who had won the Ballon d'Or.

Charlton remains an erudite link between United's past and their future. Once a superstar he is a longstanding and respected club director who has forged a close bond with manager Sir Alex Ferguson. It's perhaps easy to overlook the fact that on any criteria Sir Bobby can stake a genuine claim to being United's and England's greatest ever player. So instead of our discussing his lost and old team-mates, perhaps Bobby should be the recipient of the ultimate accolade?

So, who is United's icon and who merits cult status? Since his passing in 2005 there has been widespread support for Best as United's finest footballer. The downside to that argument is that Best's status as football's ultimate frolic-holic, on his way to becoming an alcoholic, saw him lose his career path by the time he was just 27. At times he was spell-binding, but he couldn't match the longevity of team-mates Law and Charlton or, in the modern era, the astonishing durability of Giggs and Scholes.

In fact, in the revisionist world we live in, many people – including United fans – forget that during the Holy Trinity's pomp one player stood above the rest as the idol of the Stretford End. The original king of Old Trafford back then was neither Charlton or Best, it was Denis Law. Law was the man who dispatched spectacular goals, who went to war with opponents who had fouled his team-mates, who played the game in a blur of blond-haired athleticism. Joe Mercer, the wise manager who made Manchester City champions in 1968 and regular trophy winners, was asked to sum up the differences between the two finest goalscorers of the Sixties: Law and Jimmy Greaves, the Chelsea and Tottenham marksman.

Mercer said: "The big difference is that if you put Jimmy through on goal he's absolutely lethal. With Denis you just have to put the ball into the penalty area. He'll fight off the biggest defenders, win the ball and stick it in the net." That combative spirit is why Law became the biggest star in the eyes of United fans in the Sixties. And to this day it's Denis who is named by Sir Alex Ferguson as his favourite player. Fergie knew what it took to be an aggressive striker who would go to war for his team. That was the Lawman. And let us not forget that when he finally retires as United manager, Ferguson will deservedly merit acclaim alongside the finest of Old Trafford's heroes. Indeed, when we can reflect on Ferguson's career he may become United's ultimate icon. And yet in some ways that would be wrong because, as Fergie and his predecessor Sir Matt have regularly observed down the years, a club like United needs great players to keep the dream of greatness alive.

From the modern era's succession of brilliant players Scholes can be hailed as the finest all-round footballer of his generation. To have the likes of Span's Xavi and Iniesta saluting you as their favourite player speaks volumes for Scholes' ability. In the United dressing room he is seen as a football icon.

Brian Kidd was a home-grown youngster who joined the United team of the Sixties and was the stand-in for the injured Law when United became the first English club to win the European Cup in 1968. Now the assistant-manager of Manchester City, he admits a high regard for the team he was welcomed into as well as the United side of the 1990s he coached for Ferguson. Put on the spot to name his greatest ever United player he can't deny the merits of the wayward genius from Belfast. Kidd said: "It was to be George. Besty was the best." Best was more than a footballer. Describing him as the fifth Beatle actually does him a disservice. He was the first George Best. He was the player who bridged the gap between footballers emerging from the days of maximum wages to becoming targets for the earliest forms of the paparazzi. George actually knew most of the photographers and reporters on his tail and would share drinks with them along the way. But in terms of profile, attention and public scrutiny he was the first of the modern superstars. He was at the vanguard when the sponsors realized football could be sexy and that the best young players had a following that far outweighed the numbers standing on the terraces. There is a link between Best and the likes of Keegan, Gascoigne and Beckham. My old *Daily Mail* colleague John Roberts was once asked to compare Keegan with Best and delivered this brilliant assessment: "Kevin Keegan wasn't fit to lace George Best's drinks!"

When United finally broke their title drought in 1993 I was asked to interview George. I called him to discover he was on a session in his Chelsea local. I was told to call him back the next day at noon sharp. Any later and he'd be heading to the pub. I called, we talked and George was in spell-binding form. He analysed Cantona's impact at United, where this team of United champions rated in the pantheon of great Old Trafford sides and made a bold prediction. He insisted with the first title in the bag Alex Ferguson would lead United to the greatest era in the club's history. He got that right.

So with George our icon, who should be our United cult hero? We've decided to share the honour. Eric, the French philosopher, will share it with the man crowned King Denis. As United cult heroes they are inseparable.

THE FAN'S VIEW

Steve Gill: *"Eric the King made us winners. He was brilliant for United and we shouldn't forget what Scholesy and Giggs have done for us."*

MIDDLESBROUGH

 Juninho　　　　　　　　　　　　　　　 **Willie Maddren**

Two great players are our rivals for the honour of being Middlesbrough's icon. "He was the Mozart of football – stylish, graceful, courtly, showing exquisite workmanship with the ball." Those words of tribute befit them both. The words were spoken by Sir Stanley Matthews and he was talking about Wilf Mannion, the inside-forward who emerged from Teeside poverty to become one of England's finest players. Yet Matthews might so easily have been discussing a midfielder from a very different age and a different football culture. Juninho arrived at Middlesbrough in 1995 from São Paulo, Brazil. Both players endured critical scepticism. Fundamentally, many observers thought they were too small to survive in professional football. And while they were divided by decades, there was a common bond in the street football in which both players had honed their skills. They were totally natural players, and they proved their doubters totally wrong.

Mannion was born in South Bank, Middlesbrough on 16th May 1918. He was one of 10 children, the son of Thomas Mannion, an Irish immigrant who worked at the Bolckow Vaughan blast furnace. Wilf left school at 14 and became an apprentice welder at Smith's Dock. He later revealed that his first pay packet was "six bob and four pence. I thought I'm not having that." Next he got a job in a rolling mill before signing for Boro on 17th September 1936. He was paid £3 10s a week, with a £2 win bonus for first-team duties.

There were two things that stood out when Mannion was on the field, his diminutive size and his shock of platinum blond hair. And once he had broken into the Boro first team there was little to hold him back, as his impeccable skills and choice of simple, effective passes saw him selected for an England end of season tour in 1939. But Boro manager Wilf Gallow insisted that young Mannion needed to rest, not tour South Africa. The outbreak of war and his conscription and active service in France, Africa and Italy saw his football career put on hold. In fact, Mannion was reported dead in one local newspaper in the wake of the Dunkirk evacuation. Thankfully this was untrue. Mind you, during the war his health suffered alarmingly and he contracted malaria, which took months to clear up.

By the 1946–47 season Mannion was back to his best and winning more England call-ups. England were in rampant form, thrashing Holland 8-2, France 3-0 and Portugal 10-0. Two Boro players were stalwarts in that England team. Mannion played alongside club team-mate George Hardwick, who was captain of

England in the immediate post-war games. Also wearing the Three Lions at this time were legends like Tommy Lawton, Raich Carter, Stanley Matthews, Tom Finney and Billy Wright.

Wright, who went on to become the first England player to win 100 caps, said: "Our 10-0 victory over Portugal in Lisbon was the nearest thing I've seen to absolute perfection on a football pitch. I doubt if there has ever been a greater performance by an England attack. They were all outstanding individual players but blended together so well as a unit it was a pleasure to play behind them."

Matthews agreed: "In that game, it was the best forward line I played in. They were all so skilful – wonderful players."

The fact that a couple of years later Mannion demanded a transfer, because he felt that Boro did not fully appreciate his services, became a major talking point in the game. Another club, Wilf later revealed it was Aston Villa, had offered him £3,000 to leave Boro. In the days of maximum wages the England players were well aware that some clubs found ways to beat the system by helping the players – or their wives – find second sources of income. Boro did none of these.

If Mannion had enjoyed the riches bestowed on Juninho several generations later, he would not have ended up enduring penury in later life. And yet any reflections about how Wilf found life so challenging cannot overwhelm the view of his contemporaries about his true value as a player. Tommy Lawton, in some eyes England's greatest ever centre-forward, said: "There is no question about it – Wilf was a genius."

If Mannion was a troubled soul, Juninho brought to Teeside a boyish grin and a Brazilian passion for the joys of playing football. He even went out and joined in street matches with children near his home. Like many Brazilian players, Juninho was never intimidated by the sheer size and brute force of his opponents. In fact, one of the things that endeared him to Boro fans was the way he'd admonish opponents who had tried to rough him up by wagging a finger in their faces, and invariably returning to embarrass them with his skills and sorcery.

On his arrival from São Paulo in October 1995 he made an immediate impact. His touch on the ball, dribbling skills and eye for goal were quite stunning. He would leave outstanding midfield opponents flat-footed with his dextrous drag-backs and changes of direction. He became known as TLF – the little fella. And he wasn't just an easy on the eye player. His work-rate was immense.

After Boro were relegated he left for Atletico Madrid, but part of his standing among Boro fans, who have voted him the club's greatest ever player, is that he returned twice more for spells at their club and has always professed that his time on Teeside was the most precious of his career. But in trying to choose an icon where so many years have passed since their careers it's inevitable that the young will favour the man they saw. It needs our grandparents to truly value a player like Mannion.

So if Juninho is our Middlesbrough icon, who is the Boro cult hero? One man stands out: former skipper Willie Maddren, who was forced to quit football when he was just 26 and lost his battle against motor neurone disease in September 2000, when he was just 49 years old. Maddren is widely acknowledged as the best player never to play for England. He was a stalwart of Jack Charlton's Boro team that barnstormed their way to promotion to the top flight in 1974. Maddren was in a side alongside other emerging young players like Graeme Souness, David Mills and David Armstrong.

After being forced into premature retirement Maddren eventually joined the coaching staff, and as Boro slid towards financial ruin he accepted the poisoned chalice of manager. It was in these dark days that Maddren's status as a Boro legend was enhanced. He fought tenaciously to save his club. It was a perilous episode, but Middlesbrough did not lose its football club.

Tragically, in 1995 Maddren's incurable illness was diagnosed. The typical bravery, resolution and strength he showed were inspirational. He will remain a cult figure to all Boro fans, and the words from his autobiography are a fitting epitaph. He wrote: "This is one game I cannot win but I will go down fighting. I pray to God that he will give me more and more extra-time. And yet even on the day they die, many people look back on their life and wonder what it was all for. When I go, I will do so in the knowledge that I lived life to the full and, through my wife and children, I found total happiness. No man could ask for more."

THE FAN'S VIEW

Nick Smith: *"My grandad used to rave about Wilf Mannion but I'm a Juninho fan. He brought Brazilian sunshine football to Teeside and we still love him for it."*

MILLWALL

 **Barry Kitchener**

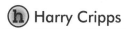 **Harry Cripps**

When we launched the research into this book I asked a friend and colleague who supports Millwall for his prediction as to who would emerge as his club's football icon.

He immediately named Barry Kitchener as *the* man. I offered a few alternatives, including Harry Cripps, Neil Harris and Lord Ted himself, Teddy Sheringham. My mate would have none of it. "I bet Lions fans vote for Big Kitch because he never left Millwall. There was no lure of a brighter tomorrow elsewhere for him."

Well, my mate was right. Millwall fans were almost unanimous in saluting the man who spent 16 years at the club, played a club record 602 appearances, and beyond any statistics, represented the true competitive values of his football club.

It was somehow typical of Big Kitch that when he passed away in March 2012 his family issued a statement expressing their thanks to the club. They said: "We would like to thank Millwall for making his dreams come true and to all their fantastic supporters for all the love they have shown him over the years. We would appreciate privacy at this time to try and come to terms with losing an unbelievable husband, dad and granddad."

Kitchener joined Millwall in August 1965. He actually made his debut as stand-in for our Lions cult hero, Harry Cripps, at left-back. But when 'Arry was ready to return Big Kitch was switched to centre-half. He stayed there, wearing the No. 5 shirt, until his retirement in 1982.

During those years there appeared to be two inseparables in football: Kitchener and Millwall.

Winger Gordon Hill, who went on to play for Manchester United and England, remembers his formative days as a young winger taken under Big Kitch's wing. Hill said: "On the field he gave you everything, he was robust, hard and there was no mucking about. Off the field he was a true gentleman.

"I would like to share a story with you about how Kitch helped me, back in the 72/73 season, when there was a shortage of sugar and petrol. I went training one day and all the country was suffering, but as I was about to leave the ground Big Kitch turned to me and asked if I needed anything. I replied 'yes, petrol and sugar'.

"He said 'come with me' and then took me to the back of his car and had bags of sugar stacked up in the boot. He loaded my little car and then said go to this garage and tell him I sent you and fill up. I have never forgotten this. I had the pleasure to have played with him and to have been able to call him my friend."

Kitchener carried the DNA of the perfect Millwall player. He was hard, uncompromising but honest. That's why we're happy to respect the wishes of so many Millwall fans in making him our club icon.

Our cult hero is Harry Cripps. There was some support for Sheringham, and his former strike partner and honorary Irishman Tony Cascarino. Some fans wanted to salute striker Neil Harris and others midfield hard man Terry Hurlock. But even after his death in 1996, 'Arry Boy remains a unique figure to Lions supporters. He actually began his career with the Lions arch-enemies, West Ham. He was in the Hammers youth team that included his good mate Bobby Moore, but Cripps didn't make the grade there. In 1961 he signed for Millwall and quickly became a popular player. Fans admired his tough-tackling approach and they loved his honesty and humour. He wasn't the quickest full-back in the business but he tried his hardest to get around. He loved delivering crosses and unleashing shots on goal. He also loved shaking up the opposition with bone-jarring challenges. His qualities of honest endeavour and accepting a few moans from the terraces when things went wrong, saw him become admired and then adored.

Cripps spent 14 years at Millwall. He made 444 appearances and scored a remarkable 40 goals. He moved across south east London to Charlton in 1974. By then he'd become a Millwall legend; he had played alongside some of the Lions finest players and etched a place for himself as one of their very best. Cripps died in 1995. He was 54.

THE FAN'S VIEW

Edo: *"Big Kitch was the finest hero a fan could wish for. He represented what MFC expect from our players."*

Graham Green: *"Our cult hero is Harry Cripps."*

MK DONS

 Karl Robinson

 Dean Lewington

This must be the hardest club to review because we're forced to address the issue of the commercial creation of a club after Wimbledon FC was transferred to Milton Keynes Dons in 2004.

Some websites and record books have attributed the Dons' historic achievements, such as winning the FA Cup in 1988, to MK Dons. That appears to be wrong and MK Dons are now widely seen as a new club whose history begins in 2004. That's how we're viewing it here. In fairness to MK Dons – and it would be smart if they dropped the Dons part of their name – they have returned the trophies won by the old club they took over.

That takeover pushed them straight into League football in Division One. Dean Lewington was one of the players who switched from Wimbledon to Milton Keynes with the takeover, and he is our cult hero. The son of Ray Lewington, the England assistant manager, Dean has been a towering presence in MK's inexorable rise. A steely left-back, who can also operate at centre-back, Lewington is acknowledged as one of the best players in the lower divisions.

He was outstanding in his club's promotion push from League Two in 2007–08. His fellow players selected him for the PFA's Divisional team that year. And he followed that up by getting in the PFA Team for League One 12 months later.

A string of Premier League and Championship clubs have kept tabs on his progress down the years, but it looks as if that kind of move will now elude him. That won't disappoint MK fans who recognize his loyalty and commitment.

Lewington became their club captain after Keith Andrews' transfer to Blackburn Rovers in 2008. He has now passed the 400 appearances mark for the club, which is a major milestone given his age.

Lewington's presence at MK Dons has not acted as a unifying force between his club and the old Wimbledon fans and players. The supporters went away and set up AFC Wimbledon. But former Wimbledon hero Dave Beasant hopes the enmity can finally end. Beasant explained: "There is a lot of bitterness from AFC fans that Wimbledon lost their League status. They think that MK didn't go about it the right way, when they should have only gained a place in the League by qualifying through non-League football.

"You understand the bitterness but it's been done, it was a while ago and the position isn't going to be changed. And MK Dons are a progressive team, having gained promotion to League Three, just as AFC have progressed into the League proper."

The man leading MK Dons in their pursuit of glory is our icon, Karl Robinson. Karl spent his playing career mainly on the non-League scene in the northwest and north Wales. But he was spotted as an outstanding Academy coach at Liverpool and was headhunted by Paul Ince, who'd seen him tutoring his son Tom.

Robinson worked with Ince as a coach at MK Dons, followed his boss to Blackburn and then landed the manager's job back at MK Dons in May 2010. Robinson was just 29 years old and became the youngest manager in the Football League. In his two seasons in charge he has taken the club into the promotion play-offs but failed to convert that into promotion.

There is a hint of Marmite to Robinson's career – people tend to love him or hate him. He clearly has immense self-belief and is convinced he will be successful. He's had a few managers along touchlines cursing his brashness and demeanour, but those incidents do not seem to have undermined him – no one can doubt the job he's done for MK Dons.

So Where Did It All Go Wrong, George?:
Manchester United icon George Best on holiday with film star Susan George in Majorca. In later life he'd joke about the fun he had while his career went into decline.

The Fiery Scots: Dave Mackay (left) makes his point to Billy Bremner. Off the field the pair were friends. On it they were ferocious competitors.

Reidy to Rumble: Peter Reid epitomized the drive and passion in Everton's fine team of the mid-Eighties.

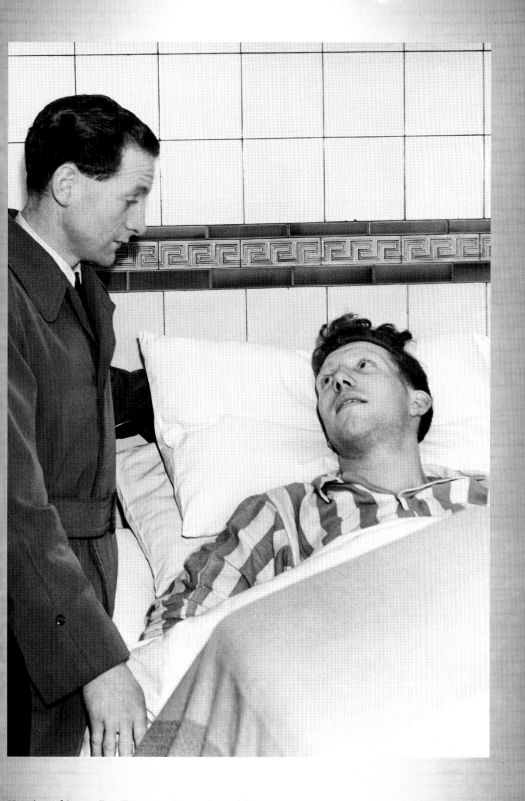

Meeting of Icons: Tom Finney, our Preston icon, visits
Sheffield Wednesday icon Derek Dooley in hospital. Dooley
had undergone an amputation of his shattered leg.

Master Blaster: The majestic Thierry Henry celebrates another goal in his record-breaking Arsenal career.

Sweet Zola Music: Chelsea icon Gianfranco Zola charms his way through another interview.

Midget Gem: Gordon Strachan celebrates Leeds United's title triumph in 1992 – the last year of the 92-club Football League.

Stan's Our Man: Sir Stanley Matthews, the first true superstar of English football, meets adoring fans on his return to Stoke City in 1961.

Nijinsky: Colin Bell was nicknamed after the race horse but it could have been the ballet star. A magnificent midfielder ahead of his time.

God on the Tyne: Alan Shearer receives a deafening welcome from his Toon disciples following his British record £15million transfer in 1996.

Brothers in Arms: Alan Hudson (left) and Peter Osgood achieved fame and some notoriety as leaders of the Chelsea pack.

Ticket to Ride: Robin Friday signs for Cardiff manager Jimmy Andrews. The striker had been arrested en route for travelling on the train from Reading without a ticket.

Transformer: John Robertson had been written off as tubby and unfit. He emerged as a creative genius as Nottingham Forest conquered Europe.

Simply the Best: When Bryan Robson retired and reflected on his career as England's Captain Fantastic, he named the man who had been his toughest opponent: Paul Gascoigne.

The Boot Room Boys: The men who made Liverpool great – Bill Shankly (left) and Bob Paisley.

Kiss and Make Up: Alan Birchenall and Tony Currie, both listed as cult heroes, prove blonds do have more fun.

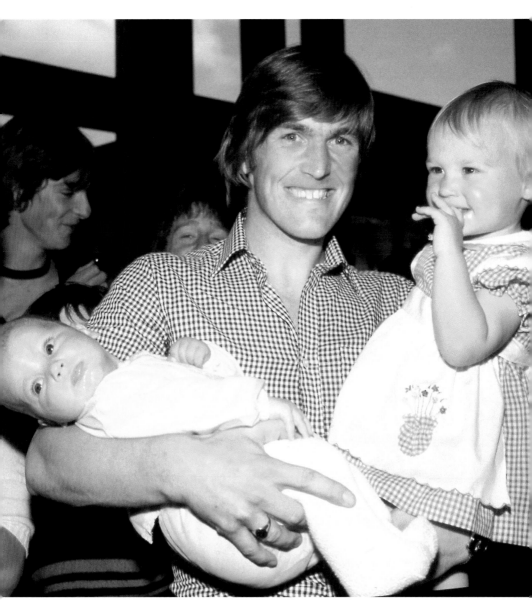

King Kenny and his Clan: When Liverpool sold
Kevin Keegan they needed a new, attacking inspiration.
Dalglish surpassed even his predecesor's greatness.

Mr Blue Sky: Birmingham City's finest player and football's first £1 million man, Trevor Francis.

Posh and Becks Mark 1: The original footballer and pop star duo; Billy Wright, his wife Joy (on his right) and her twin sisters who made up the Beverley Sisters.

History Boys: Tottenham manager Bill Nicholson shares the champagne with his players who in 1961 became the first Double winners of the 20th century.

**A Penny For Your
Thoughts?:** Brian Clough
joked he could walk on
water. Here he is in a
moment of contemplation.

Clown Prince: Sunderland's Len Shackleton, famed for flicks and tricks that mesmerized opponents and delighted the fans.

Frankly Elvis: Frank Worthington (above right) was nominated as a cult hero by more clubs than any other player. He did a good impersonation of Elvis Presley, too.

Three Amigos: Three football legends onboard the Manchester United team coach, Boxing Day 1986. (From left) Alex Ferguson, Bryan Robson and Bob Paisley.

MORECAMBE

ⓘ Jim Bentley

ⓗ Barry Roche

Jim Bentley graduated through the playing ranks at Morecambe to become one of the youngest managers in the Football League in 2011 when he was just 34. When the Morecambe skipper took over the managerial reins from Sammy McIlroy he had made 329 appearances for the Shrimps, scoring 34 goals.

Former Manchester City trainee Bentley developed into an inspirational captain after signing for Morecambe from Telford in 2002. McIlroy handed him his first coaching role in the 2010–11 campaign, when he looked after the reserves as Morecambe just managed to stay in the League. Bentley, who was a Conference play-off winner with the Shrimps in 2007, stepped up to replace the Northern Irishman and has proved as totally committed as a manager as he was as a player.

Our Morecambe cult hero is Barry Roche. The 6ft 4in Dublin-born goalkeeper has become a firm favourite with fans at the Globe Arena after developing into one of League Two's outstanding keepers.

Twice voted by the supporters as Player of the Year, Roche has made Morecambe's goalkeeping position his own with consistency over five seasons that have seen him amass more than 230 appearances.

Roche's career began at Leeds United, before he left to follow his mentor, Paul Hart, to join Nottingham Forest in 2001. Hart understands why Roche is so popular with the Lancastrians. "Barry is a smashing lad, a very gifted goalie and a great man to have around your club. Leeds had a great scouting operation in Ireland and Barry was a great recruit. I really thought he might have made the grade to be Forest's No. 1. We had a lot of faith in him. I'm pleased by the career he's carved out with Morecambe."

Roche was an understudy at Forest, playing just 10 senior games before signing for Chesterfield in 2005, where he finally established himself.

He moved to League Two Morecambe in 2008 – just a year after they had won promotion to the Football League. In 2010, the year he won his second Player of the Year award, Roche was made club captain. On 21st January 2012, Roche signed a new contract that keeps him at Morecambe until June 2014.

THE FAN'S VIEW

Bill Morrison: *"Barry is a giant of a goalie and has been great for us."*

NEWCASTLE UNITED

 **Alan Shearer**

 **Tony Green**

The Geordie nation has always had a special affinity with their local football club. Few areas can match Newcastle in producing world-class footballers. The perpetual dream at St James' Park is to see a team of Geordies representing Newcastle United – ideally with a Geordie as their manager. Even the much-travelled and much-lamented Sir Bobby Robson admitted this was his ultimate sporting goal when he was Newcastle manager.

Newcastle fans know their football – and what they want from their heroes. And lethal, exciting centre-forwards are the foundation of many Geordie football fantasies. Their names are woven into the tapestry of Geordie folklore. The common link is that they wore the Newcastle No. 9 shirt with panache. They scored goals, led the attacking line with style, and provided thrills and entertainment for some of the most knowing fans in British football.

Hughie Gallacher, Jackie Milburn, Malcolm Macdonald and Alan Shearer all fitted the bill to perfection and were so popular on Tyneside that they inevitably dominate the debate for Newcastle's idol. Some fans might also suggest that we should include Wyn Davies. The towering Wales international led the attack when United won their last major trophy, the Inter Cities Fairs Cup in 1969, but while he was brave, honest and provided a commanding aerial presence, he could not match his rivals as an all-round player.

In fact, you couldn't create a bigger contrast between Davies, the towering Welsh battering ram, and Gallacher, the 5ft 5in bundle of energy who revelled in going to war with the brutal defenders who attempted to kick him out of a game. Gallacher's goals per game ratio remains the best by any Toon striker. The career goals total accumulated by Jackie Milburn, and later broken by Alan Shearer, sets a remarkable standard, and yet when it came to goals per game the diminutive Scotsman beat the lot.

Gallacher joined Newcastle for £6,500 in December 1925. He ended that season as the club's top scorer with 23 League goals in 19 games.

For the 1926–27 season Newcastle made Gallacher their skipper, and he led them to the title for the first time since 1909. That season he scored 36 League goals in 38 appearances, a club record that still stands.

Gallacher's time at Newcastle was controversial, too. Already married in Scotland, he met and fell in love with Hannah Anderson, the daughter of a landlord of one of his favourite watering holes. Divorce was rare and frowned upon back then, and Hannah's family tried to warn him off. But Gallacher eventually got his divorce and he married Hannah. They had three sons together and formed a powerful union for the rest of their days. During his Newcastle career Gallacher scored 143 goals in 174 appearances.

Malcolm Macdonald arrived on Tyneside from Luton in a club record £180,000 deal in 1971. The London-born striker won instant acclaim by scoring a hat-trick against Liverpool on his debut. Macdonald was an explosive crowd pleaser. He had the power-packed shape of a boxer, a searing change of pace and ferocious shooting power – especially in his favoured left foot. For five consecutive seasons Supermac was Toon's top scorer. It was during his days with Newcastle that Macdonald made his England debut, and on a famous night at Wembley scored all England's goals in a 5-0 victory over Cyprus. Ironically, he won 14 caps in total but only scored a single goal in the other 13 appearances, and later revealed his belief that manager Don Revie didn't really want him in the England side.

For Supermac life on Tyneside was a case of so near, yet so far. He lost two Cup finals with Newcastle, another with Arsenal when he moved to Highbury. He was the kingpin of a Newcastle team that promised much but couldn't quite deliver the silverware. In the end he fell out with Gordon Lee, the Toon manager of the time. Macdonald was sold to Arsenal for £333,333. Predictably Macdonald was the Gunners' top marksman for the next two seasons, yet still failed to win a major honour in the game.

Until the arrival of Alan Shearer in 1996 one legendary name dominated the history of Newcastle United – the goal king of the Forties and Fifties, Jackie Milburn. A self-effacing man with an impeccable football pedigree, Milburn actually wrote to the club asking for a trial. He had grown up in the Northumberland mining town of Ashington, 15 miles north of Newcastle. When he was invited for his trial he turned up with borrowed boots, but made enough of an impression to be asked back. In his second trial game he scored six goals and was duly signed up, although the Second World War ensured he still worked in the mines while turning out for Newcastle in wartime League games from 1943 to 1946. He was handed the iconic No. 9 shirt in October 1947, and the proud Geordie described the moment as being "fortunate enough to wear Hughie Gallacher's shirt".

While Bobby Mitchell danced down the left wing and Joe Harvey led the team with steely aplomb, Milburn was the key man as Newcastle won the FA Cup three times in five years – 1951, 1952 and 1955. With his dark hair swept back and his rapier thrusts in attack, he was a thrilling player to watch. "Wor Jackie" was blessed with a predatory eye for goals that few in any era could match. Despite being the goal king of Tyneside, Milburn never got carried away by the trappings of fame – even if the maximum wage ruling prevented him from ever chasing his fortune. Like many other British stars of his day Milburn could have moved abroad in pursuit of more money. His modesty ensured that he gained even more respect from Newcastle fans. And Milburn's 200 goals in 353 games for Newcastle set a record that everyone regarded as unique – until another thrilling England striker hit town.

It's important to remember that in the summer of 1996 Manchester United, who had just won a Premier League and FA Cup Double, were favourites to land Shearer from Blackburn Rovers. The era of Alex Ferguson-inspired domination had been launched in earnest at Old Trafford. By that summer the Red Devils had won the title in three of the previous four seasons. The one blank had been when a Shearer-inspired Blackburn had won the title in 1995. Shearer's fee was a world record £15million. He was by some distance the best striker in England. For three consecutive seasons he had scored over 30 League goals: a feat achieved for the first time since Jimmy Greaves in the early Sixties.

So, for manager Kevin Keegan to persuade Shearer to turn his back on Old Trafford and head home to his northeast roots was a major coup. The Toon faithful appreciated the significance of the transfer. After all, they had become accustomed to talent draining away from Newcastle and moving south. The Shearer homecoming was significant and the lethal striker did not disappoint. At times perceived as diffident and aloof, Shearer had a warm side he was prepared to display with his friends and those he trusted. Sometimes, in retrospect, it's easy to criticize Shearer for his blandness as a television pundit, yet he does possess strong opinions, a sharp humour and real knowledge of the game. And, more importantly, when we're analysing iconic status nobody could doubt what Shearer delivered on Tyneside. Remember he even managed to top Wor Jackie's goalscoring records by claiming 206 goals in 395 appearances for Newcastle.

As for our Geordie cult hero, we'll nominate a Scotsman who arrived on Tyneside in October 1971 in a £150,000 transfer from Blackpool. Tony Green became a huge fans' favourite at St James' despite his career being tragically cut short with a knee ligament injury after just 33 League games. Toon were locked in a relegation battle when he arrived, but his silky skills, jinking runs and powerful shooting soon excited St James' Park in the way another Tyneside idol Peter Beardsley would do in the following decade.

But an injury sustained in his prime at Crystal Palace ended the Scotland international's career in 1973, causing manager Joe Harvey to admit: "It was the saddest day of my life. He was my best buy."

The Geordie fans took to Green with an enthusiasm few other Newcastle players have enjoyed, and he is always given a rapturous reception whenever he returns to St James' Park.

Newcastle historian Paul Joannou said of him: "Simply to become the idol Tony Green did in such a short space of time was a remarkable achievement in itself."

After retiring from football, Green became a teacher and was a member of the Pools Panel.

THE FAN'S VIEW

Gary Linney: *"For the Toon Army our icon's got to be Alan Shearer."*

NORTHAMPTON TOWN

 **Joe Kiernan**　　　　　　　　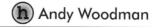 **Andy Woodman**

Northampton Town had one of the great legends of football management in their team when they achieved a club record triumph. Herbert Chapman, a serial winner with Huddersfield Town and Arsenal and the man who introduced the Gunners' white sleeves, was playing when the Cobblers beat Sutton 10-0 in the FA Cup in 1907. Chapman scored twice in that win but his playing days at the County Ground were not as illustrious as his later career.

Our Town icon is Joe Kiernan. He was a sophisticated, silky Scot whose wing-half play was a crucial feature of Northampton's sensational rise to the top flight in 1965. Joe probably didn't get the plaudits he deserved wider afield.

Coatbridge-born Kiernan was understudy to another Scot, Jimmy McNab, at Sunderland and managed just two senior appearances. But he made his mark in one of those scoring twice in a League Cup tie against Oldham.

But after a £2,000 transfer to Northampton, Kiernan made the left-half position his own, clocking up 308 appearances for the club during the era when they marched through the divisions in record time, only to fall back down again. The rise and fall of the Cobblers lasted nine seasons. And Kiernan holds the unique distinction of being the only Cobbler to play in all of their 42 top-flight games in 1965–66 and was later voted Northampton's greatest player in a PFA poll. Joe died in 2006. He was 63.

Our Northampton cult hero is Andy Woodman. The extrovert keeper developed a marvellous relationship with Cobblers fans and has few rivals in the popularity stakes with Town heroes of the Sixfields era. The larger-than-life Woodman became a huge favourite when his saves helped Northampton to win the Division Three play-offs against Swansea City in 1997 when John Frain scored the winner. Woodman was also part of the Northampton side that were Division Two play-off runners-up the following year, losing to Grimsby Town.

All told he made 160 appearances for the Cobblers between 1995 and 1999. An account of his life as a junior player at Crystal Palace alongside his long-time friend Gareth Southgate entitled *Woody & Nord: A Football Friendship*, written by *Sunday Times* sports writer David Walsh, won critical acclaim.

Woodman is now goalkeeping coach with Newcastle United, having previously worked for Toon boss Alan Pardew at West Ham.

NORWICH CITY

(i) Bryan Gunn  **(h) Grant Holt**

Bryan Gunn has earned his status as Norwich City's iconic figure for far more than just the 12 years he spent at Carrow Road as a goalkeeping hero.

In sporting terms Gunn was brave, strong, gifted and approachable. He was aware of his status as an ambassador for his club – whether that was at Aberdeen in his formative years or Norwich for the bulk of his career. But the way he, and his family, handled heart-breaking adversity during his Carrow Road career elevated the young Scotsman to new heights in the esteem of many people, even those with no great affection for Norwich City.

Gunn grew up in the north of Scotland on a farm and joined Aberdeen during Alex Ferguson's reign at Pittodrie. Gunn's progress was blocked by Jim Leighton's presence. It's one of those true, but slightly embarrassing facts, that a young Gunn was invited to childmind for his manager when Alex and Cathy Ferguson had a night out. The babysitting duties didn't get young Bryan any favours from his boss. I'm sure he never expected any and it was because of his lack of first-team opportunities that Gunn decided to ship out of Aberdeen.

Gunn's life was transformed by his move south. He actually beat Ferguson by a month in moving to England. Ferguson had promised to help the young goalie in his pursuit of regular first-team football. Aberdeen agreed a £100,000 fee with Norwich in the summer of 1986 but the deal was delayed due to an injury to Leighton. By October Gunn was allowed to move to Carrow Road. Within weeks Fergie would be heading to Manchester United.

Gunn savoured the chance to grab first-team football. Ironically, his steady progress at Norwich was in direct contrast to his old mentor, Leighton. Jim joined Ferguson at Manchester United but endured a difficult time, including being dropped for the 1990 FA Cup final replay against Crystal Palace. Leighton has gone on record to say that that selection bombshell destroyed his professional career – and his relationship with his manager.

Ken Brown was the Norwich boss who signed Gunn. He made the new boy wait a few weeks for his chance, but once in the team there was no stopping the Scotsman. City finished his first season in fifth place in the old First Division. These were pre-Premier League days. At the time it was the club's finest League campaign. But they were going to get better and some of the greatest games for Norwich and Gunn came in Europe. Yes, Norwich, for so many years dismissed as also-rans in the

Euro qualifying stakes, were being pitched against Europe's finest.

Gunn recalled: "The major highlights of my time at Norwich were the UEFA Cup run and qualifying for it. Norwich finished third in the first ever Premier League season to get there."

Perhaps the high point of Gunn's career came in their UEFA Cup victory over Bayern Munich. The triumph was described as "the pinnacle of Norwich City's history". Gunn was called on to make a series of saves that kept his team in the tie. In fact, one particular save to deny Adolfo Valencia has been described as the finest of his career.

Managers came and went at Carrow Road, but the club had become established in the Premier League. Proof of Gunn's value came when he was sidelined with a fractured dislocation of his ankle when playing against Nottingham Forest. At the time City were seventh in the League. Without their dependable goalie City's fortunes plummeted. They won just one of their final 17 games and were relegated.

But in any assessment of Gunn's time at Norwich you have to review your take on football and life. Defeats on a football field can spark headlines of crisis. That might be vaguely true in the microcosm of sport. In the real world people have to face real crises, and these struck the Gunn family in 1992.

In the autumn of that year Bryan and Susan Gunn endured the bereavement of their 2-year-old daughter Francesca, who died of leukaemia. The family were devastated. But out of that family tragedy Bryan vowed to move forward by establishing in 1993 the Bryan Gunn Appeal. The fund helps research into childhood cancer and leukaemia. It also provides emotional help and advice to those dealing with these kinds of issues.

When he reflects on his life and times at Carrow Road Gunn may harbour one or two regrets. Becoming manager in the summer of 2009 might be one of them. He didn't enjoy the most glorious of reigns. But the esteem he is still held in transcends his goalkeeping greatness. He made 478 appearances for Norwich. He was voted the club's Player of the Year twice, in 1988 and 1993. And when the club granted him a testimonial Sir Alex Ferguson took his all-conquering Manchester United team to Carrow Road to salute his old charge. The city of Norwich recognized Gunn's unique status and charity work by naming him Sheriff for 2002.

A number of Gunn's team-mates were nominated as potential cult heroes for the club. Jeremy Goss, the stylish midfielder who dispatched some sublime goals, was among them. From a slightly more modern era there were calls for Iwan Roberts and Darren Huckerby to be recognized. Very different in size and style, both enjoyed successful spells with the Canaries. But our cult hero comes from the current team. We're saluting Grant Holt.

Winning the club's Player of the Year award three years running since moving to Carrow Road does prove both his remarkable impact at the club and his enduring consistency. In music parlance Holt paid his dues before even getting to Norwich – the 11th club of his nomadic career. The travails he has endured have helped shape him both as a footballer and a man. It's fair to say Holt does not suffer fools gladly. Both externally, in terms of opponents and internally, when he thinks his employers should reward him with a new contract. There was alarm in the summer of 2012 when Holt climaxed a fine first Premier League campaign by asking for a transfer. Norwich fans couldn't believe their attacking warhorse would leave. A few weeks later a new contract was signed.

You sense that, as a man who had turned 30 by the time he was playing in the top flight, Holt intends to make the most of his opportunities. He has travelled a career path that started with rejection at his home-town club Carlisle and has led him through such hot spots as Workington, Halifax, Barrow and Rochdale. Mind you, we should not scoff at suggestions that Holt was made in Rochdale. That's where his career showed real signs of promise and the goals began to flow.

But you sense the prickly resilience, that combative "Don't mess with me or my mates" approach, was shaped on his way up to the top flight. Now that he's there he isn't going to give it up lightly. And Norwich fans adore him for it.

THE FAN'S VIEW

Neil Shaw: *"I loved watching Darren Huckery terrorizing opponents with his speed but Grant Holt is my cult hero. He's done brilliantly for us."*

NOTTINGHAM FOREST

 **Brian Clough**

 **John Robertson**

One of the oldest clubs in world football, Nottingham Forest was formed in 1865, three years after neighbours Notts County. Known originally as Forest Football Club, in 1865 they bought red caps to wear on the field.

One man deservedly dominates any debate about icons and cult heroes of Nottingham Forest. As Martin O'Neill put it: "Without Brian Clough Nottingham Forest would never have been the major force they became in European football. Without Brian Clough there would have been no European Cup triumphs. He made them."

It's impossible to argue with the Sunderland manager who was at the City Ground as a young player to witness the arrival of the football miracle worker called Clough. Brian had previously sparked a revival at Derby County, and led them from the old Second Division to become English League champions. At Forest Clough inspired even greater glories. He wasn't content with seeing his provincial club hailed as champions of England; he took them the next step – not only to conquer Europe but also to retain that crown.

When you consider the years and investment clubs across Europe had put into lifting that giant trophy with big ears, the Clough-inspired glory train put together at the City Ground was little short of a football miracle. And Clough didn't have a wealthy benefactor splashing the cash to recruit Europe's best available talent. Apart from some shrewd signings, like Peter Shilton from Stoke City, Clough arrived at a club, assessed his inheritance and got on with the task of exploiting the existing players' untapped potential. His man-management skills were extraordinary.

In the mind's eye it is easy to remember Brian Clough only from his latter years, when the precocious, handsome manager of his younger days had morphed into a bloated old man troubled by ill health and alcoholism. That kind of pigeon-holing is unfair to the man and his legend.

At a tribute night by the League Managers Association staged at Wembley last year, footage was shown of Clough down the years and then Forest old boys O'Neill and Frank Clark spoke about the great man. The video archive produced some gems before the ravages of alcohol had afflicted him. You remembered how captivating Clough was on screen with his wit and self-confidence; his teasing of interviewers or fellow panellists; he was sharp, funny, eloquent and massively self-assured.

Both Clark and O'Neill recalled the way Clough inspired his charges by placing his faith in players to do the job he expected of them. If they couldn't meet those standards they would be discarded, because as well as being an inspirational boss who led his teams to glory Clough had a ruthless streak, too. His temper would see him physically assault emerging players like Roy Keane and Nigel Jemson. Forest players throughout Clough's reign either accepted they worked for an eccentric boss and prospered – or moved on. When he reflected on punching Keane, Clough said: "I only ever hit Roy once. He got up so I couldn't have hit him very hard." Later in his life Keane reflected: "It was the best thing he ever did for me. It's good to get angry. It's an emotion and part of the game."

I recall writing an FA Cup semi-final piece about Paul Hart a few months after the centre-back had left the City Ground. Clough had gone on holiday in the belief that Hart would be trying his hand as a player-manager at either Peterborough or Tranmere Rovers. Instead Howard Wilkinson had stepped in and persuaded Hart to join top-flight Sheffield Wednesday – as a player. Harty, an old mate, assured me Clough would contribute to the piece I was writing for a national newspaper, and even told me the best way to make contact with the Forest boss.

So on the evening of a home game at the City Ground I spoke to Carol, the Forest manager's PA, and explained I was looking for help in a piece I was writing about the former Forest centre-back. Carol said she'd put it to Mr Clough, and if I called back in 20 minutes she'd have an answer. When I called she told me the Forest boss was happy to oblige. There was then a pause, so long I wondered if the line had gone dead and I should hang up, before the great man spoke. "Hello, sh*t head," was his friendly greeting. "What can I do for you?" I explained the outline of the article, fearful that Hart's defection might spark a bitter response from his old boss. Far from it.

"Have you got your pen ready, sh*t head?" he asked. "The biggest mistake I've made in my time at Forest is giving a free transfer to that big, ugly centre-back Harty. How we've missed him this season. But if I had one wish for this season it's that big Harty wins the semi on Saturday and gets to Wembley for the final and I'll be there to support him – if he puts a ticket on for me!" He paused, and I came up with my next question, which was along the lines that some people thought Hart might have played for England if he'd had a yard more pace. The manager spotted his chance. "Are you a coach or a journalist, sh*t head?" I told him I was a journalist. "Right," he continued. "If Paul Hart had a yard more pace he would have played for England, but he didn't. He's made the most of what he had and he's a fine man. All right, sh*t head?"

And there, in a nutshell, was the essence of Clough: fiercely loyal to a player who had served Forest well. Hart's regard for Clough remained undiminished through his playing days to his time as Forest manager, when he brought through a posse of home-grown youngsters from the club academy he had been asked to run by Clough.

With Clough as our Forest icon we turn to the club's cult hero. In Forest life BC – before Clough – Ian Storey-Moore stood out as their most accomplished player. A goalscoring winger, he was their star in the late Sixties before a messy transfer saw him perform a U-turn on a move to Derby County and join Manchester United.

From the Clough era Stuart Pearce eclipses Peter Shilton among the fans' on-field heroes. Pearce, a ferocious left-back, played the game with the kind of zeal that warmed the hearts of fans. He was as committed to the Forest cause as they were, and that meant a lot to them. Pearce was at Forest when the club went into decline and was eventually relegated, but even then he didn't defect to calmer waters: he stayed at Forest to join the fight-back. And that loyalty meant so much to the Forest faithful.

But our cult hero has to be the little fat guy who Clough exquisitely harnessed into his team of European champions. Forest's cult hero is John Robertson. Clough said: "Robbo was a scruffy, unfit, uninterested waste of time. But something told me he was worth persevering with." That was hardly the warmest salute to the Scottish winger who smoked cigarettes and never hinted at being the finest trainer in the business. Some of his Forest team-mates sincerely believe that Robertson was a football genius. He was the release pass for them under pressure. He could retain possession on the left wing, make yards down the flank and then, at the critical moment, pick out a team-mate with a killer pass from the flank. Of course, Robbo's defection to Derby County was controversial, but he returned to extend his Forest connection.

In his book *The Great and the Good* John Giles assesses the truly great players of the modern era and what separates them from those who are just very, very good. Giles reveals that it's when he names Robertson alongside Bobby Charlton as one of the truly great players, he sometimes sparks looks of disbelief from the listeners. However, the former Leeds midfielder is a total believer in Robertson.

Perhaps the last word, as ever, should come from Old Big 'Ead. Asked to review Robbo's ability, Clough said: "Give him a yard of grass and he was an artist; the Picasso of our game."

THE FAN'S VIEW

Fiona Kitchen: "*Brian Clough gave us some great teams and happy times and John Robertson stands out as our greatest player. He was so unpredictable.*"

NOTTS COUNTY

ⓘ Jimmy Sirrel

ⓗ Tommy Lawton

The oldest professional League club in the world, Notts County are the original Magpies. Formed in 1862, they were founding members with 11 other clubs of the Football League in 1888.

In 1903, when Juventus wanted a new kit, they were given as a gift a black and white County outfit, which became Italy's most celebrated club's colours.

One man stands out as Notts County's icon, and it's Jimmy Sirrel, a man who was ahead of his time. That statement is easy to make, but there's hard evidence to prove the point.

It's over 30 years since Sirrel and County chairman Jack Dunnett came up with their blueprint for running a football club. The chairman would run the finances; Sirrel would effectively become the director of football; and they would recruit a young, talented coach to take charge of first-team coaching and day-to-day training. Admittedly it was a plan that had been deployed on the Continent, but Notts may well have been the forerunners in England when Sirrel invited Howard Wilkinson to become his first-team coach at Meadow Lane.

Wilkinson revealed: "I was sceptical about joining Notts because it was football legend that at Brentford, Aldershot and Notts Jimmy took charge of the laundry, the pitch, the treatment of injuries as well as the team. He then vowed if I took the job he would replace the tracksuit with a lounge suit. On that basis I became County's first team coach and with Jimmy forged a relationship that stood the test of time.

"Jimmy's waspish tongue could inflict serious damage. I agreed that after I had delivered the main team talk Jimmy would add his own personal thoughts. It goes without saying he always found it necessary. We used to take the players to the National Watersports Centre at Holme Pierrepoint before matches. On this particular occasion we were due to face Tommy Docherty's QPR in a League Cup tie. I casually mentioned to Jimmy that I wanted to have a quiet word with striker Trevor Christie who, I sensed, needed a little gee up.

"Unfortunately, Jimmy's wee word to the squad became a few wee words and then a few more until we were running late and had to dash to Meadow Lane. In the dressing room he asked whether I'd had a chance to speak to Trevor and when I told him I hadn't he advised me to leave the matter to him. He invited Trevor into the medical room and declared: 'The manager wanted a word with you, son, but time has not been kind so I shall speak with you instead. Big fellow, you're an effing coward!'

"My heart sank. I could see Trevor taking three months or more to get over this. I thought our chances were doomed and I would face a major challenge rebuilding a relationship with a key player. Instead, in his broad Geordie Christie simply said: 'I'll prove you wrong.' To my utter surprise he went out, played like a hero and scored a goal as we won 4-1."

Sirrel arrived at Meadow Lane for the first time in November 1969, when County was languishing in the basement division. There was a nucleus of a team that Sirrel would lead to the old Division Four title the following season.

Among that squad were men who became club heroes, like Don Masson, Les Bradd, Brian Stubbs and David Needham. Two years later another promotion was won from the old Third Division. Don Masson's tribute to the Scot emphasizes this impact, with the former County play-maker stating: "I owe everything in my football career to Jimmy – he was fantastic."

Two years later Sirrel accepted the job of managing top-flight Sheffield United. But his spell in Yorkshire was short-lived. By 1978 he was back at the Lane for his second stint in charge – and this time the glory game became even more glorious. He recruited that smart young FA coach called Wilkinson. County started the 1980–81 season as complete outsiders for promotion, but finished runners-up and went back into top-flight football for the first time in 55 years. They stayed up for three seasons, but Wilkinson left for Sheffield Wednesday and even a return into front-line management by Jimmy could not save the day.

Sirrel sadly passed away in 2008, but he will never, ever be forgotten by those that populate the terraces at Meadow Lane. There's a stand named in his honour. He's a true Notts County icon.

A few players can claim cult County hero status. There's Charlie Palmer who enjoyed a terrific spell under Neil Warnock's management at Meadow Lane. County won consecutive play-offs and appeared in an Anglo-Italian Cup final against Brescia. But perhaps Palmer's two greatest claims to fame were the match-winning goal he scored to beat arch-rivals Forest in a derby match and the County fans' favourite chant of those days: "We've got Charlie Palmer, he smokes marijuana!"

Don Masson, a cornerstone of Sirrel's teams, was not the most popular player inside the Meadow Lane dressing room. He set exacting standards and could be withering in his criticism of lesser mortals, but he was a brilliant midfield general. I remember seeing him play in 1971 when Third Division County beat the holders, Stoke City, in a League Cup tie at Meadow Lane. Masson was imperious. I'd never seen a player before who appeared to demand to take every free-kick, corner and throw-in. He didn't dictate play; he was the dictator of play. But even the great Scotland international pales alongside one of the true giants of English football and our County cult hero.

The football world was astonished when Tommy Lawton, the finest centre-forward in the game, opted to leave top-flight Chelsea to join County of the third tier in 1947. He was a few months short of his 28th birthday, in the prime of his career. He cost £20,000. He made 166 appearances for County and scored 103 goals, achieving cult status with the fans during his five years at Meadow Lane.

In later life Lawton was not the easiest person to get along with. His post-football world was beset by financial problems, and he became bitter about the riches on offer to the later generations of footballers. He died in 1996, aged 77. But those sad latter days cannot take away what he achieved as a true cult hero at Meadow Lane.

THE FAN'S VIEW

John Burgess: *"While Cloughie hogged the headlines across at Forest we knew we had a great manager at County in Jimmy Sirrel. His achievements with Notts were outstanding."*

OLDHAM ATHLETIC

 Andy Ritchie

 Roger Palmer

When the Premier League was launched in 1992 Oldham Athletic were among the founding members. They lasted only two years in the new top division of English football but their status as a top-flight club was testimony to Joe Royle's inspirational management.

Paul Scholes must surely rank as Oldham's most famous fan. Indeed, many Latics supporters have hoped down the years that the ginger-haired Manchester United star would choose to finish his playing career at Boundary Park, a venue he has visited consistently since his childhood days.

So when a man who ranks among Manchester United's greatest players announces who his footballing heroes are, and they played in the blue of Oldham, they surely take some topping in any battle to be the club's ultimate icon. The self-effacing Scholes doesn't do press conferences often or easily. He prefers to let his boots do his talking.

But in the countdown to England's clash with Argentina at the 2002 World Cup finals in Japan Scholes attended a press conference and was asked to name his favourite players. Given the setting at a summit of world footballing superpowers, the media in attendance presumed he would salute the likes of Zidane, Van Basten or maybe older heroes like Maradona or Pelé. Scholes needed no prompting. "Frankie Bunn," was Scholes' reply.

The journalists were silenced. They all asked "who's Frankie Bunn?" When pressed for another name, perhaps more mainstream, Scholes answered: "Andy Ritchie." Yes Scholes revelled in being unpredictable, but he was telling the truth. His two favourite players played for his favourite club. Not many big-time England stars would bother responding to a request for an interview for the Yeovil Town match programme, but Scholes did. He then made his declaration clear about his Oldham icon. He said: "My hero was Andy Ritchie – always was and always will be," before extolling the virtues of Frankie Bunn, Andy Barlow and the rest of Joe Royle's brilliant side.

Ritchie was one of those players who everyone knew was truly gifted, but who never seemed to get the right platform to display his talents – until Royle took him over the Pennines from Leeds in 1987. That route over the M62 had proved an excellent scouting path for Oldham, with Ritchie arriving from Elland Road a year after Denis Irwin and Andy Linighan. Irwin, in particular, proving to be a master-stroke signing by Royle.

But strikers do tend to grab the glory and Ritchie, who had played for Manchester United, Brighton and Leeds, emerged as the goalscoring king of Oldham in the greatest era of the club's history. Two managers stand out for their efforts at Boundary Park – Royle, and from an earlier era Jimmy Frizzell. Frizzell's achievement established a real degree of pride at a club that had spent too long in the doldrums. When he took over in 1970 they were in the lower reaches of the Fourth Division, facing the real threat of applying for re-election to the Football League. He guided them to safety and over the next 12 years not only won promotion but established them as a stable, well-run lower division club.

Coincidentally, Royle was also in charge of Oldham for 12 years. He arrived in 1982 and left to take charge of his beloved Everton in 1994.

So it was Royle who masterminded a brilliant recruitment policy for cut-price deals and free transfers. He also encouraged a high-tempo, attacking style that delighted the fans and proved a major problem for opponents. Add to this the controversial plastic pitch – which Oldham laid in 1987 – and you had a compelling recipe for an unfashionable club grabbing a stack of back page headlines.

Ritchie was the Latics' leading marksman in the sensational 1989–90 campaign when they reached the League Cup final and FA Cup semi-finals. Boundary Park was rocking as Oldham swept away higher division opponents like Arsenal and Southampton in a series of memorable Cup ties. But getting Oldham into the top flight must surely rank as the greatest achievement of Royle's reign at Boundary Park, and Ritchie was a central figure in that 1991 triumph. Despite criticism from opponents, Oldham could play on grass as well as their plastic pitch.

So our Oldham icon is Andy Ritchie. Perhaps his attacking sidekick Frankie Bunn should be our cult hero? Admittedly, there are a gang of rivals from the Royle era, including the manager himself and some notable heroes like Dennis Irwin, winger Rick Holden and midfielders Mike Milligan and Neil Redfearn.

But our Oldham cult hero is another astute signing and, coincidentally, a man out of the Paul Scholes mould who preferred a low profile and quietly declined most requests for interview: Roger Palmer, Oldham's record goalscorer. Palmer played for Manchester City before finding chances there limited and moving to Oldham in 1981. He spent 13 years with the club and scored 141 goals. He was a lethal finisher who favoured his right foot but dispatched some superb headed goals – a worthy cult hero.

OXFORD UNITED

 John Aldridge

 Ron Atkinson

If you ever wanted living, breathing proof that the art of goalscoring can be transferred across different levels of football, look no further than John William Aldridge.

Before he became internationally famous with Liverpool and the Republic of Ireland, Aldo was scoring goals for fun with little Oxford United. He was signed from Newport County in 1983–84 for £78,000 but was used sparingly in Oxford's run-in to the old Third Division title. But the following campaign saw Aldridge form a deadly partnership with Billy Hamilton, becoming the first Second Division player for 19 years to reach 30 goals.

And Aldridge hit six goals to help Oxford win the League Cup in 1986, the only major trophy they've won in their history. Aldridge also famously scored one of the goals in a 2-1 win over Manchester United that wrecked Alex Ferguson's 1986 debut as manager. All told he scored 90 goals in 141 games for Oxford before joining Liverpool for £750,000 in 1987.

There was a time when one man epitomized Oxford as a club. Nicknamed "The Tank", Ron Atkinson was a vital part of Oxford's progress through the Sixties and early Seventies. Big Ron and his younger brother Graham were both rejected by their home-town club Aston Villa and found salvation in non-League football at Oxford – then known as Headington United.

The Atkinsons were outstanding stalwarts in building the foundations that lifted the club from their Headington United days to eventually become a First Division outfit who actually won a major trophy.

As a player Ron holds the club record for the most overall appearances for Oxford United with 500, while younger brother Graham is the club's top all-time marksman, with 107 goals. Graham had the distinction of scoring Oxford's first-ever Football League goal in 1962 against Barrow. But his big brother was the bigger favourite with the fans. Both Atkinsons later left for Kettering before Ron became famous in management and as a leading, if at times controversial, television pundit.

PETERBOROUGH UNITED

 Terry Bly

 **Ken Charlery**

Terry Bly became an instant hit in Peterborough's first-ever Football League season of 1960–61 when he scored an incredible 52 League goals as the newcomers ran away with the Division Four title.

Bly made his debut as Posh played their first-ever League game against Wrexham on 20th August 1960, following his £5,000 transfer from Norwich City. He showed his scoring ability by netting the third goal in the inaugural 3-0 victory at London Road.

The tall, brave East Anglian just couldn't stop scoring that season, and his total of 52 League goals has never been bettered in the post-war era. Only four men in English League history have topped Bly's tally: Dixie Dean's 60 for Everton in 1927–28 remains the all-time best total.

Stepping up a level in 1961–62 lessened Bly's strike rate but he still managed 33 goals.

All told, Bly scored 81 goals in 88 games in those fabulous two seasons at Peterborough. He died in 2009 from a heart attack at the age of 73.

While Bly's goalscoring heroics make him our irresistible Posh icon, our cult hero is widely known around London Road as King Ken. Stepney-born St Lucia international Ken Charlery grabbed legendary status in his first spell at Peterborough United by scoring two goals at Wembley in the 1992 Third Division play-off final against Stockport, the second an 89th-minute winner. He totalled 26 goals in that memorable campaign.

Ken first left Posh in the 1992–93 season to sign for Watford, rejoining the following year for a second spell at London Road.

He was named skipper for the 1994–95 season and was voted Player of the Year – the second time he'd received the accolade. Again he was on the move, joining Birmingham in 1995. But was back for a third spell with Posh in 1996. In the 1996–97 season he endured a run of 24 scoreless games, but in all Charlery scored 80 goals in 228 games during three eventful spells at Posh.

PLYMOUTH ARGYLE

 Tommy Tynan

 Paul Wotton

He was football's original reality star. Long before TV came up with *The X Factor* or *Britain's Got Talent*, the *Liverpool Echo* ran a competition to find a football hero and a 16-year-old kid called Tommy Tynan won an apprenticeship at Anfield as first prize.

Sadly, the nearest he got to playing for Bill Shankly's champions was a run-out in Ron Yeats' testimonial. But the chance to learn alongside legends helped him forge a career scoring goals for Swansea, Sheffield Wednesday, Lincoln and Newport before in 1983 he arrived at Plymouth Argyle.

It proved a dream move both for him and the club. Settled in the surroundings of the Devon city he became an instant hero of what was arguably the club's most successful era. He was the star of the side which reached the FA Cup semi-finals in 1984, scoring the goal that beat First Division West Bromwich Albion in the fifth round. In the next season he was even more prolific, collecting 31 goals to be joint top scorer in all four divisions of the Football League.

He moved on that summer to Rotherham, but was back in less than a year, scoring nine in as many matches in a thrilling climax to the season to help clinch promotion to the old Division Two.

He played with a smile on his face, and the fans loved him. He trained the same way. He was a goalscoring machine. He told anybody who would listen that he'd rather score three goals from a yard out than one spectacular one from 30. And by the time he left the club at the age of 35 he'd scored 126 in all for The Pilgrims in 262 games.

Tynan continued to live in Plymouth when his playing days ended. He had become an adopted son of the West Country city, but the club's cult hero was born and brought up there. Powerful defender Paul Wotton only ever wanted to play at Home Park, and he got his wish when then manager Neil Warnock signed him straight from school.

In 1998, when the club were relegated to the bottom tier, Wotton was asked about his future and answered with the pledge that he would be part of a side that won promotion. His words came true four years later as he captained the team which won the Division Three title in 2002 with a record haul of 102 points. Two seasons later and he was holding silverware again, this time the trophy for Division Two champions as the club reached the Championship.

Released by Argyle in 2008, he played for Southampton and Yeovil before being asked by then manager Carl Fletcher if he fancied returning to Home Park. His answer? "I'd walk over broken glass to get there." At a club now fighting to retain its Football League status he brought experience and commitment as he moved into the top three of their all-time appearance figures.

Revered for his passion and his commitment to his home-town team, Wotton has also always been loved for the way he takes free kicks and penalties – thumping the ball with a rocket shot that has brought him more than 50 goals in his two spells for the club.

THE FAN'S VIEW

Ged: *"Tommy Tynan equals goals. Says it all."*

PORT VALE

 **Robbie Earle**  **Neil Aspin**

Robbie Williams and Howard Wilkinson may be very different but they have one thing in common: they're both avid fans of our Vale cult hero, Neil Aspin.

That might surprise people who recall it was Leeds boss Wilkinson who decided to let Aspin leave the club he'd supported all his life in order to move to the Potteries in a £150,000 deal after making over 200 appearances for Leeds.

It was at Vale Park that Williams, following the club before he became a pop superstar, joined the Vale fans who adopted Aspo as their perfect anti-hero. He was prematurely bald and the platinum blond wisps of hair he retained didn't get spotted on a football pitch. He was a junior Bobby Charlton. A Leeds coach once said: "Neil looked about 70 when he was 17." But while he looked old before his time there was never any doubting Neil's commitment or athleticism.

His managers lost count of the number of strikers who thought they could knock the ball past Aspo and out-sprint him. They were so misguided: as well as being muscular, awkward and hard, Aspin had real pace. In a sprint he'd flip his turbo switch and surge past the surprised attacker.

Wilkinson sold him on yet thought so much of Aspin he always wanted to help him. I recall getting calls from Leeds when Wilkinson and his assistant Mick Hennighan wanted to support Aspin's testimonial. In that game there was a guest appearance from the Take That star Williams, who counted Aspin among his friends. The two seemed incongruous buddies, but there was something straightforward about the Gateshead-born defender that made you feel Robbie would be enriched by having Aspo as his mate.

When writing about Aspin in 2012, Robbie Earle commented: "Aspo was one of those guys who played with a very basic philosophy. Either the ball or the player could pass him, but never both – and he often preferred to clear the player rather than the ball."

And it's Earle who wins our title as Port Vale icon. It's widely accepted that the player who was released by arch-rivals Stoke City became Vale's finest player. Stoke released him after he'd broken his leg. Vale grabbed the opportunity to sign the local boy. Initially he was seen as a utility player, operating in virtually every position bar goalie. But eventually Earle proved to be an outstanding attacking midfielder.

Under the expert tutelage of John Rudge, one of the great lower division managers of his time, Vale became a dashing, attacking team with Earle at their heart. Vale Park boasted one of the biggest pitches in English football and the home side used that to the full. No top-flight team relished visiting Vale for a Cup tie.

Earle spent nine years at Vale Park. He helped the club win two promotions and he was saluted by the Vale fans as their favourite player. Robbie made 357 appearances for Vale and scored 90 goals. But his ready smile, erudite manner and stylish football made him much more than a set of impressive statistics.

THE FAN'S VIEW

Stevie Watt: *"Robbie Earle was our goalscoring pearl. Great bloke. Great player."*

PORTSMOUTH

(i) **Alan Knight**  (h) **Micky Quinn**

"This lad is one of the warmest people you could wish to meet." Those are the words that described our Portsmouth cult hero, Micky Quinn.

They were uttered by Alan Ball, Pompey's manager back in January 1987. His sentiments were sincere, if the setting was slightly strange: Ball had to declare his belief in the chubby Pompey striker as Quinn prepared to serve 21 days in prison after twice being convicted of driving while banned.

These were interesting times for Ball. He had put together a team that would eventually win promotion to the top flight. Euphemistically it would be claimed that the Pompey team was "full of characters". Quinn himself described that team as "football's Dirty Dozen".

There have been many contenders for cult hero down the years at Fratton Park. Paul Merson, Kanu and Micky Kennedy can all stake their own claims. Micky grabs our prize for a specific showdown in the crazy world of Bally's bad boys. It came when Wimbledon visited Fratton Park and the police were forced to break up a ruck between warring players at half-time in the tunnel. It was the day that John Fashanu hit the deck.

Quinn recalled what happened next. "Ball went berserk. 'That was disgraceful. You've behaved like animals and let the club down. I want to know who started it.'

"I stood up and said: 'It was me Boss. I chinned Fash because he dropped Billy Gilbert in the tunnel.' Bally yelled: 'Is that right Billy?'

"'Well I did go down in the tunnel,' Billy replied. 'But Fash didn't hit me. I tripped and fell down the stairs.'

"The manager was apoplectic. But he shouldn't have been surprised. At Portsmouth Ball had a team that were the footballing equivalent of the Dirty Dozen. And I fitted the bill perfectly. I came from a hard background and was never afraid to dish it out if required. John Fashanu was known as Fash the Bash but reputations didn't bother me."

Ball recruited Quinn in a £150,000 deal from Oldham. The Liverpool-born striker never looked like an athlete. He was always on the portly side of hefty. But he knew how to dispatch goals with a clinical zeal that suggested he could play at the highest level. At times, though, he just gave off the air of a lazy, fat layabout. His run-ins with the law came early in his Pompey career but he still established himself as Portsmouth's top goalscorer. He claimed 24 goals as Pompey finished the campaign as Second Division runners-up and finally moved back into the top flight in 1987. Sadly, Pompey were relegated after just one season. Quinn stayed at Fratton Park and scored 20 goals in the 1988–89 campaign, but Pompey struggled and Ball was replaced by John Gregory. The new boss appointed Quinn as skipper but when his contract expired at the end of the season Quinn moved on to Newcastle.

Quinn was well aware of the terrace taunts he was subjected to. He explained: "There was a lot made of my weight and size, but you don't play 600 League games if you're unfit. That's the way I was built – it was my strength. I would laugh off the chants of 'Who ate all the pies?' and just put one in the back of the net. Then the fans questioned my parentage and not my weight!

"I had a sense of humour. I remember at West Ham once we were waiting for a corner and some fan shouted the chant and threw a pie at me. I actually managed to catch a bit of it and I just ate it in front of him! I didn't make a fuss and his mates started giving him stick. Laughing it off is always best."

Our Pompey icon is the goalie who made 801 appearances for the club – Alan Knight. He actually holds the record for the number of appearances by a goalkeeper at a single club. Between 1978 and 2000 he was the cornerstone of the Pompey defence.

Knight's value to the Pompey cause saw him nicknamed "The Legend" by his fans. He was that good and earned immense respect. But football has an awful habit of exploiting a man's failings. Knight's career was over when he revealed he was enduring major alcohol-related problems and issues with his personal finances. The fact that these crises engulfed an apparently level-headed hero simply emphasized his humanity in the eyes of his supporters.

Knight explained: "I grew up in a drinking culture and it was normal to go out drinking with the lads. Football and drinking used to go hand in hand, but slowly my drinking increased to a point where sometimes I felt I needed up to eight pints at night just to be able to sleep. Although I drank heavily at this time, it wasn't until my football career finished and all that structure was taken away that my life fell to bits. My drinking was starting to impact on my life in so many ways. My relationship with my wife and then my new partner fell to pieces, my health started suffering and I was in debt."

Knight sought professional advice and regained control of his life. In a sense his plight stressed the point that even club icons have to deal with their own demons.

PRESTON NORTH END

(i) Sir Tom Finney   (h) Graham Alexander

Sometimes you meet a sporting legend and are left disappointed. Perhaps they've become sour and disaffected by their sport, frustrated by the salaries on offer to players they know are their inferiors.

Anybody who met the great Sir Tom Finney realized that he was a truly special man. He appreciated the past and his achievements but he still marvelled at the joys of football and particularly his beloved home-town club Preston North End.

I never saw Sir Tom play, but I met him first in the Seventies when I was a young reporter. The first meeting was a chance encounter on the staircase at Deepdale after a game. Tom's old team-mate Bobby Charlton was managing the club at this time.

I'd been taught to introduce myself politely to my elders and betters. I couldn't believe that Tom spent 10 minutes chatting away about that day's game, the relegation battle Preston were facing, the state of English football and finally, at my pressing, his career. Tom's bright blue eyes sparkled as he aired his views. The way he was so animated and friendly in sharing his thoughts with a young journalist always astonished me. And yet whenever we met at Deepdale he'd come over for a chat, always remembering my first name and always showing absolute courtesy. He was never looking around the room to join the more famous faces. He was charm personified – apart from the day when I called him to discuss allegations of betting coups and match-fixing in football. Tom was then outraged and outspoken; so people should not perceive the great man as an angel who lives in a sporting paradise.

But in terms of his ability as a footballer, he had been blessed with sublime gifts. My first awareness that Tom must have been a supreme player was hearing Liverpool manager Bill Shankly discuss the identity of the greatest player he'd ever seen: Shanks had played alongside Finney at Preston and was adamant that Finney was that man.

Tommy Docherty also played for Preston behind Finney. And in terms of making a modern comparison the Doc was inspired. He said: "In his day Tom was like Lionel Messi of today. He was that good. And he played the game in the same way. He was a model pro, Preston North End through and through. He was the perfect model as a footballer and as a person."

During his illustrious career in which he made 473 appearances for his home-town club and won 76 caps for England, Finney was also twice crowned as

Footballer of the Year. Bobby Charlton was an emerging young England player when Finney was in his pomp. Charlton's regard for the man known as the Preston plumber is informed and unstinting. Bobby said: "He was one of the greatest, arguably the greatest, that there has ever been.

"I used to gain great pleasure watching Tom play. I used to dream about controlling the ball, dribbling, passing with left and right feet like he did. I remember playing against Scotland with him in the England team and we beat them 4-0. Tommy got the ball, got to the dead ball line. I'd always been told to support the attacking player. I dashed like hell to get into the area. I didn't have to check my stride. Tom beat the Scotland full-back, crossed the ball and it came to me about two feet off the ground. I smashed my shot and it flew into the top corner.

"Tommy had so much in his locker. He could be right-footed, left-footed, deliver a pinpoint cross, head the ball and tackle. Stanley Matthews, for example, didn't really tackle. Stan was a wonderful player but Tom could do everything Stan could do and more.

"Tom could have played in any era, in any tactical system and on any pitches. He was just magic."

Nobody connected with Preston will expect any name beyond Sir Tom Finney to be listed as their club icon. But, given the immense rivalry among the Lancashire clubs, it may surprise some of them to hear the salute from a club not too many miles east of Deepdale. Jimmy McIlroy, acknowledged as Burnley's greatest ever player, was an international star with Northern Ireland when they reached the 1958 World Cup finals.

McIlroy was regarded as one of the great creative thinkers in the game. To this day McIlroy insists: "Tom was the greatest player I've ever seen – and I include Pelé when I make that observation."

Finney has dwarfed any other North End player, but there are still some potential cult heroes left. There was Alan Kelly Snr, the Republic of Ireland international who played for them in the Sixties and Seventies and whose career was ended by a severe elbow injury. And a talent scout called Jim Scott sent a posse of gifted Scottish players south to Deepdale that included the likes of Archie Gemmill, Alex Bruce and Mel Holden.

But we'll nominate as Preston's cult hero the grand old man of English football, Graham Alexander.

Alexander had two spells as a player at Deepdale, with a spectacular cameo at Burnley in between. He ended up playing beyond his 40th birthday and with Tony Ford is one of only two outfield players to make over 1,000 appearances.

QPR

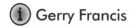 **Gerry Francis**

 **Stan Bowles**

Queens Park Rangers are the most nomadic club in League football. It's acknowledged that with 16 different venues they've had more changes of home ground than any other. Rangers had spent most of their days living in the third tier of English football but were always a friendly, welcoming club that attracted support from west London locals committed to the cause. Then, in 1967, a double event happened that changed everybody's perception of the club that wore the famous blue and white hoops.

Rangers achieved a remarkable Double that season when they combined promotion from the Third Division with a thrilling 3-2 fight-back victory over West Bromwich Albion in the League Cup final. It was the first time a Third Division club had won a Wembley final.

At a stroke people were taking notice of QPR, the squad put together by manager Alec Stock and astutely coached by Bill Dodgin Jnr. As so often happens when an unsung club suddenly bursts to prominence, the basis for success was a youth development programme that had been patiently nurtured and was now reaping rich rewards. The likes of Frank Sibley, Roger and Ian Morgan and Mick Leach were aided and abetted by astute signings, like 21-year-old Rodney Marsh from Fulham, for just £15,000 in March 1966.

Any assessment of icons and cult heroes at Loftus Road has to include Rodney. In his first full season he scored 44 goals in 53 games as that remarkable Double was achieved. Then, in the following season, Rangers marched through the old Second Division to reach the top flight for the first time in their history. Marsh was a maverick. He had fallen out with manager Vic Buckingham at Fulham and was always ready to offer his own views on a variety of subjects. Yet that self-confident, opinionated attitude earned his affection at Loftus Road. He was a one-off who played his football that way. He brought a skilful, continental approach to the QPR number 10 shirt.

QPR were on a roller-coaster during Rodney's days, and struggled to establish themselves as a top-flight club. That achievement would come after their talisman had been sold to Manchester City for £220,000 in 1972. And the income from Marsh's sale was used wisely, as a group of players was assembled that would take QPR to the greatest high in their history. The man who was to succeed Rodney as their creative genius eclipses him as the club's cult hero. Stan Bowles was even more unpredictable than his predecessor. He certainly got into more scrapes off the field, with his penchant for gambling.

Gerry Francis, the young QPR skipper of the Seventies, recalls a memorable visit to share a meal at chez Bowles. He said: "We were sitting down eating lunch, Stan's wife at the time went to answer the door and it was the bailiffs. They came in, took the table we were eating at, the chairs we were sitting on and the television we were watching. After they left, our plates of food were on the floor. That was life with Stan."

Bowles was born in the Collyhurst area of Manchester. This was a breeding ground for fine footballers and comedians, with the likes of Nobby Stiles, Brian Kidd and Les Dawson being born there. Perhaps Stan was blessed with both sets of skills. He was a contemporary of Kidd, and while Brian joined Manchester United, Stan headed to City. But whereas Kidd was to enjoy an immediate breakthrough at Old Trafford, Stan set off on his wanderings. He was released by City and headed to Bury, Crewe and Carlisle before joining Rangers for £112,000. Six months after the sale of Marsh, Rangers had their new attacking talisman. He spent seven years at Loftus Road in what must surely still be accepted as Rangers' greatest ever side. They had a real tilt at winning the title in 1976 only to be beaten at the death by Liverpool. It remains one of football's great ironies that Dave Sexton, the manager who had fallen out in such spectacular style with Peter Osgood and Alan Hudson at Chelsea, could develop such a fine working relationship with Bowles. But they undoubtedly helped each other.

And then there came another prodigious home-grown talent. Gerry Francis was so good that after only four senior international appearances he was named England captain. Sadly, he never played in the same England team as his Rangers colleague Bowles, because the link between the midfielder and striker was uncanny and so productive. Certainly, the careers of Bowles and Francis are linked. Put together at Loftus Road, they formed a partnership that in Gerry's own words "was telepathic".

Bowles explained: "Me and Gerry hit it off straight away. Terry Venables said at the time we'd only played in one five-a-side game together, we'd never met each other before but we just hit it off. I loved playing with Gerry and he loved playing with me."

Francis, the epitome of the modern box-to-box midfielder, agreed: "It was such a great understanding. It was telepathic. I could play things blind and he could do the same and we really, really enjoyed playing with each other." There was an intriguing balance to the Rangers team as they hit new heights in the mid-Seventies. Frank McLintock was the elder statesman at the back: a man who'd seen it all as skipper of the Arsenal Double-winning team of 1971, as well as his time in and around the Scotland team. McLintock's verdict of Bowles? "Stan was a little bit unique. Dave Sexton understood him quite well. He thought the world of Stan, because he knew he was a great player. People say to me, when I do after dinner speeches: 'Who is the best player that you've ever played with?' Well, Stan would rank with some of the best I've ever played with. He was a superb player at Rangers."

Sadly, the fact that Francis and Bowles were kept apart on England duty leaves Francis frustrated to this day. To a degree Stan blames himself and his attitude. Bowles: "I could be very arrogant when I felt in the mood – without a doubt. That's why I didn't get on with the England squad and didn't get so many caps. They didn't really want to talk to me. Where I'd be taking the mickey in League games, they didn't talk to me at all – Emlyn Hughes and that lot." As new England manager, Don Revie had persuaded the FA to increase the match fee from £100 to £300, and passed on what he thought was the good news to the players. Hughes, the Liverpool legend, went on record to say he wasn't bothered about money. When it came to representing England it was all about pride – not money.

Bowles recalled: "Don Revie tried to get the money put up. Emlyn Hughes stood up, when there were no staff around, and said in a players meeting we should play for nothing for the Three Lions. Jokingly I shouted out that I'd have his extra money then! Nobody spoke to me for the next three days and I didn't get picked for the next game."

Stan the Man, the maverick striker of QPR, wins our award as cult hero of Loftus Road. With it comes a citation from another seasoned pro who played alongside him for the Rs. David Webb said: "Stan's vision of the game was second to none. I used to find myself applauding some of Stan's magic moments." That's how Bowles, on his good days, could make any lover of fine football feel.

So who should be our QPR icon? Undoubtedly Les Ferdinand must be considered. He arrived for just £5,000 from non-League Hayes in 1986, and over the next nine years made himself a sporting hero in west London. Such was the acclaim heaped on him, as much for his unpretentious, friendly manner off the field as his goalscoring heroics on it, that the Rangers faithful nicknamed him "Sir Les". In his early days Rangers were invariably fighting to avoid relegation from the top flight. Ferdinand's 10 goals in 23 games in the 1991–92 season saw him established as a first-team regular, and his club guaranteed a place in the new Premier League. In the debut season of the new set-up Les got even better, with 20 goals in 37 games. Rangers finished fifth that season – London's top side.

If not quite back to the heady heights of Dave Sexton's team, these were happy days for Rangers. Ferdinand was accepted as one of the hottest strikers in English football, and yet he was still happy to sign a new two-year deal in 1994 to stay with his first senior club. That meant a lot to Rangers fans. Inevitably the time arrived where a big enough bid was going to prise Sir Les away. In 1995 he was sold to Newcastle for £6million: that deal remains Rangers' most expensive sale.

But our Rangers icon is the man with the mullet, Gerry Francis. The breakthrough he made and some of his performances for club and country were quite extraordinary. He was the Steven Gerrard of his era. Given the dominance of Liverpool, Manchester City and Derby players at this time, it is astonishing that one so young, and from QPR, could be selected to skipper his country.

Francis, of course, went on to manage Rangers too. He'd proved his worth at Bristol Rovers before becoming Loftus Road boss in 1991. He was the man in charge as they ensured they were part of the Premier League and became London's top team in 1993. The fact that Gerry resigned from his post and quickly became the Tottenham manager midway through the 1994–95 season disappointed the Rangers' faithful. He returned in 1998 but the club was unstable by then, and he resigned in early 2001. So there were some splendid highs – such as a 4-1 New Year's Day victory at Manchester United in 1992 – as well as some frustrating failure.

But Francis represented something special at QPR. A persistent back injury prevented him truly fulfilling his astonishing potential, but he wins our icon status because he was the real deal. The complete midfielder.

THE FAN'S VIEW

Pete Smith: *"Stan Bowles was the man who made us laugh, cry and sing. What an entertainer. He must be our cult hero."*

READING

 **Steve Coppell**

 **Robin Friday**

It's incredible to think that if Robert Maxwell had won his battle for power Reading FC would have ceased to exist 30 years ago.

Given the club has twice hit the heady heights of Premier League football in the last seven years, the advent of Maxwell's ill-judged Thames Valley Royals and demise of Reading would have been a sporting catastrophe. It was back in the spring of 1983 that the autocratic millionaire businessman, who already owned Oxford United, announced his intention to merge the clubs and create a new home stadium, probably at Didcot.

It was a sensational story. Other clubs had been linked with proposed mergers in the past. In 1967 Brentford and QPR had discussed a potential union, but supporters' groups objected vehemently and insisted on protecting each club's unique identity. With the passage of time we now know Maxwell would become a discredited, dictatorial businessman. Back in 1983 he presented the merger as a done deal. He owned Oxford United, claimed he had a watertight deal in place with the majority owners of Reading, and his route to creating Thames Valley Royals would not be diverted by anybody. He had not taken into account the ill-feeling he would generate among both sets of supporters.

When we debate cult heroes at Reading we shouldn't forget the role former player Roger Smee played in torpedoing the Maxwell masterplan. While Maxwell's fellow directors at Oxford believed there was no alternative, the supporters launched their counter-attacks. Smee galvanized efforts at the Elm Park end with relish. Maxwell, ever ready to bully the opposition into defeat, rounded on his critics. He said: "If they wish to oppose it they can get themselves a new chairman for Oxford United and let somebody else pick up the tab. The option they have is to have the Thames Valley Royals to carry on the great tradition of Oxford United and Reading football – or to have no football in Oxford." He also claimed that the campaign to stop the merger was like "trying to make the Thames run backwards". Little did he know what would happen next.

With Smee launching a counter-bid for Reading, the Elm Park board's unity began to unravel. It proved a critical blow when Roy Tranter, a key Reading director behind the takeover, admitted he did not have a controlling number of shares to sell to Maxwell. A legal injunction followed and the takeover gradually disintegrated. Smee, a former Reading and Chelsea player, was hailed as a hero for his stance.

He took charge from 1983 until selling out to John Madejski seven years later: Smee accepted his pockets weren't deep enough to take Reading further, but Madejski guided them to the Premier League in 2006. It was the first time in their history that Reading had competed in the top flight. Madejski had also overseen the move from Elm Park, the club's home for 102 years, to the brand new Madejski Stadium in 1998. There's no doubting the popularity Madejski enjoyed from his historic reign as chairman and owner, and yet Smee's success in blocking the Maxwell takeover is seen by many followers of the Royals as even more significant. You can understand why.

Our Reading icon is a man that Madejski appointed as his manager. Steve Coppell has endured a roller-coaster reputation as a manager. Widely saluted for his work in developing Crystal Palace and Reading, Manchester City fans still wonder why he walked away from their club after a few weeks in charge. Reading were in good shape when Coppell succeeded Alan Pardew as manager. But what he achieved was quite astonishing and remains in the record books of English football.

Coppell's team didn't just win promotion from the Championship in the 2005–06 season. They annihilated their rivals by scoring 99 goals, only losing two games and accumulating a record 106 points to be crowned champions. Coppell wasn't just voted Manager of the Year for the Championship. He won the award for the entire Leagues – including the Premier League. That was the regard in which his achievement was seen by his rivals. Reading, classically perceived as a homely club from the third level of the English game, had hit the top flight. Coppell had overseen a football miracle – and it didn't end with that moment of promotion glory.

Reading were widely tipped to face relegation after just one Premier League campaign. How they silenced their critics. They finished the 2006–07 season in eighth place. It was a wonderful return for Coppell and his hard-working team. Coppell was again voted the League Managers Association's Manager of the Year. Manchester United boss Sir Alex Ferguson said: "I think it's totally deserved. It's a marvellous contribution he's made. And what's encouraging for the Premiership is that it's mostly British-based players in his side, with some Irish players thrown in. I think that says a lot for the way he has gathered his team together."

But even Steve could not keep working miracles, and the 2007–08 campaign ended in relegation. The following season, back in the Championship, saw Reading start with a 15-match unbeaten home run, but eventually they slipped into a play-off place and were beaten by Burnley in the semi-finals. Within hours of that set-back Coppell quit. But he remains an iconic figure to Reading fans. Many still refer to him as Sir Steve, so we'll hand him the status as being Reading's football icon.

As to their cult hero, there are a few contenders. Ronnie Blackman must be considered. He remains the club's most lethal marksman. He dispatched 39 League goals in the 1951–52 season when Reading were competing in the Third Division South. His Reading career total of 158 goals has never been surpassed.

And there's the man we salute as our cult hero – Robin Friday. The Acton-born striker had been signed and released by Crystal Palace, QPR, Chelsea and Reading as a youngster before he made his way in non-League circles. He was signed by Reading when they were a Fourth Division club in 1974. His impact was immediate as he emerged as a star performer in the promotion-winning, 1975–76 season. He was an impressive sight. Highly combative and clever at leading the line, he could produce moments of creative magic to bamboozle opponents and delight the fans. He was twice voted Reading's Player of the Year.

Welsh referee Clive Thomas was in charge of a Reading game against Tranmere when Friday dispatched an audacious goal from around 30 yards. Thomas insisted: "Even up against the likes of Pelé and Cruyff that rates as the best goal I have ever seen."

It was Friday's off-field persona that ensured his notoriety. He was known for his heavy smoking, drinking, involvement with a string of women and, eventually, drug abuse. It was the latter that sparked his transfer to Cardiff City. Friday's form had dipped, and Reading decided to shift the player who was becoming an increasing problem. He could hardly have made a more spectacular start at Cardiff. Friday had not bought a rail ticket for the journey to South Wales and was apprehended at Cardiff station, where the stunned Cardiff manager had to bail him out. Friday stopped playing when he was just 25. He died of a suspected heroin overdose in 1998. He was 38.

THE FAN'S VIEW

Roger: *"Robin Friday wasn't with us long but those who saw him will never forget him. He was truly astonishing."*

ROCHDALE

(i) Reg Jenkins

(h) Adam Le Fondre

It's fair to state that Cornwall has hardly been a fertile breeding ground for footballers. England international goalie Nigel Martyn is probably the most famous and Mike Trebilcock was a match-winner for Everton in the 1966 FA Cup final. But Rochdale fans will justifiably claim that their club signed a Cornishman who became their best ever player.

Reg Jenkins was born in Millbrook, Cornwall, in 1938. He started his career in Devon with Plymouth Argyle and Exeter and then moved to Torquay. He appeared to be on a football tour of the South West. But the making of the man, and his club, came when Jenkins travelled north to join Rochdale in 1964. It proved to be an inspired move as Jenkins, described in those days as a goalscoring inside-forward, went on to become Dale's record marksman and, at the time, set up an appearance record.

Every boy was told the story about a man who could shoot so hard the ball broke the back of the net. That man was Reg Jenkins and the story was factually correct – not another football legend. That's how Reg became known as unfashionable Dale's very own Roy of the Rovers. He made the incredible happen.

Reg scored 119 goals in 305 League appearances. He was a key member of Dale's first ever promotion-winning side. He was renowned as a tough, forceful player who competed hard – but fair. Jenkins scored 13 goals as Rochdale finished third to climb out of the Fourth Division in 1969.

Reg passed away in Tenerife in January 2013, aged 74. In an interview he said: "That was obviously the highlight of my time at Rochdale. The best bit was seeing the smile on Fred Ratcliffe's (chairman) face because he was such a big part of the club. The day we went up was a little bit of a dream."

Rochdale had to win or draw against Southend to win promotion. Reg scored twice in a 3-0 win to ensure history was made.

So, with Jenkins established as our icon, we turn to cult hero and there are a number of strikers who've played for the Lancashire club in their formative years. Alan Taylor, who became a West Ham FA Cup hero is one. And more recently Dale fans have saluted the combative Grant Holt (who is hailed as Norwich's cult hero) and our Dale cult hero, Adam Le Fondre.

Le Fondre, who is universally known as Alf (an abbreviation of his initials), will hate any reminder of this fact, but it's true. In Reading's Premier League campaign of 2012–13 he became typecast as a supersub. That's nothing new to Alf. He was consigned to the same kind of cameo appearances at Spotland. And, invariably, he came on and delivered goals.

He originally joined Rochdale on loan from his home-town club, Stockport County. He scored four goals in seven games on loan to excite the Dale fans and convince manager Keith Hill he should sign the young Manchester United fan. Alf revelled in life at Spotland – apart from the fact he was still too often named as a sub. But from the bench he was so effective. He scored 17 goals in his first full season and 21 in his second when Dale reached the promotion play-off final. Unfortunately, Le Fondre lost to his first club, Stockport 3-2. To help cover their Inland Revenue debts Le Fondre was sold to Rotherham, but he left behind many happy memories and the knowledge that Dale fans had seen a clinical finisher who would ply his trade at a much higher level.

THE FAN'S VIEW
Bob Johnson: *"Reg Jenkins is our best ever player. He must be our icon."*

ROTHERHAM UNITED

 Ronnie Moore

 John Breckin

What do Leeds United and Rotherham United have in common – apart from being Yorkshire football clubs?

Well, both clubs have famous presidents who sport facial hair. And two of the three are comedians. So step forward Leeds president Ken Bates and Rotherham's Paul and Barry Elliott, otherwise and professionally known as the Chuckle Brothers.

Our Rotherham icon is also a man with a sharp sense of humour. Ronnie Moore is loud, proud and a wicked mickey-taker, ever ready to wind up his players, staff and opposing fans. Big Ronnie loves a laugh and enjoys life to the full. He played for the Millers and our Rotherham cult hero was a contemporary of his. John Breckin was a dependable, stylish left-back who also worked as Moore's assistant-manager during some of the club's glory days.

Ronnie arrived in south Yorkshire for the first time as a player in 1980. In his first spell Moore spent three successful years there but there was the hint of a nomad in his career as he moved to Charlton, Rochdale and back to Tranmere until he retired in 1989. He worked at Tranmere as assistant-manager to John King, had a brief spell as manager of non-League Southport and then headed back across the Pennines to become Rotherham manager. He was an amazing success.

Moore led his team to consecutive promotions, taking them from Division Three to Division One between 1999 and 2001.

He was a larger-than-life presence around the club and the fans loved his personality. He had eight years in charge before leaving in 2005. Four years and three managers later, Ronnie was invited back. He began his second stint in September 2009, much to the delight of the United supporters. In his first season he guided his team to the League Two play-off final at Wembley, only to see his team lose 3-2 to Dagenham and Redbridge at the new Wembley. The following season Rotherham started well but fell away and, after a run of five games without a win, Ronnie left the club by mutual consent. It was hardly a disaster though. Rotherham were sixth in the table.

He remains the most successful manager in the club's history but he was more than that to Millers' fans. That's why he's our icon.

Breckin, our cult hero, had a different personality from Ronnie's but was also a club stalwart. He was in the teams that won promotion in 1975 and 1981. He briefly managed United in 1987, but he was more suited as an assistant and he did well in that job during two stints – the first time he worked with Ronnie Moore and the second with Mark Robins. Breckin's status as Mr Reliable ensures he's our Rotherham cult hero.

THE FAN'S VIEW

Steve Tanner: *"Ronnie Moore was an iconic man in the leadership he showed."*

SCUNTHORPE UNITED

ⓘ Alex Calvo-Garcia　　　　　　　　**ⓗ Peter Beagrie**

It's always troubled me that one of the hospitality lounges at Glanford Park is named after England cricket legend Sir Ian Botham.

I do know that in order to stay fit during the winter Both, a local man, used to turn out for The Irons; but you wouldn't get Yorkshire CCC naming an executive area at Headingley after David Batty. And he's a Leeds lad born and bred who became a hero with his home-town United and played for England.

Scunthorpe actually had three former England captains in their ranks – Ray Clemence, Kevin Keegan and Botham. But if we're looking for one man's iconic status at Scunthorpe there can be no disputing Alex Calvo-Garcia's claim to that title.

When he arrived in England in 1996 many people doubted if he'd make any significant impact. The claim was that English football would be too physical and fast for the Basque who failed to make the grade at Real Sociedad, the club from San Sebastian on the northern Spanish coast. How wrong that claim proved to be.

Calvo-Garcia's fame in this part of Lincolnshire was secured when he scored the winning goal in the 1999 play-off final against Orient at Wembley to bring some glory to Scunthorpe fans. But continental signings were still rare in those days and Alex did much more than win matches for United. He had the intelligence and personality to win over the fans, not just as an import but as a new player arriving in England for the first time and unable to speak a word of English. He displayed a wonderful keenness to understand English sporting culture and then went out of his way to please the fans, who took him to their hearts.

Calvo-Garcia explained: "The best thing I achieved at the club was the relationship with the fans. The biggest difference between Spanish and English football is at the lower levels people are very loyal and take their team to heart. People still love their own team.

"In Spain I would not be asked for an autograph on the street. In Scunthorpe they always want to talk to you about football and you can see there is a lot of passion, in the kids, in the old people. All those things make you feel you have a privileged job."

Calvo-Garcia delighted the fans, loved his time in England and even learned to dismiss old gags about life in Scunthorpe. He was happy there.

Our Scunny cult hero is also a skilful attacking player, but definitely English. When Peter Beagrie arrived at Glanford Park, in his veteran days, he still had two or three consistent parts to his game – some of which frustrated the fans but somehow the regulars at Glanford Park grew to indulge him. For instance, Beags was known as king of the drag-backs. He operated on the left wing, went past his man but, instead of crossing, checked back. On occasion he'd either lose possession then or the best opportunity to cross had been missed – because of his damned drag-back. And yet, when he did deliver, he could be a match-winning player and carve open opposition defences. He also did a tidy line in back flips to celebrate goals, although as his career approached its twilight days these became less frequent – probably for medical reasons.

But Beags could play and the Irons fans realized that. For all the fun, entertainment – and frustration – he delivered, Beagrie is our Scunthorpe cult hero.

THE FAN'S VIEW

James Smith: *"My Dad used to go mad watching Beags when he delayed his crosses. It was great seeing him get so wound up. Then when he was about to explode with anger Beags would do something brilliant and we'd all turn and tell my Dad to shut up."*

SHEFFIELD UNITED

ⓘ Jimmy Hagan  **ⓗ Tony Currie**

Those who remember Bramall Lane as a home to Yorkshire CCC as well as Sheffield United will be able to guess the roots of the football club. In March 1889 members of the cricket club formed Sheffield United a few days after an FA Cup semi-final between Preston North End and West Bromwich Albion convinced leading cricket men that professional football had a future.

It's brutally simplistic, but your choice as Sheffield United's football icon is largely dependent on your age. The old-timers, who saw the great Jimmy Hagan in action, insist Tony Currie wasn't fit to lace his boots. The younger brigade – now not too youthful – insist TC brought a style, vision and fun to Bramall Lane that no other player has matched before or since his halcyon days of the Seventies.

Hagan joined the Blades from Derby County in 1938 when he was just 20 years old. The Second World War undoubtedly prevented him from exploiting his sporting ability for five of the prime years of his career. National service saw him based at Aldershot and selected by England for a series of wartime internationals in which he frequently starred. One of these was the 8-0 demolition of Scotland at Maine Road. Hagan scored two of the goals.

Tommy Lawton, among an elite band who could claim to be England's greatest centre-forward, raved about the supply of pinpoint passes delivered by Hagan. In fact, both Lawton and England goalie Frank Swift described the England line-up that day as the best they ever played in. The front five read Stanley Matthews, Raich Carter, Tommy Lawton, Jimmy Hagan and Denis Compton.

Hagan played with a minimum of fuss, an almost understated awareness of what was happening around him. He was wonderfully two-footed, and rarely appeared troubled by the hurly-burly of a game or the over-physical approach of opponents in a day when physical contact was much more prevalent and accepted. Hagan's approach was almost serene.

He probably cemented his status in the immediate post-war years as United's superhero by rejecting the chance to leave the Lane. In February 1951 the United directors accepted a British record fee of £32,500 for their 33-year-old star. The deal had been struck with arch-rivals Sheffield Wednesday. Hagan refused to move. Wednesday were relegated that season. Hagan kept playing for United until the 1957–58 season and the approach of his 40th birthday.

Tony Currie, universally known in football as TC, joined United 30 years after

Hagan, in 1968. He cost £26,500 from Watford and was 18 years old. TC was recruited by one of the most unsung but admirable managers of that era, John Harris. Harris was a non-smoking, non-swearing disciplinarian. He didn't feign at being a hard man with a rough, tough, brusque approach. He exuded authority towards his players and the media, who all learned to respect him. Indeed, Gentleman John set up the kind of attacking tactics that suited TC to a T.

John Harris didn't do verbal blasts. He admonished you with an intensity to his voice and demeanour that made you quickly realize you'd better do as he said quickly – or else! I recall asking TC for an interview after training as the players returned to the dressing rooms at Bramall Lane. Ever affable, TC grabbed a quick shower and returned with a towel tied to his midriff to conduct the interview. John Harris didn't do explosions of temper; he always simmered just below boiling point. TC and I were never sure who the manager was bollocking the most as he seethed through gritted teeth: "You don't do interviews here with a player who's only just had a shower. Understand?" We sure did. TC cleared off to get changed and the interview took place in the United social club, in those days underneath the old cricket pavilion at Bramall Lane.

Currie was part of a United team that had a few players who could be deemed Blades cult heroes. There was the goalscoring winger Alan Woodward and powerful centre-back and skipper Eddie Colquhoun. With Harris's astute leadership this gang was establishing itself as a decent top-flight squad. Currie broke into the England squad during his days in Sheffield, but he won the bulk of his international caps after his £250,000 transfer to Leeds in June 1976.

Other nominations for United hero status have included Joe Shaw, who still holds the record for most League appearances for the club between 1948 and 1966, as well as more recent heroes like goal king Keith Edwards. Perhaps the length of Hagan's United career makes him a justified icon. But nobody who saw him will forget the fun and style TC brought to the Blades. He must rank, unquestionably, as United's ultimate cult hero.

THE FAN'S VIEW
Mike Oliver: *"No assessment of the Blades can fail to recognize the talent of Tony Currie. He was our brightest star."*

SHEFFIELD WEDNESDAY

 Derek Dooley    Chris Waddle

The city of Sheffield was one of the bastions of the new sport of Association Football in the 19th century. The club was formed by the Sheffield Wednesday Cricket Club in 1867, and both Sheffield's professional football clubs had their roots very firmly in cricket.

It's impossible to think of anybody who gave as much in the service of their club as Sheffield Wednesday's icon – we'll hear more about that unique football man later.

The Owls have had some exciting players down the years. For instance, Albert Quixall was acclaimed as the Golden Boy of English football after bursting onto the scene at Hillsborough in the early Fifties. He was lured away to Manchester United in 1958 when Matt Busby needed to rebuild a club shattered by the loss of eight players in the Munich air disaster. Quixall cost United £45,000 – a British record – but he had blossomed early and Wednesday had seen the best days of his career: it was during his time as an Owl that he won his five England caps.

In latter years Chris Waddle and Paolo Di Canio have graced Hillsborough with some sublime skills. Waddle, in particular, became a firm favourite with the Wednesday fans. He was 31 when he arrived at Hillsborough in a £1 million move from Olympique Marseille. He was the creative inspiration behind Wednesday reaching both domestic Cup finals in the 1992–93 season. Unfortunately, they lost both. In 1993 Waddle was named as the Football Writers' Footballer of the Year.

But the candidate who stands out as their football icon is a man whose commitment to the club, together with the pain, anguish and heartbreak he endured, surely makes him one of the great football men of the past century.

Derek Dooley was Sheffield born and when he left school at 14 began work in a hearing aid factory while playing football as an amateur for Sheffield YMCA. A year later he was invited to play for Lincoln City in the old Third Division North and joined them as an amateur so that he could still turn out for the local YMCA team.

Lincoln eventually offered Derek a contract, but he turned them down to stick to his Sheffield roots. Eventually he came to Wednesday's notice, and his barnstorming style and eye for goal saw him bulldoze his way (he was now 6ft 2ins tall) through the junior and reserve teams. Ironically he made his League debut against Preston North End in March 1950. Once he was handed an extended run in the first team he didn't just grab the opportunity, he produced a rich seam of form that remains the most lethal period of goalscoring by any Wednesday player.

In one run of just nine matches he scored an astonishing 22 goals. He went on to score 46 goals in his first senior season. That goal return remains a Wednesday club record and helped the club win promotion back to the top flight. His career ended in tragedy at Deepdale on St Valentine's Day, 1953. He was 23. Dooley collided with Preston goalie George Thompson and suffered a double fracture of his leg. As he was being discharged from hospital a nurse noticed that he did not react when his toes were touched. The plaster was removed and it was discovered that a wound on the back of his leg had become infected. It was gangrenous and the gangrene had spread. After fighting the infection Dooley, the power-packed striker with the red hair and never-say-die attitude, was told he would have to have his right leg amputated just six inches below his hip.

In the circumstances lesser men might have turned away from football. Dooley was made of sterner stuff. Despite his awkward gait and physical limitations he became an inspirational youth coach at Hillsborough and also worked in the club's development office. Dooley was a Wednesday man through and through and very much part of the club. It was no surprise when he was appointed manager in February 1971. Nobody could doubt his commitment to the Wednesday cause. He wasn't a bad manager either, but a change of regime in the boardroom sparked his dismissal. The timing, though, must rank as one of the most manipulative, cynical acts to heap disgrace on the murky world of professional football. The new Wednesday directors decided to dispense with their club's most loyal servant on Christmas Eve 1973. A few years later I was able to challenge one of the board members about the appalling timing of the Dooley dismissal. The shame-faced director admitted they had chosen Christmas Eve in an attempt to limit the backlash they expected to face. Their misguided logic was that with no newspapers published until 27th December, and a full Boxing Day programme, they might escape condemnation for their brutal insensitivity to a man who had done so much for Sheffield Wednesday. Wednesday fans could not believe how their old hero had been treated. Dooley vowed that he would never set foot inside Hillsborough again.

He accepted a job at Sheffield United and progressed from their staff to become chief executive and eventually chairman. And after 19 years he did finally return to Hillsborough for a Sheffield derby. Both sets of fans gave him a standing ovation. And when he died in March 2008 both clubs saluted the work of a fine, straight-talking, proud Yorkshireman. A worthy Wednesday icon.

As for their cult hero, it's hard to look beyond the Eighties and early Nineties. John Sheridan assured his hero status by scoring the only goal of the 1991 League Cup final as Wednesday beat Manchester United at Wembley. It was their first major trophy for 50 years. Wednesday won promotion that year as well to set up a couple of great seasons of exciting football. Chris Waddle was at the centre of much that they achieved and was saluted by the fans for his efforts. For that, the man who started his working life in a sausage factory is our Sheffield Wednesday cult hero.

THE FAN'S VIEW

Ron White: *"Derek Dooley must be the Sheffield Wednesday icon. He was an old-fashioned No. 9 who scored for the fun of it."*

SHREWSBURY TOWN

(i) **Arthur Rowley** (h) **Joe Hart**

Arthur Rowley holds the record by some distance as the most prolific League goalscorer in English football history. The striker affectionately known as "The Gunner" scored 434 goals in Football League outings.

He arrived at Shrewsbury from Leicester City in the summer of 1958 to become the club's player-manager. He was famed for the number of goals he dispatched and the power of his left-foot shooting. Even though he was 32 and approaching the end of his career, Rowley did not disappoint the Gay Meadow fans.

In his debut season he achieved a feat he'd managed three times at Leicester. He set a new club record for the most goals in a season. The 38 he notched for the Shrews in that opening campaign remains a club record. Rowley's first season in player-management also saw him guide Shrewsbury to promotion from the newly formed Fourth Division, the first promotion in the club's history.

He almost went one better in the next campaign. The Shrews missed back-to-back promotions by just one point. They established themselves in the Third Division while Rowley maintained his incredible goalscoring feats.

He retired in 1965 with the distinction of scoring more League goals than any other player, a status that makes him our Shrewsbury icon. Rowley passed away in December 2002, aged 76.

Our Shrewsbury cult hero launched his career with the club, England goalie Joe Hart. He made his debut in the season Shrewsbury spent in the Conference. It came the day after his 17th birthday. From the age of 18 he was Town's established first-choice keeper – and how he revelled in the role! He played a full 46-match League season, and won rave reviews. He won recognition with the England Under-19 team and the word was out that the Shrews had a goalkeeping prodigy.

Premier League clubs starting trailing him around the country and checking his form. It wasn't a question of *if* he'd hit the big time – it was a question of *when*. Everton appeared to be leading the chase but then Manchester City overtook them.

In 2006 he was named in the PFA's League Two Team of the Season – proof that his fellow pros and opponents had recognized his burgeoning talent. At the end of that season Hart was snapped up by City. Initially the fee was speculated to be £600,000, rising to £1.5million. There was some disagreement about this, but the £600,000 figure has remained with the player to this day. It was a great return for the Shrews for a home-grown youngster. And it was a snip for Premier League City.

SOUTHAMPTON

(i) Matt Le Tissier   (h) Mike Channon

Alan Ball's defection to Manchester City in 1995 was probably ill-conceived, and to his death in 2007 was never fully forgiven by some Saints supporters.

But Bally was a passionate football man. He would hold court and deliver opinions laced with humour, anecdotal evidence and fiery assessments. Fence-sitting was not Ball's forte. He was opinionated and usually willing to share his views and prejudices in captivating style.

I remember spending time with him after his controversial departure from Southampton and move to work for his old friend and England team-mate Francis Lee, who had become chairman of Manchester City. Ball, who revelled in confrontational banter, demanded: "Who is the most valuable player in the Premier League?"

To each of the following names the red-headed manager snorted in disagreement or, on occasion, disgust – forget Cantona, Shearer, Keane. And it wasn't Adams, Ince or Fowler either. Bally delivered his considered opinion: "The best, most valuable player in the Premier League at the moment is Matthew Le Tissier. Nobody can compare with what that lad is delivering for Southampton."

Ball then provided the stats and facts to back up his assertion, showing how Le Tissier had scored 45 goals in 64 games from midfield when the duo had worked together. Ball then insisted: "But the goals don't tell you the whole story. Let's look at his assists. The free-kicks he takes that create chances for others, the passes he's delivered, the creativity that lifts others. I'm telling you, Le Tiss is more important to his club than any other player in the Premier League. He's priceless to Southampton. Imagine what he'd be like in a team of potential champions!"

Given the troubles Ball endured at City, perhaps he regretted his move to be reunited with an old pal and the return to his Lancastrian sporting roots. But the other side of the Le Tissier coin is provided by the great man himself, the player many Southampton fans still refer to as Le God.

Le Tissier is unequivocal. "The 18 months that Bally was in charge were the best time of my career. Bally let me get away with a lot more than other players. There were players who didn't like him but if you weren't producing Bally would get on your back. It would have been the same for me."

The connection and mutual admiration between the duo is uncanny. Le Tissier, who successfully converted 47 of the 48 penalties he took in his career, has gone on record explaining that part of the reason for his success was being the focal point of attention within the stadium. As he put it: "My penalty record was a mixture of confidence, a little bit of ego because I knew the whole stadium was looking at me and I liked that, and positive mental attitude. I used to visualize the crowd erupting as the ball hit the net."

Turn back the clock to Alan Ball's career with Arsenal in the early Seventies. He had joined them as a £220,000 club record signing from Everton. At 26 he was at the top of his game; five years earlier he had been the youngest member of England's World Cup-winning team. Ball, hated at Anfield for his success and ultra-positive approach to playing for arch-rivals Everton, knew he would be the target for non-stop terrace abuse. So what did the Arsenal skipper do? He led his team out and flouted convention. Instead of turning left from the tunnel towards the Kemlyn Road end of Anfield, Ball turned right and led the visitors towards the towering Kop where Liverpool fans directed a deafening torrent of vitriol at the ginger-haired midfielder. As he walked towards them Ball raised his arms in salute, fists clenched, he punched the air as if he'd just scored the winning goal – and the game hadn't even started. I have to say I have never seen a player set himself up for the most embarrassing of falls as Ball did that day. If we thought he was demented in the pre-match warm-up he played like a man possessed during the game. Ball was brilliant as Arsenal won. Just like his protégée, Le Tissier, he revelled in being the focal point of attention – even if most of the people inside Anfield that day were baiting him.

Ball, of course, had been an important signing as a player for the Saints. He was among the steely band of senior professionals (okay, some were veterans) recruited by the canny Lawrie McMenemy. He offered the likes of Ball, Peter Osgood, Frank Worthington, Dave Watson, Chris Nicholl and the exceptional Kevin Keegan the opportunity to enjoy their football at a friendly club where they were much loved and skilfully managed.

Keegan's signing from SV Hamburg in 1980 was a massive coup. A superstar at that time, Keegan had spent three years in Germany and been voted European Footballer of the Year for the first two of them. It spoke volumes for the impact McMenemy had enjoyed at the club that he was able to persuade players of this stature to move to the Dell. Allied to their FA Cup final triumph over Manchester United in 1976 this must rank as a golden era for the Hampshire club.

But while the big names offered cameo roles, the factor that endorses Le Tissier's status as a club icon is his devotion to the Saints. In 1990 a deal was set up to sell him to Tottenham – but he declined the move. He remained a one-club man. On one hand he was adored by the Saints fans. On the other he missed the opportunity to win trophies he would have gained by joining bigger, more successful clubs. Le Tissier has no regrets about his career path. "I knew I probably wouldn't win any honours but when you're at a club of that size, staying in the Premier League for 16 years gave me as much pleasure as winning a medal if I'd gone somewhere else. No one expected us to stay up that long. I was so chuffed to be part of it."

It's hard to look beyond Le Tiss as Southampton's icon, but Terry Paine must be recognized as an outstanding candidate. He remains the holder of the most League appearances. During the course of 18 years at the Dell he made 713 League appearances. He was a stalwart of the Saints sides of the Sixties, mixing a blend of skilful play on the right flank with some pinpoint crosses and an approach to winning the ball that saw him gain some notoriety. His ability to deliver inch-perfect passes and crosses helped him win 19 England caps and he also helped Martin Chivers and Ron Davies emerge as lethal predators. Their supply line of ammunition was top quality.

So, with Le God as our icon, who can be our cult hero? Undoubtedly, the likes of Keegan, Peter Shilton and manager McMenemy deserve salutes for what they brought to Southampton. But it's one of the players from the victorious 1976 FA Cup final team that beat Manchester United at Wembley who wins our cult hero status. This was at a point in the club's history when McMenemy was charged with getting them back into the top flight. They were still in the Second Division when they beat Tommy Docherty's United thanks to Bobby Stokes' goal. Our Saints cult hero, Mike Channon, was up-front that day.

Channon of the whirling arm goal salute was a massive hero to Saints fans. His goalscoring record saw him become an England regular through the Seventies. One of the most disappointing aspects of his career was that he even dispatched 21 goals in 1974 and those strikes were not enough to prevent Southampton being relegated. But Channon stayed loyal for another three years to the Saints' cause. He was a few months short of his 29th birthday when he joined Manchester City in 1977. City had finished the previous season in second place and had aspirations of becoming champions. Channon's move north did not really work for either party. Two years later he headed back to the Dell.

He has remained prominent in the sporting world through his success as a racehorse trainer. That did not surprise those who had dealings with him in his playing days. It wasn't just his interest in horses that stood out. For a footballer Channon had a rare attitude that saw him see the world differently and express personal opinions that, at times, didn't go with the flow but seemed obvious to him. There was always a sporting intellect ticking away. The West Country burr perhaps kidded people that here was some country bumpkin. They were wrong. Channon was an astute man and a sharp thinker. He wasn't a bad footballer either as 21 international goals in 46 England appearances proves.

THE FAN'S VIEW

Philip Strange: *"I've been supporting Southampton for over 47 years and would like Terry Paine to be recognized in your book."*

SOUTHEND UNITED

 Chris Powell

 Roy McDonough

Chris Powell is in distinguished company even if he can't quite eclipse the status of one of the knights of English football.

Sir Stanley Matthews is the only man to be nominated as an icon for two clubs, in his case Stoke City and Blackpool. Powell is nominated here as Southend's icon. He's also nominated in the Charlton area as the Addicks cult hero – not a bad achievement for a self-effacing fellow who operated as a left-back.

But Powell was a fine footballer and perhaps he should have won far more than the five caps for England he won towards the end of his career when he was a Charlton player.

Chris arrived at Roots Hall on a free from Crystal Palace in 1990 and his outstanding ability soon made him a huge favourite with the Southend faithful. In six seasons he was hailed as a gentleman of football, having made 290 appearances for Southend. He left for Derby County in January 1996 in a £750,000 deal. Later he became PFA chairman.

He rejoined Charlton, where his international career had belatedly taken off when Sven Goran Eriksson stunned the media by selecting him. But while some journalists belittled him there was no doubting the affection fans had for Powell. He's an honest, friendly guy who cares about people and his profession. No fans love him more than those at Roots Hall.

Our Southend cult hero is one of the toughest men to walk on a Football League pitch.

Roy McDonough is regarded as one of the wildest men in football and perhaps even England's dirtiest footballer ever!

Red Card Roy is the name of a book about "terrace cult hero" McDonough – whose notoriety was lapped up at rival Essex clubs Southend and Colchester. McDonough was sent off a record 22 times in a career of more than 650 games, 100 goals, thousands of beers and, reportedly, 400 daliances with women.

From his first red card, aged 15, when he tried to strangle the referee in a school's Cup final to his infamous drop-kick on Tony Pulis that saw him dismissed in the first 10 minutes of a Cup clash, McDonough was a sucker for an early bath.

But "Donut", as the Southend fans called him, was always admired by some for his commitment in more than 200 games for Southend, although disliked by others for his self-destructive traits.

THE FAN'S VIEW

Bob Harling: *"Nobody will top Roy McD as our cult hero. He was crazy but brilliant, too."*

STEVENAGE

 Ronnie Henry

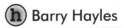 Barry Hayles

Ronnie Henry's place in football folklore was assured when he became the first captain to hold aloft a trophy at the new Wembley Stadium in 2007. The defender, the grandson of former Spurs full-back Ron Henry, skippered Stevenage to a thrilling 3-2 victory over Kidderminster Harriers at the new national stadium in front of an FA Trophy final record crowd of 53,262.

His outstanding displays in that memorable season won him the Stevenage Player of the Year award for 2006–07. He had joined the Conference national outfit on a six-month contract after a spell playing in Irish football.

Henry, who failed to make the grade at Spurs, was again a Wembley winner in 2009 when he was in the Stevenage team that beat York City 2-0 in the FA Trophy final. A year later there was more success for Stevenage and Henry as the dream of playing in the Football League was finally achieved and he was also in the side that won promotion to League One.

Henry's seven years at Stevenage, during which he played 329 games and scored four goals, coincided with the best period in the club's history. He left for Luton in 2012.

Barry Hayles was without doubt one of the best strikers ever to play for Stevenage during their non-League era. But the Broadway Hall outfit were cruelly deprived of his services as he approached his peak when the club's promotion to the Football League was blocked by the authorities in 1996.

Lambeth-born Hayles began his career with Willesden Hawkeye, before moving to the Isthmian Premier Division outfit, then called Stevenage Borough, in 1994. During his time with the Borough he scored 73 goals in 154 League games.

Hayles was a big hit with the Stevenage fans and was part of the side that won the Football Conference in the 1995–96 campaign. Promotion to the fourth tier of English football should have secured the partnership.

But Hayles' ambitions to play in the Football League continued, and with Stevenage's way barred because their ground facilities were deemed to be below standard, Hayles decided he would have to move on.

He won a move to Bristol Rovers in 1997, where he was an immediate success. That led to a switch to Fulham, where he was again a success – in 2000–01 he hit 18 goals to take Fulham into the Premier League.

The much-travelled Hayles won 10 caps for Jamaica after originally being called up by the Cayman Islands. But FIFA ruled Hayles was not eligible for the Caymans.

STOKE CITY

 Sir Stanley Matthews    **Denis Smith**

Founder members of the Football League, the Potteries was one of the cradles of Association Football and also gave the world one of the most famous English footballers of the 20th century. Sir Stanley Matthews was a man of Stoke who began and ended his career at his home-town club.

We have football club owners, managers and players as our icons, but only one man wins the remarkable status of being the icon of two clubs. That man is Stanley Matthews.

"Stanley Matthews was a footballing genius. A product of the Potteries, Stan became England's favourite sporting son, the game's first true superstar. The maestro played to a supreme standard for 33 years, filled grounds all over the world and didn't retire until he was 50. The English football public adored him."

That's the assessment of Matthews delivered by his contemporary and fellow great Tom Finney. There is a rich irony about Finney's assessment in that for many years a rumour developed that the two great England internationals and wingers did not get along. It is a myth that Finney goes out of his way to silence once and for all in his book *My Autobiography*.

The first true superstar of football is quite an assessment given the way the likes of Pelé, Maradona and Johan Cruyff have been lionized in the post-Matthews era. But Matthews was the vanguard in so many ways for the modern game. In 1948 he was the first ever winner of the Football Writers' Footballer of the Year award; the inaugural winner of the European Footballer of the Year; and the first footballer to be knighted while still playing.

Matthews was a man of the Potteries, born in Hanley, yet fêted around the world. Undoubtedly his talent as a right-winger, blessed with exquisite dribbling skills and the ability to deliver pinpoint crosses, put him on the road to fame. But there have been other wingers who could beat opponents and pick out team-mates with inviting centres. Matthews took the art of wing play to a whole new level. Finney explained: "Stan would always rise to the biggest occasion. The greatest ball player of our generation, he showed no mercy to defenders. I have never seen another player who could take the ball so close to his opponent and still manage to retain possession. It was almost hypnotic as he invited a challenge, but while the full-back dithered and deliberated, Stan would drop a shoulder, wiggle his hips and disappear down the line."

Undoubtedly part of the Matthews legend is the fact that here was a man who enjoyed a career spanning 33 years. He was 50 years old when he finally retired in 1965. He remains the oldest player to appear in the top flight of English football and the oldest man to represent England. He was 42 when he made his final international appearance against Denmark in Copenhagen in 1957. There were calls in the media for his inclusion in the England squad that travelled to the 1958 World Cup finals in Sweden. The calls were resisted. But it's still some achievement to consider he won his last England cap some 23 years after his full international debut.

He had made his debut for Stoke at Gigg Lane, Bury, in March 1932. He was 17 years and 1 month old. He was paid £5 a week, which was reduced to £3 a week in the summer. That is a significant statistic; more about it later.

Stoke won promotion to the top flight in Matthews' first season. He made 15 appearances and won a Second Division champions' medal. Matthews spent 15 years at the Victoria Ground in his first spell at Stoke, but it cannot be overlooked that the Second World War denied him six prime years of his career, from the age of 24 to 30. Matthews became disenchanted by life at the Victoria Ground; club politics disturbed him and he twice asked for transfers. On the second occasion his wish was granted. Stoke clearly thought they'd seen his best days when they sold him to Blackpool in 1947 for £11,500. He was a veteran of 32. But the normal ageing process and use of calendars did not apply to Stan. He was unique. Elsewhere you can read about the impact Matthews had with the Seasiders, including having a Cup final named after him despite the fact that one of his team-mates scored a hat-trick in a 4-3 win.

Matthews returned to Stoke in October 1961 in a £3,500 deal. City were in the old Second Division, but with fellow veteran Jackie Mudie and former Manchester United star Dennis Viollet, Matthews played a significant role in their promotion campaign in 1962–63 season. He was voted Footballer of the Year again – 15 years after first lifting the award. As well as playing his part in the team's success he had been a massive box office success. Stoke's attendances trebled.

Matthews made his final competitive appearance in February 1965. It's worth repeating that he was 50. For most of his career he had seen his earnings potential limited by the maximum wage rule. The fight to break the antiquated contract retention rules and the maximum wage truly escalated in 1960. The clubs' rejection of players' requests saw the PFA, the players' union, call a series of meetings around the country. Perhaps the most important took place in Manchester, when Stanley Matthews came out in support of the threatened strike action. If the veteran superstar was on the PFA's side surely nothing could stop them now. Jimmy Hill, chairman of the PFA at the time, described Matthews' support as the finest thing Stan had ever done for English football.

Hill explained: "All England wondered what Stan was going to do. We soon found out. I'm sure the public thought the basis of our struggle was Jimmy Hill and his soap box. After those meetings, and with Stanley Matthews voicing his support, the situation had changed."

Stoke awarded Matthews a testimonial at the Victoria Ground which was supported by some of the world's greatest players, including Russia's legendary goalkeeper Lev Yashin and Ferenc Puskás, the creative genius of Real Madrid and Hungary. At the end that famous duo carried Matthews from the field on their shoulders: a fitting tribute to round off a truly extraordinary and unparalleled career. So if Matthews is our undisputed Stoke icon who wins their cult hero status?

One man who is often overlooked these days is the manager who decided that a band of veterans could take Stoke back into the big time and establish them there – manager Tony Waddington. The Mancunian wanted skilful players who could express themselves, and saw age as no barrier to quality. So through the Sixties his team became established in the top flight with the likes of George Eastham and Peter Dobing as cornerstones.

Waddo also spotted the potential of a tough, uncompromising centre-back called Denis Smith. Another son of the Potteries, Smith joined Stoke from school and spent 14 years at the Victoria Ground. Nobody could or would ever dispute his commitment to the cause. His bravery was the stuff of legend. He was part of the Stoke team that finally won silverware at Wembley, when they lifted the League Cup in 1972. It was a truly historic day for everyone connected with the club. And he also made the *Guinness Book of Records* when he was recognized as the most injured man in football. His list of serious injuries might have broken a lesser man, but I recall interviewing Denis at his home and always finding him absolutely positive and desperate to play again. The list of injuries included five broken legs, breaking his nose four times, a cracked ankle, broken collarbone, broken fingers and enough stitches around his face and eyes to suggest he must have been a boxer in his spare time. Denis was a genuinely hard man. Hard in the real football sense of the word – brave, uncompromising and totally committed. He is rightly acclaimed to this day as a Stoke City legend.

That's a status that has also been earned by current City boss Tony Pulis, who has enjoyed the most extensive League success of any Stoke manager.

But we're looking beyond Pulis for our Stoke cult hero. We salute Denis Smith.

SUNDERLAND

ⓘ Jim Montgomery  **ⓗ Len Shackleton**

A Scottish schoolmaster called James Alan had the smart idea of forming a football club, and in 1879 set up the Sunderland and District Teachers' Association FC. The club hit financial problems so they decided to open the membership to people outside the teaching profession, and in October 1890 Sunderland AFC was born – the pride of Wearside.

The FA Cup's loss of status in recent times is a source of deep sadness to many football followers. If you're under 15 you probably have no awareness about how many fans used to place winning the FA Cup at the summit of their club's ambitions for any season. After all, there was the glamour of the big day out at Wembley, the minute-by-minute television coverage. And we're not talking about match analysis; we're talking about the cameras following the Cup final players around their hotel hideaway, hours before the kick-off. Oh, and the kick-off was always at 3pm on the final Saturday of the domestic season. All domestic League issues had been resolved a week earlier. It was the good old days for the FA Cup. The status of the world's oldest, most prestigious club knock-out tournament has been grievously undermined by recent events.

Yet try telling that to Sunderland fans. The impact of their 1973 FA Cup final triumph over Leeds United remains a matter of immense pride on Wearside and to Sunderland fans around the world. Ian Porterfield scored the only goal as the Second Division team destroyed the form book and the bookmakers' odds to defeat mighty Leeds – the Cup holders and one of the most powerful forces in English football at the time. The 1973 FA Cup remains the only major trophy Sunderland have won since the Second World War.

Porterfield, the goalscoring hero, was a good man and a dear friend. He was just 61 when he died from colon cancer in 2007. During his time as manager of Aberdeen I joined him on a UEFA Cup trip to face Feyenoord in Rotterdam. More than a decade had passed since his famous Wembley exploits, and yet Dutch journalists and football fans who'd never been near Roker Park invariably greeted him with the words: "Ian Porterfield – you're the man who beat Leeds in the Cup final." Ian would self-effacingly point out: "Well, it wasn't just me. It was the Sunderland team."

But then Porterfield would always deliver a follow-up point, singling out a team-mate for special praise, and that man is a front-runner for our title as Sunderland's icon. He's Jimmy Montgomery, the goalkeeper whose brilliance ensured Sunderland pulled off the most memorable FA Cup final shock.

But is Monty our Sunderland icon? Any debate must also include the man who was voted by Sunderland fans as their club's greatest player of the 20th century. Legendary centre-back Charlie Hurley is still affectionately known as The King. He arrived at Roker Park from Millwall in 1957 and spent 12 years with the club. Hurley was a cornerstone of the team that eventually won promotion to the top flight in 1964. He was a massive presence in the heart of the Sunderland defence. The famous red and white stripes, which seemed to be stretched to their limit to cover his bulging chest, emphasized his power-packed physique. And when Sunderland won a corner the crowd would chant "Charlie, Charlie" as he ran up field to either launch a header on goal or cause mayhem in the opposition defence. Hurley was much more than a big, bruising centre-back. He had a deft touch and an eye for a pass, but his sheer presence on the field caught your eye. He still had this sense of presence even when his career was winding down at Bolton.

So who is the Sunderland icon? Monty, the Cup king, or Charlie the king of Roker Park? We're going with the voters in the *Sunday Mirror* poll, and their man was Montgomery. As for cult heroes, they tend to be audacious forwards such as Charles Buchan, who joined Sunderland from Leyton in March 1911 and spent 14 years with the club, although his career was severely affected by the First World War. In later life he worked as a sports writer, was a founding member of the Football Writers' Association in 1948 and launched his own football magazine in 1951. Buchan died in 1960 and his eponymous magazine closed in 1974.

Buchan, the tall, slim, elegant centre-forward, was tactically astute and a lethal predator. His 209 goals still make him the club's most prolific marksman. He was a key member of the Sunderland team that won the League Championship in 1912–13 and almost clinched a Double. They lost the FA Cup final in 1913 to Aston Villa.

Sunderland have never been major trophy hoarders. In fact, there have been times when the pickings have been lean. And it's from these darker days that Michael Brunskill of the Football Supporters' Federation nominates his personal cult hero. Michael pointed out: "The temptation is to choose the best player you ever saw. For Sunderland that pretty much narrows it down to two players who'll always be linked – Niall Quinn and Kevin Phillips.

"I doubt we'll ever see another European Golden Boot winner at the Stadium of Light like we did with Super Kev. And what more can you say about Niall Quinn? Not only a vastly underrated player on the pitch but a legend off it, who hauled the Black Cats back from the abyss. But those choices are too easy and too obvious.

"My cult hero only spent four or five years at the club, including just one season in the top-flight, and spent most of his career in the second tier. Nonetheless he grabbed a goal every other game for the lads and was a constant ball of energy, aggression and pace.

"As a kid I loved him so much I even tried to convince my mam to let me change my name to his – I was nine-years-old and she laughed at me. Since then I've seen dozens of supposedly better players wear the red and white shirt but youthful naivety trumps experience and logic every time. In my mind, no one will ever be better than Marco Gabbiadini."

But our Sunderland cult hero is the self-styled Clown Prince of Football – the unique Len Shackleton. In modern parlance he could be described as Gazza on acid! Sadly there was no television coverage in Len's days to truly capture the genius of the man. Shack, as he was widely known in the game, was plying his trade in the Forties and Fifties. In his case this meant producing tricks, flicks and skills that bamboozled opponents and had the fans roaring with delight. Sunderland fans loved him even though he was in a team that promised so much but won so little. England fans loved him, too, even though he only won five full caps for his country.

Shack, who died in 2000 aged 78, knew why fans loved him but many managers and coaches didn't: "I got the name the Clown Prince because I went out to enjoy the game. I wasn't as good a competitor as I might have been or as I should have been. But results weren't all that important to me." Bob Stokoe, a team-mate of Shacks during their days together at Newcastle and later the Sunderland manager, was equally succinct. Stokoe said: "If Len had been more of a dedicated team player than an entertainer he'd have been a world beater."

But cult heroes are made from different ingredients than reliable trophy hunters. I grew up in journalism hearing tales of incredible Shack's genius that at times bordered on madness. For instance, Brian Redhead, the late award-winning journalist and former editor, recalled as a youngster seeing Shack take a penalty for Newcastle against Manchester City. He was astonished when Shackleton kept retreating until he was virtually on the half-way line to start his run-up. As Redhead recalled: "Shack set off like a train on this long run and as he reached the ball took an almighty swing and Frank Swift, the great City goalie, dived in anticipation. But Shack hadn't touched the ball, he turned around and back-heeled the ball into the net. Swift walked out, grabbed Shack's head in those huge hands and kissed him."

Playing one-twos off the corner flags, beating a player, then turning back to beat him again, going around the opposition goalie, stopping on the line, sitting on the ball and then tapping it into the net: these were Shackleton's regular party pieces. Walter Winterbottom was the England manager of this era. Admittedly he didn't pick the England team, that was done by the FA's selection committee, but he did work with the players. Sir Walter delivered a telling insight into Shack. "I remember when we played West Germany, then the world champions, at Wembley. The England fans rose to Shack for his performance. It was like when Gazza played for England against Scotland in Euro '96. He was quite exceptional."

THE FAN'S VIEW

Graham Trotter: "My dad put on a DVD of the 1973 FA Cup final and I saw Jim Montgomery's double save. I knew from that moment I was a Sunderland AFC fan."

Clive Lee: "Jimmy Montgomery is the all-time icon for Sunderland. He is famous all round the world for his unbelievable, fantastic double save at Wembley.

"To this day, many still cannot believe that he managed to save the day for Sunderland. First he saved a diving header from Trevor Cherry pushing the ball across his goal, then hot shot Peter Lorimer hammered the rebound on target towards goal (from just 6 yards out). Miraculously somehow Jimmy managed to push himself up off the ground to divert the shot onto the underside of his cross bar and away. Many experts have said to this day, no double save has ever matched it."

SWANSEA CITY

Ivor Allchurch was the original Golden Boy of Welsh football, his blond hair accompanying his awesome range of attacking talents. His name is still spoken of with reverence in his native Swansea.

And proof of his lasting legacy came in 2008, when Swansea City fans were polled in their thousands to name the club's greatest cult hero. It was 40 years since Allchurch last played for them, 11 years after his death. Yet an overwhelming 76 per cent voted for him. Most would probably have been too young to have even seen him play. But such was his legendary status that stories of his wondrous skills have passed through the generations.

Allchurch, born in 1929, was a 16-year-old playing in a public park kick-about when Swansea scout Joe Sykes was impressed enough to invite him for a trial. He was signed immediately but had to serve two years in the army before making his debut in 1949.

The story thereafter is the stuff of legend. He played 445 League games in two spells for the Swans, scoring 164 goals. He struck 46 goals in 143 games in his three-year spell at Newcastle United, played 118 games and scored 40 goals in three seasons with Cardiff. Add the 68 games he played for Wales – scoring 23 goals, a record eventually surpassed by Ian Rush – and that, with Cup games, takes his tally to well over 800 senior games, spread over nearly 20 years.

"I just loved playing. That's all I ever wanted," he once said with masterly understatement. Football was his obsession. He was 39 when he kicked his last ball for Swansea. And he went on to play in the lower Leagues for Worcester, Haverfordwest and then Pontardawe, where he finally hung up those golden boots for good when he reached his 50th birthday!

If Allchurch had one frustration, it was that he was never able to play for Swansea in the old First Division. They remained in Division Two for the 11 years of his first spell with them. "I loved the club but I really wanted to play at that top level, just to test myself regularly against the best," he declared.

He was 29, probably just a little too old, when Newcastle paid £28,000 to sign him. He certainly repaid them – and Geordies still remember him with genuine affection – but Allchurch regretted waiting so long before making the move, acknowledging that he "should have gone a couple of years earlier".

If he played most of his football outside that top level, it did not affect his status in the game. "He didn't need that blond hair or even a number on his shirt to be recognized – his polish, his class made him stand out. To me he was up with the great players of all time," was the glowing testimony from Sir Matt Busby. That tribute was mirrored when he was named in the top 100 British footballers of all time.

Even the great John Charles, who played alongside him many times for Wales and for Cardiff, said: "He was just so perfect on the field. He had a great shot, he could score goals from either foot. But his vision, his passing, his dribbling skills – Ivor had it all."

Ironically John Charles himself, the greatest Welsh player, could also have become a Swansea legend. He was born in the town (as it was then) and signed on apprenticeship forms by the Swans. But he was never given his big chance there. Instead he was allowed to leave for Leeds – and for his matchless career.

In terms of longevity, Alan Curtis' record and his enduring popularity take some matching. Like Allchurch, Curtis was an inside-forward of adroit skills. He was a son of the Rhondda Valley, born in Pentre in 1954, but Swansea snapped him up from school and he had three spells at the club in all, a total of a dozen years at their old Vetch Stadium.

Since he retired in 1990 he has never left the club, coaching at first team and junior level for most of that time, as well as being stand-in manager nearly a dozen times when they have been in-between bosses. And he's done it all with a ready smile – he only gets embarrassed when his name is mentioned in legendary terms. But a cult figure he truly is.

John Toshack will always have his special place in local folklore for piloting Swansea's magical ride from the bottom division to (fleetingly) top of the First Division between 1978 and 1982. Nobody captured the swashbuckling spirit of that side more than the James Boys, Robbie and Leighton, both seasoned Wales internationals, both cavalier footballers.

Half a century ago, Harry Griffiths earned the title Mr Swansea, playing with verve in defence and midfield, managing the team briefly and going on to perform any other job he was ever called on to do.

Lee Trundle joined Swansea in 2003 and became such a folk hero in his five years there that he became the first player outside the Premier League to set up his own image rights company. His fellow players loved his Scouse wit, supporters cherished his outrageous skills and his showmanship – though showboating was the word rivals used!

Leon Britton has never been one to shout, but he has earned his own legendary status as the one common thread of their unbelievable journey from the brink of oblivion to Premier League high fliers in the past decade. Those who also played major roles in getting them there, from Michu to Michael Laurdrup, Brendan Rodgers to Ashley Williams, will also surely earn their place in time.

THE FAN'S VIEW

Billy Pride: *"I'd like to nominate the James Boys – Robbie and Leighton – as our cult heroes."*

SWINDON TOWN

 Don Rogers    Steve White

If ever a footballer was playing quite brilliantly in the wrong era that man was Don Rogers. The finest player to wear the Swindon Town shirt was a sensational attacker in the Sixties and early Seventies. Even the heaviest of pitches and the most ferocious tackling could not detract from Rogers' purpose and intent. He was a thrilling winger with the most outrageous sidestep and body swerve that left the most experienced defenders trailing in his wake.

Despite producing a string of impressive displays he never gained full international honours for England. The fundamental problem was that wingers were out of favour in those days. The success of Sir Alf Ramsey's 1966 World Cup-winning wingless wonders had created a blueprint many clubs followed. So while all the major clubs monitored Rogers' progress from the Swindon youth ranks they shied away from a big money transfer and left the exciting winger to ply his trade in the old Third Division – now League One. Ironically, in these days when managers are searching for players who can start in wide positions and then join a central striker – or even play off him – Rodgers would be tailor-made for the task.

He was thrilling to watch. His speed over the ground with the ball at his feet was akin to George Best. He could transform defence into attack with a couple of quick passes and a 50-yard dash past opponents. He really did have fans on the edge of their seats whenever he received possession.

The poor pitches in those days should have chronically undermined a player of Rogers' pace and style. Yet he seemed to accept the mud and ruts: this was a golden era for the club and Rogers was the inspiration behind much of their glory. The evidence of his fleet-footedness can be seen in one of the greatest days in Town's history when they beat Arsenal 3-1 to win the League Cup final in 1969. The Wembley pitch had been reduced to a ploughed field after staging the Horse of the Year Show. The appalling playing surface did become one of Arsenal's excuses for their embarrassing set-back as Swindon defied the form book and the bookmakers by winning after extra-time. Rogers scored two of their goals, including the third where he coolly ran through on Bob Wilson's goal before side-stepping one of the bravest keepers in the business and sliding the ball into the empty net.

Winning the League Cup should have ensured European qualification, but Swindon's Third Division status barred them from entry. Instead, admittedly as a sop, they were invited to take part in the Anglo-Italian Cup, which they won. And they did subsequently climb out of the Third Division, but financial problems beset the club. Bert Head, the manager who had signed Rogers as a teenager and moved on to Crystal Palace, spotted his chance. After 490 appearances and 181 goals in all competitions Palace signed Rogers for £147,000 in 1972. In one deal Swindon's greatest crowd pleaser, brightest star and most lethal attacking weapon had been sold. It was of no consolation to Swindon fans when Rogers won ITV's Goal of the Season in 1973 playing for his new club. Guess what? It was a muddy, bobbly pitch when Rogers sprinted from his own penalty area against Stoke to dispatch the wonder goal.

Unquestionably, Rogers must rank as one of the finest uncapped players in British football history. He is the worthy Swindon icon.

The debate over their cult hero, however, revolves around two players. John Trollope epitomized loyalty and long service. In fact, the reliable defender holds the record for Town appearances having played 889 first-team games between 1960 and 1980. In terms of League games Trollope holds the Football League record for a player at one club in turning out on 770 occasions. So for loyal service and longevity Trollope takes some beating.

But there is a view that a cult hero from the greatest promotion campaign in Swindon's history deserves special mention. Steve White came on as a substitute when Swindon played Leicester in the promotion play-off final at Wembley in 1993. Town had tossed away a three-goal lead and the odds seemed stacked on a Leicester victory. But player-manager Glenn Hoddle spotted White's forward run and the ever-willing striker earned a penalty amid the confusion in the City defence. Paul Bodin stepped forward and slotted home the winning goal.

White was a player with many failings as well as virtues. What nobody could doubt was his level of effort and commitment. To this day some Swindon fans claim they knew White would win a penalty because he'd have shot wide if he'd had the chance to score himself. There is a certain crazy logic to that thought. Anyway, striker Steve White is our Swindon Town cult hero.

TORQUAY UNITED

ⓘ Sammy Collins   **ⓗ Derek Dawkins**

The fact that Torquay played their first Football League game in 1927 makes many people think United are a relatively young club. But it was in May 1899 that the agreement by old boys from Torquay College and Torbay College to set up a football club came to fruition.

The 1950s saw Torquay United reborn as the sunshine club. They had entered the Football League in 1927 as a sort of mini Newcastle – playing in the same black and white stripes and even known as The Magpies.

But after the war the club's owners wanted to change their image to reflect the town's booming status as a holiday destination. And it was Sammy Collins who was probably the greatest of the players to help make that happen. Born in Bristol, and christened Ronald, he collected the nickname of Sammy at a young age. The stockily built inside-forward began his career at Ashton Gate as a right-winger, although he never quite made the grade. But when Torquay's manager John McNeil signed him in 1948 and asked him to play in a more central role he blossomed.

His impact was immediate: Torquay had never finished in the top 10 of the old Third Division South until his arrival, but in his very first season his goals helped them through that barrier. Clever in possession, and a neat passer of the ball, he perfected the art of the late run into scoring positions, coming alive with power and strength when he had even half a chance.

He scored 204 goals in 356 League games across 10 seasons, and his growing reputation helped the club gain agreement to the change of colours in the 1954–55 season to the yellow and blue stripe they wear now, reflecting the sun and sand of the seaside town. That year he played his part in a 4-0 FA Cup win against Leeds United, which then saw a record 21,907 crowd cram into Plainmoor for a fourth-round tie with Huddersfield.

Collins still holds the record for most League goals in a season – an amazing 40 in 1955–56. He began the following season scoring a penalty after only 10 seconds in a game against Walsall, and set another record which still stands by scoring in seven games in a row.

As for the cult hero, firebrand 1980s Scottish striker Dave Caldwell was loved for an aggressive attitude that got him sent off several times, while Barbadian international Rodney Jack brought flair and skill.

But the player loved most by Gulls fans was Derek 'The Dude' Dawkins, part of the Cyril Knowles' team of the 1980s. A midfielder who joined from Weymouth in February 1984, he was stylish on and off the field, loving fashion and cool clothes when he was out and about in the seaside resort. Yet Dawkins brought substance as well as style. He was able to pick a pass as well as win a crunching tackle, and in the home game against Crewe on the final day of the 1986–87 season that saved the club's Football League status he heroically played out of position at centre-half, keeping the defence together to hang on to a 2-2 draw that avoided relegation on goal difference.

THE FAN'S VIEW

Tony Atwood: *"Ralph Birkett (1913–2002) played for Torquay, Arsenal (during the Chapman era) and England. For this reason I would suggest he is unique for Torquay. The club found him playing for Dartmouth United as an amateur, and he played 95 games scoring 19 times, before going to Arsenal for what was then a record fee for Torquay of £1,500."*

TOTTENHAM HOTSPUR

(i) **Bill Nicholson**   (h) **Paul Gascoigne**

The Hotspur Football Club was formed from an older cricket club in 1882. After a couple of moves the club ended up at White Hart Lane in 1898. Years later their stadium would become one of the most passionate theatres for European action. Visiting teams were stunned by the noise level created. Perhaps people had forgotten that in January 1901 Tottenham played a German Association team from Berlin. Tottenham won 9-6. The Euro bug was born.

It must rank as one of the most illogical oversights in the history of English football. A flaw within the DNA of our national sport that Tottenham fans of a certain age know is a serious miscarriage of justice.

While the likes of Bill Shankly, Matt Busby and Brian Clough enjoy iconic status, not just at the clubs they built but in the wider national sporting perspective, few people beyond White Hart Lane mention the name of a brilliant, inspirational Yorkshireman in the pantheon of architects of successful football clubs. Yet, as every Spurs fan knows full well, the status of a football genius sits very handsomely on Bill Nicholson's square shoulders.

Bill Nick, as he was known throughout the game, was really a one-club man. He devoted his life to Tottenham Hotspur as a player, coach and manager. He had played for Spurs with some distinction in Arthur Rowe's push and run side of the early Fifties. He then coached the club and was promoted to manager in 1958, a job he performed with massive success until his resignation in 1974.

In some of his observations on life Nicholson could be almost as quotable as Shankly. He was certainly as inspired and decisive in the transfer market as Busby and as clear in his vision of what makes a winning football team as Clough. Nicholson was actually a forerunner. He set standards with his beloved Spurs that his contemporaries struggled to follow, such as guiding his club to the League and FA Cup Double in 1961 – the first time it had been done in the 20th century. That was a feat beyond rivals like Busby, Shankly and Wolves' highly successful boss Stan Cullis. But rather than publicly dissecting and debating his success, Nick was a firm believer that actions always spoke louder than words. He was never one to court the media – either with charm or controversy. He kept his head down and worked.

Bill Nick's players and colleagues have often declared their devotion to him, but still talked about his exacting demands, brusque manner and, put bluntly, miserly approach in contract talks. The Sixties were the early days when the maximum wage limit had only just been officially lifted. Yet, like Manchester United's Busby and Celtic legend Jock Stein, Nicholson saw it as his duty to extend the directors' parsimony when it came to dealing with the players' wage demands. Bill Nick was brutal in deciding what a player merited in the club's expenditure master plan and ensured he stuck by those tight guidelines. He was unbending.

Yet this was the same man who would willingly listen to the opinions and tactical ideas of players like his Double-winning skipper Danny Blanchflower, and allow his men to offer ideas in team meetings. Blanchflower, an erudite Northern Irishman who could charm or firmly argue his way to gain support in any forum, was Nick's perfect skipper. It was Danny, the brilliant wing-half and cornerstone of the Tottenham team of the late Fifties and early Sixties, who famously declared: "It's not about the money. It's about the glory." That ethic was music to Billy Nick's ears. He truly appreciated honesty, integrity and hard work from his players and coaching staff.

He was also a quite brilliant judge of a player. While he inherited some outstanding players like Blanchflower, Bobby Smith and Maurice Norman, he went out and bought the likes of Dave Mackay, John White, Les Allen and Jimmy Greaves. Such was the attacking brio of his Double-winning team that they scored 115 goals in the 42-match season. Alongside Blanchflower, Mackay can lay claim to being considered a Spurs icon too. Mackay's assessment of Nicholson is perceptive. "He was quite simply an excellent man and manager who was completely focused on the club. He wasn't like some of the modern managers who are always in the papers. For him the game was the most important thing, not talking about it." Nicholson would never think of socializing with his players. On rare occasions they invited him to join them for drinks. He would never do it, and they knew he'd prefer it if they didn't go out to the pub either. He went to his end terraced house in Tottenham, to his devoted wife Darkie, and planned the next stage of his Tottenham crusade. As Mackay hinted, the media never took to Bill Nick in the way they did to some of his contemporaries. Yet some of his pearls of wisdom were gems. It was Nicholson who said: "There's no use being satisfied when things are done wrongly. I want perfection." He also said: "It's no use just winning, we've got to win well." And given that by the end of his life he had spent 60 years at White Hart Lane in one capacity or another, it was fitting he should say: "It's been my life, Tottenham Hotspur, and I love the club."

He resigned as manager in the autumn of 1974, outraged by the hooliganism that besmirched Tottenham's UEFA Cup final against Feyenoord in Rotterdam. He was appalled by the wage demands of players he did not believe were special yet demanded the pay of superstars. He left with a £10,000 pay-off from the club.

In effect, the club had been as tight-fisted with him as he had been with so many players down the years. The situation had turned full circle.

So perhaps it's justice that we elevate Bill Nicholson to the status of Tottenham icon. He's always deserved it. But what about the cult heroes? We've already mentioned two contenders – Blanchflower and Mackay. The shrewd, intelligent, wise Blanchflower who played tiki-taki keep ball before the world had discovered Barcelona. And there's Mackay, a swashbuckling wing-half who possessed incredible raw power, drive, determination and a canny intelligence to match. He was also skilful, too. Jimmy Sirrel, the legendary Notts County boss, once reflected on the great players he'd seen, and selected Mackay as among the greatest. The Scottish duo became firm friends later in life, and Sirrel would reflect on Mackay's football skills with the words: "Davie could pass, tackle, dribble, shoot, the lot." He would then pause before adding with real emphasis: "And he was a hard bastard, too."

Hard men invariably make their mark on fans, and when the Football Supporters' Federation offered their input to this book there were Spurs followers who immediately cited Graham Roberts as their cult hero. Roberts, a tough centre-back, served Spurs with some distinction between 1980 and 1986. He played a key role in them winning two FA Cups and the UEFA Cup. But would it be right to hand the status of cult hero to a mainly destructive player when down the years Spurs have craved attacking style and verve?

We must look at two attacking midfield players who on their day could stand comparison with any players in the world. In terms of skill, invention and the ability to win big matches it's impossible to ignore the merits of Glenn Hoddle and Paul Gascoigne. During their peak years they were the finest creative forces in English football. Hoddle could transform a game with a scintillating pass or deft volley. Gazza had more power and a physical edge to his game. Both were masters of the art of taking free-kicks and proved match-winners with their skills.

When Bryan Robson retired after 19 years at the summit of English club football and almost a decade as England skipper I remember interviewing him, and asking him to name the finest opponent he had faced. Robbo, the Captain Fantastic for club and country, delivered an immediate response. It could have been Platini or Tardelli or Bonhof. He ignored them all. "The best player I've faced was Gazza. He had everything. It's just a tragedy about the knee injury he got when Spurs won the 1991 FA Cup."

Our Spurs cult hero is Paul John Gascoigne – always to be known as Gazza.

THE FAN'S VIEW

David Scripps of the FSF: "Gazza is my cult hero for the following reasons. What an entertainer. It was worth the admission fee just to watch him play. What a character. As Bobby Robson said, he's as daft as a brush! And what a player! He could win a game single-handedly, and did that on numerous occasions during our 90–91 FA Cup run. And finally, and for me this makes him a cult hero just on its own: scoring that superlative free-kick against the other (and smaller) team from North London in the FA Cup semi-final at Wembley. What a moment, what a game, what a player!"

TRANMERE ROVERS

ⓘ John King    **John Aldridge**

There's something about Tranmere Rovers that appears to get into a football man's DNA and forces him to have a long-term link with the Birkenhead club.

Maybe it's because Prenton Park is situated across the Mersey on the Wirral side of Liverpool. Maybe it's the challenge of trying to run a successful club with the giants of Liverpool and Everton attracting the bulk of support just over the water. There's an inherent challenge in being a Rovers player, manager or supporter. You're always going to be derided as the little team from Birkenhead. And yet down the years that kind of dismissive talk has brought the best out of some strong, inspirational people.

You don't have to be a Scouser to be acclaimed around Prenton Park. For instance, Dave Russell was a Dundonian who arrived as manager in 1961. He won promotion from the old Fourth Division before moving upstairs to be general manager and stayed with the club for 17 years. He was a wonderful ambassador and few clubs or administrators offered a warmer welcome than Dave, who was widely respected in the game. He died, aged 86, in 2000.

Our Tranmere icon was signed by Russell. John King had started his career with Everton, failed to make a major impact and headed south to Bournemouth. But he headed back to his Scouse roots and became a cornerstone of Russell's promotion-winning team. He was a hard-working wing-half and while he was good it wasn't as a player that King won salutes from the Rovers fans.

King became Tranmere manager in 1975 and in his first full season won promotion from the Fourth Division. John was popular and well respected and the big boys across the Mersey spoke of their admiration for the way he operated. But that didn't prevent him from being sacked by Rovers in 1980. Far from being undermined by that dismissal, King joined non-League football with Northwich Victoria and Caernarfon Town. He enjoyed success with both. Vics won the FA Trophy in 1984 and Caernarfon enjoyed some splendid FA Cup giant-killing moments.

And Tranmere was already in King's DNA. In 1987 he returned as Rovers were in real danger of dropping out of the Football League, and he guided them to safety, in the following season even to promotion – a spectacular turnaround in fortunes. This era is acknowledged as a golden age for Rovers. They won the Football League Trophy in 1990, reached the final of that tournament a year later as well as promotion from the Third Division via the play-offs. But then came a run of form that reflected King's outstanding talent as a manager and the pain of near-miss failure. Three times between 1993 and 1995 Rovers reached the promotion play-offs as they pursued a remarkable promotion to the Premier League. They also reached the semi-finals of the League Cup. But somehow they couldn't break through that final barrier to achieve the astonishing feat of seeing Tranmere Rovers in the top flight of English football.

King was admired throughout football for the organization he brought to his teams, the fighting spirit they showed and the fact that they made Prenton Park a happy hunting ground, enjoying some memorable Cup wins there. But he couldn't guarantee long-term success, and in April 1996 he moved upstairs as director of football.

One of the joys in researching this book has been the discovery of previously unknown statistics. For instance, I must be the only person who didn't know that since the Second World War the player in Football League and Premier League football with the highest goals per games ratio is our Tranmere cult hero, John Aldridge. In 889 career appearances, Aldo scored a record 476 goals.

I had the privilege of covering the Republic of Ireland when Aldo, thanks to his Irish parentage qualifications, was playing for the boys in green. Given his track record for every other team he represented it's incredible to think that he played in 20 internationals before scoring his first international goal for Ireland. Whenever the squad met up Aldo would spot the press and immediately joke: "Don't even ask me if this is the game when I'm going to break my duck." What Aldo didn't know is that a few of his team-mates were involved in a wind-up to ensure we did keep asking that question, such was the fun and banter around the Ireland squad in those days. Jack Charlton encouraged a regime where the players and regular media could share a pint of the black stuff on the Sunday or Monday night, then do their work for the match and enjoy being part of the Ireland scene. I can assure you there were very few cry-offs from those internationals – and the club managers back in England realized it!

Aldo scored goals throughout his career. His spell at Liverpool won him most acclaim. Although he'd done well in Spain with Real Sociedad for two years, his family had not fully settled in the Basque Country and in 1991 he moved back to Merseyside and joined Tranmere in a £250,000 deal. You can predict what happened next. Aldo, aged 32, scored a club record 40 goals in his first season at Prenton Park. He stayed with Rovers until his retirement at the end of the 1997–98 season. Typically, he marked his farewell game as a professional player by scoring twice against Wolverhampton Wanderers. He made 294 appearances for Rovers and scored a remarkable 174 goals.

You will have noticed that the Aldo reign of goal terror coincided with Rovers' three tilts at reaching the Premier League – proof, if any was necessary, of the value to any team of an accomplished, reliable marksman. Sadly, they lost on each occasion in the play-off semi-finals. They also took Aston Villa to a penalty shoot-out in the 1994 League Cup semi-finals. But, yet again, the game ended in heartbreak.

Aldo became Rovers player-manager for the last two years of his career before concentrating on management. He did well with those successes in the League and a series of impressive Cup runs. But Tranmere were relegated in 2001. Before the dreadful drop was confirmed, Aldridge resigned as manager. To some people that disappointment may taint Aldo's record at Prenton Park. We feel he still deserves to be acclaimed as a cult hero.

THE FAN'S VIEW

Jim Sanderson: *"Aldo was a veteran when he joined us but he still played with his heart on his sleeve and scored goals for fun. He was lethal in front of goal."*

WALSALL

 **Alan Buckley**    **Colin "Cannonball" Taylor**

It is 29th August 1973. Walsall, having lost 2-0 away to Wrexham on the opening day of the season, are playing a first-round League Cup tie at home to Shrewsbury.

The few hardy souls who had travelled to North Wales a few days earlier are full of worries about what the season will bring. The only promise, they say, was a brightish display from a left-winger called Alan Buckley, signed after being released by Nottingham Forest. And then 90 minutes later the new kid has scored a hat-trick in a 6-1 win and a Saddlers legend was born.

If Buckley's impact at Fellows Park was instant, it was also enduring. First, as player his goals shaped the side through the 1970s, and later as manager he kept the place alive during a period of deep debt and fear before new ownership eventually steered Walsall to their current Bescot Stadium home.

Born in Mansfield in 1951, he played only 18 times at Forest before being shown the door – but with Walsall he immediately flourished. Switched quickly from the wing to a central role by manager Ronnie Allen, he got 21 League goals in his first season and went on scoring. He was small in stature, but lightening quick in the 6-yard box with tricky and nimble movement that would help him find space to make a chance. He also had superb balance, enabling him to react to any opening.

But most of all he was obsessive about goals and confident he could score them. On one occasion his shot was heading for the corner flag before it deflected off a defender into the net. However, he went into a rage at the local newspaper man on hearing it was being recorded as an own goal.

His success in his first spell at Walsall, with 125 goals in 241 games, saw him transferred to Birmingham in 1978; but he was back a year later and the £175,000 fee remains the club's record. It was well justified: he played another 178 games, scoring 49 more times in the process.

Promoted first to be player-manager and later manager, he was an inspired leader and his Walsall side played some of the most attractive football the club has produced, winning 2-1 at Arsenal in an amazing 1984 League Cup run that culminated in scaring that year's champions Liverpool by drawing 2-2 at Anfield in the first leg before a 2-0 defeat at Fellows Park.

Buckley's final total of 174 goals, however, still left him 10 short of the man who jointly holds the club record and gets the vote as our Walsall cult hero. Colin "Cannonball" Taylor shares the record set by Tony Richards in the 1950s, but then

Taylor not only scored as many but, in his position as an old-fashioned left-winger, also set up a good deal of those scored by Richards.

Taylor, born in nearby Stourbridge, spent three spells in all with the Saddlers, leaving to join first Newcastle then Crystal Palace before each time being lured back to the club he loved most.

His first spell was the most successful, under the guidance of manager Bill Moore achieving successive promotions by scoring 102 goals on their way to winning the Fourth Division in 1960 and then finishing second a year later to reach the second tier of English football for the first time since the early 1900s.

He got his nickname for the stunning shooting power in his left foot – he'd fire ferocious shots from right out on the touchline that left goalkeepers beaten by sheer pace. Was it a fluke? "No," he would say. "I do it every week."

THE FAN'S VIEW

Bruce Taylor: *"I nominate Alan Buckley as our icon. The great thing about him was his super confidence. Sometimes it might have seemed misplaced but he never lacked self-belief."*

WATFORD

 **Luther Blissett**

 **John Barnes**

John Barnes was the most gifted player to play for Watford in living memory. That's the view of Luther Blissett. So if that's true, why are we nominating Blissett as our Watford icon and reducing Barnes to the ranks of a cult hero?

The duo have much in common. They share Jamaican roots and were key parts of the astonishing charge through the divisions masterminded by Graham Taylor. Taylor's reign as England manager may have been widely criticized and ended in ignominy, but there can be no doubting the impressive way he transformed Watford's fortunes and led them from the Fourth Division to the top flight for the first time in their history.

Luckily for Blissett, Taylor arrived at Vicarage Road to succeed Mike Keen. Luther recalled: "Mike Keen had actually made noises about getting rid of me, and it was being discussed by all sorts of people at the club. Tom Walley, who was still a player but had involvement in the youth team, said to Graham Taylor that he should keep me and give me a chance. Thankfully, Graham listened to that advice.

"At the end of the season Graham arranged a meeting with everyone, and wanted to meet every single player on an individual basis. We had about 15 minutes each with him. I got called in and he told me to sit down. He was in this great big chair and I was on a little stool, so he was really looking down on me. I was only 17 so I was as nervous as anything. With a new manager coming in you don't know what's going to happen, and everything seems in slow motion. He had a piece of paper in his hands and he was reading that as we sat in silence. He then looked straight at me and said my full name three times with a couple of seconds pause in between each time. After the third time of saying it, he then said 'Well, son, with a name like that you are going to have to be a star aren't you!'

"He then told me that the previous manager was going to let me go but Tom Walley said I was worth giving a chance so that was what they were going to do. The rest is history!"

Blissett had three spells as a player at the club and later joined the coaching staff. But it was in his first incarnation that Watford stormed through the divisions and he proved his prowess as a powerful centre-forward. He was aided and abetted by the brilliant supply lines provided by Barnes on the left and Nigel Callaghan on the right. Cally was part of an England Under-21 team that became champions of Europe in the early Eighties. If truth be told, unlike Barnes and Blissett he never fully exploited his natural ability. Blissett broke into the Watford team in 1977–78 as they gained promotion from the Fourth Division. They won back-to-back promotions the following year and this time Blissett chipped in with 21 goals. There was a period of consolidation until Watford made the top flight for the first time in their history in 1982. This time Blissett had delivered 19 League goals.

Watford took the top flight by storm. Early on in the campaign they were at the summit of English football. In the end the title was won by Bob Paisley's Liverpool but Watford finished runners-up. This was a remarkable achievement and Blissett was the division's leading marksman with 27 goals. That's when AC Milan entered the equation and prised Blissett out of Vicarage Road in a £1 million deal.

Life in Italy was not kind to Blissett, though. Milan were recovering after being relegated following match-fixing allegations. The only star name in their ranks was a budding teenager called Franco Baresi.

Legend has it that they signed the wrong Watford player; they really wanted Barnes, made a mistake and ended up with Blissett. That story is a myth. While nobody would dispute Barnes is by far the more technically gifted, Milan desperately wanted a proven marksman. Blissett fitted the bill. But they never played to his strengths and after a miserable year he was happy to return home to Vicarage Road.

Luther's second and third spells at the club couldn't match his spectacular opening, but he never lost the affection of the Watford fans, even though their club was slipping from the highs of the early Taylor regime. The statistical fact remains that Blissett holds the club's all-time records for appearances and goals, having played 503 games and scored 186 goals.

He was invited back as a coach when Taylor was general manager and Kenny Jackett was team boss in 1996. But Gianluca Vialli's arrival as manager five years later saw the Italian insisting on appointing his own backroom staff. Blissett was sacked – a decision that provoked criticism from Taylor.

John Barnes had always been the attacking gem in the Watford ranks. On his best days he was unstoppable. He was a Watford player when he slalomed through the Brazil defence to score one of the greatest ever England goals in the Maracana Stadium in June 1984. Sadly, there were National Front racists following England who taunted Barnes rather than salute him for his brilliance.

After their success in charging through the Leagues Watford also reached the 1984 FA Cup final where they lost 2-0 to Everton, but it was another sign of a club developing real stability at the top level. A queue was forming for Barnes. Eventually, in the summer of 1987, he joined Liverpool in a £900,000 deal. He really was a complete attacking talent, a virtuoso in creative play.

We had nominations for Watford's cult hero for Stewart Scullion, a winger from the Sixties, and Cliff Holton, a centre-forward of the Fifties with one of the most ferocious shots in the game. Of course they have their merits. But it's impossible to look beyond Barnes and the moments of magic he delivered for Watford.

THE FAN'S VIEW

John Navin: *"Stewart Scullion was our George Best. In a way he defined Watford. John Barnes justifies his inclusion as a club legend. And Luther Blissett, although not as sophisticated as Barnes, was our best player."*

WEST BROMWICH ALBION

 Tony Brown  Darren Moore

There can be few players so woven into the fabric of a club as Tony "Bomber" Brown. It is more than three decades since his record-breaking career of 279 goals in 720 games drew to a close, but he is still to be seen at every West Bromwich Albion game, home and away.

He's there doing radio work, but you suspect his media commitments are just an excuse. Talk to him about that day's team, last week's game, a star player from the first team or a bright young prospect among the kids, and his enthusiasm for the club – his club – still bubbles over. Quiet, understated, sensible and measured in his views, he is absorbed in Albion for the here and now, and not just for the memories of his own glory days. And as a succession of managers and team-mates will confirm, "The Bomber" was a fantastic player.

There's been a lifelong love affair since he turned up at The Hawthorns for a trial at the age of 15, persuaded to give the club a try by their Manchester-based scout John Shaw. A United fan as a boy, he had agreed to sign for Manchester City. But, in his words, "as soon as I stepped into The Hawthorns I just knew this was the club for me. I've never quite known why, but I just knew."

Albion just knew, too. He scored a hat-trick that day and was immediately offered the chance to become an apprentice. It was a decision that neither club nor player would ever regret.

With his goals record and nickname, it would be easy to assume that "Bomber" was a big centre-forward. Not so. He stands just 5ft 8in tall, and played first as a wing-half and then an inside-forward – what you'd call midfield these days. But his ability to break forward, his instinct to arrive in the right position, and his cool talent for clinically finishing the most difficult of chances, made him way ahead of his time. He was a stealth bomber, arriving unexpectedly to do the utmost damage to defences – or producing a shot from out of nowhere from the edge of the box.

He scored on his debut a few days before his 18th birthday – away to Ipswich – and again on his home debut against Aston Villa. And the goals kept coming, most notably in the 1965–66 season when he was the top scorer. Some 17 in the First Division – Albion finished sixth – were topped up by at least one in every round of a journey to the League Cup final and a 4-1 win over West Ham in the second leg of a 5-3 aggregate triumph, which he considered the best team performance of his career.

Arguably the greatest moment came in 1968, part of a closely knit team that went to Wembley and beat favourites Everton to win the FA Cup. Albion, who hadn't won a trophy since 1954, now had two in two years, and there were trips to Wembley for League Cup finals in 1967 and 1970, too.

Ironically it was in the 1970s, as Albion's team began to go into decline, that Brown's legend was written largest. He dropped deeper to play a key role in struggling teams, providing telling passes to Jeff Astle as well as continuing to score goals – he got 12 of the 38 in all that the club scored during their 1973 relegation season. Then, at a time when he had won his only England cap, he stayed loyal and fought through three seasons before helping secure promotion back to the top flight.

There was one more key role for him, as the senior player to set the tone for Ron Atkinson's flamboyant side. As the likes of Bryan Robson, Derek Statham, Cyrille Regis and Laurie Cunningham emerged in Big Ron's swashbuckling style, it was Brown and skipper John Wile who provided the experience and leadership. The youngsters emerged as real stars of the future aided by Brown's guidance. The likes of Valencia – including World Cup-winning striker Mario Kempes and West Germany midfield star Rainer Bonhof – were overrun in a famous UEFA Cup triumph. That was the European tie that helped secure Cunningham's move to Real Madrid.

Those players held Brown in the highest esteem. Atkinson, his manager, always maintained that "The Bomber" was the finest, clinical finisher of his era bar none. He was that good. By the time his career at Albion ended Brown had smashed almost every appearance and goalscoring record. They are unlikely ever to be broken.

Albion's glory days came in the Fifties with the likes of striker, and later manager, Ronnie Allen, midfielders Ray Barlow and Bobby Robson, and full-back Don Howe among their stalwarts. In 1954 they won the FA Cup and almost became the first team of the 20th century to win a Double, but finished runners-up in the League to Wolves. They finished in the top five of the top flight for three consecutive seasons up to 1960.

But cult heroes are not always spawned from the glory years; some arrive on a more circuitous route. There were no records attached to the player Baggies fans named as their cult hero. In fact, Darren Moore made just 116 appearances in six years with the club.

But it was Moore, Big Dave, Dazzler, who was the rock on which the club's current status as a top-flight fixture was built. At the start of the "boing, boing" decade, with successive promotions and relegations to and from the riches of the Premier League, the giant defender provided leadership. He grew up in nearby Handsworth, but had played for Torquay, Bradford and Portsmouth before Gary Megson paid £750,000 to sign him in September 2001. There was little style to his play, but there was no shortage of substance. He was a rock who won headers, flung himself into tackles and put his body on the line to block shots, his whole-hearted example spreading through the team.

Fans loved his commitment. And they loved how he enjoyed fighting for their cause, that huge grin signalling his love for the club. Nobody fought harder to try to preserve their Premier League status, and nobody gave more in the cause of winning it back again. Even when, under Bryan Robson's management, he was drifting out of the team he came on as a substitute to play a pivotal role in the 4-1 win at Charlton, which inspired the club's "Great Escape" season.

He's back at Albion now working with the youth teams – a great example to young players that commitment, determination and courage are factors every bit as vital in football as skill and talent.

THE FAN'S VIEW

David Allen: *"Tony Brown remains the ultimate Baggies legend to everyone at the club. We make sure even the youngsters growing up as Baggies fans know about him."*

WEST HAM UNITED

ⓘ Bobby Moore   **ⓗ Julian Dicks**

The forerunner to West Ham was the Thames Ironworks FC, which was established in 1895. Five years later the club was reformed as West Ham United, and their home was the Boleyn Ground, where they remain to this day.

But names, statistics and landmarks do not reflect the true majesty and meaning of West Ham United. The pride of the club is in the personnel, their style and their deeds. And the Hammers have plenty to be proud about, epitomized by Bobby Moore.

He climbs the Wembley steps, pauses briefly, looks along the front of the royal box to see the Queen wearing pristine white gloves, and wipes his own hands on his shorts before drying them on the velvet balustrade. To any football fan who has watched the grainy, black-and-white footage of the moment England's captain stepped up to collect the Jules Rimet trophy, it is the defining image of Robert Frederick Moore. It can be summed up in one word: class.

To West Ham fans it was the moment their club won the World Cup. The statue, which now stands around the corner from Upton Park and shows Moore held aloft by Everton defender Ray Wilson and his West Ham team-mate Geoff Hurst, while another Hammer, Martin Peters, looks on, simply confirms the belief that this was an East End triumph as much as an English one. After all, while Bobby was the skipper that day, all four England goals came from Hurst and Peters.

Indeed, Moore was the golden captain of a golden age for the Hammers. You can't measure his or his team's success in trophies. There was the FA Cup in 1964, and the European Cup Winners' Cup at Wembley a year later. But the 1960s was a unique decade for West Ham United because it was the time that established a tradition. It was never a code of win-at-all-costs. The way of winning was more important to the Hammers and their followers than victory itself.

It was an age where the club's youth scheme began to produce local players of the highest quality; it was a time when Ron Greenwood laid the principles of a style of football and a way of playing; and Moore was the iconic figure who represented all those values on the field. In more modern, troubled times the club may not have always reached those standards, but the supporters have always aspired to them.

There were those who said Moore had no pace, was poor at heading the ball and lacked aggression. Even the scouting report produced by Jack Turner, the man given the task by manager of the time Ted Fenton to check up on a young lad playing for Leyton Boys, was less than enthusiastic: it contained the immortal phrase "Whilst he would not set the world alight ..."

What he did have was an ice cool brain, brilliant positional sense, an incredible knack of timing in the tackle, and a sense of calm in the deepest crisis which spread to those around him. If you grew up paying your money to go through the turnstiles at Upton Park he was the rock you could rely on.

Jack Charlton tells the story of England's glory day against West Germany in 1966. The clock's ticking down and the home side are winning 3-2. Moore collects possession in his own half and, as big Jack explained: "I screamed at him to belt it down into the Germany corner flag to waste time. What did Bobby do? Pick out Geoff Hurst with an exquisite pass, my words stuck in my throat as Geoff runs through for his hat-trick goal and the game was all over. That was Bobby at his best."

Ron Greenwood became manager of West Ham in 1961. He instinctively knew that Moore, whom he had coached with England's youth team, would be his leader. Within a season he was appointed captain, and his influence was so immediate that at the age of 22 he was captain of England for the first of 90 occasions. On good days Moore's leadership would turn draws into wins for West Ham; on others it would scramble a point from a match that seemed lost.

He was brilliant at Wembley in a topsy turvy 1964 Cup final that finished in a 4-3 win, and then magnificent again the following season as the Hammers played their swashbuckling football across Europe.

My abiding memory, though, isn't of any of the famous moments for club or country. It's of a run-of-the-mill League game at Upton Park – I think it might have been against Leeds – on a day when West Ham were hanging on to a single goal lead with a few minutes left, and defending frantically. I can still play in my mind my personal film of seeing a mad goalmouth scramble, shots and blocks with the ball bouncing round like a bagatelle, until Moore, standing on the goal-line, stopped it under his foot. He looked up for what could only have been a millisecond but seemed like an eternity, weighed up whether he could pick a pass that would turn defence to attack, decided he couldn't and calmly pushed the ball the other side of the post to concede another corner. Around 30,000 fans were suffering heart failure; Bobby had simply picked the best option.

Moore has to be unopposed as West Ham's icon. He was just 17 when he made his debut against Manchester United. The Hammers won 3-2, and reports of the day speak of the "composed" performance of the young blond lad taking his initial steps on the First Division stage. It was a word used time and again through another 542 League appearances across 15 years.

In every one of those games there seemed to be a moment when he did something special – pulled a ball from the sky and controlled it dead with a magic touch, picked a perfect pass that sent one of West Ham's wingers on to the attack, or arrived at just the right place at the right time to snuff out danger before it began.

If he was genius on the field, he also had a magic touch off it. He owned a sports shop opposite West Ham's ground in Green Street and would often spend an afternoon serving behind the counter. He always had time to talk, always signed autographs, always made his customers – however young – feel they were far more important than him.

West Ham supporters understood the special bond between their greatest captain and the club, even if those who ran the show failed to make the link – until, tragically, it was too late. Since his untimely death through bowel cancer at the age of 51 his name is immortalized in a stand and behind the scenes at Upton Park. Should he have been welcomed after he retired from playing to give more as a coach or manager? Unquestionably. Have West Ham ever had a better or more influential player? Never.

Maybe that's why all the great players since Moore's era can compete only to be considered the cult hero. Billy Bonds was a buccaneering, tough-tackling midfield man, Frank McAvennie provided goals and glamour in a side that almost won the League title in the early 1970s.

And then there was Julian Dicks, the left-back who looked as if he had stepped out of the Chicken Run to pull on a shirt, and played with the same passion and ferocity of the supporters who most idolized him.

Born in Bristol and brought up as a footballer with Birmingham, he was signed by John Lyall for just £300,000 in 1988. Fiercely competitive, he collected too many yellow and red cards, but the fans identified with his burning will to win as he set the tone for a team that brought the Hammers back into the Premier League in 1993, following relegation a year earlier.

A brief spell at Liverpool didn't go well, but Harry Redknapp made it one of his first priorities as manager to bring back Dicks' leadership and determination. The strategy paid off, and Dicks spent another six years fearlessly playing on despite the pain of a crippling knee injury which ultimately forced his early retirement from the game. In all he spent 11 years at West Ham, playing 315 competitive games and scoring 64 goals – many of them penalties, thumped firmly into the back of the net with a single-minded desire for success that had become his hallmark as a player.

WIGAN ATHLETIC

 Roberto Martínez    Dave Whelan

Wigan Athletic are the youngest club in the Premier League, having been formed in 1932. And it's a measure of their impact as a senior club that they've become a Premier League outfit after being elected into the Football League at Southport's expense as late as June 1978. In those days there was no automatic promotion from non-League football. Clubs had to be re-elected to the Football League and after the first vote was tied the Latics beat Southport on a second vote.

I'll never forget attending Wigan's first Football League game. Springfield Park, their old home, had a healthy crowd and the main stand was packed with fans keen to see history being made at the start of the 1978–79 campaign.

One particular Wigan fan had brought his girlfriend with him to savour the moment. It was a noisy, passionate occasion. Unfortunately, the aforesaid lady slightly spoiled the event by digging out of her bag a paperback book she was reading and burying her nose in it while all those around her revelled in the novel occasion. She was the target for some verbal banter and one WAG even joked: "You won't be reading a book when we're playing Man United in the top flight!" Little did the joker know – or even suspect – how that prophecy would come true.

But in selecting icons and cult heroes for Wigan we do have to acknowledge two basic facts. At heart Wigan is a rugby league town. In fact, it has one of the richest seams of rugby history of any place in the world.

The other fundamental truth is that without Dave Whelan's benevolent ownership the Latics would never have made it to the Premier League in 2005 – or successfully clung on to their top-flight status since then.

Whelan bought control of the club in February 1995 when they were in the Third Division, the fourth tier of English football at the time. Whelan was derided when he announced that his ambition was to take Wigan into the Premier League inside a decade. In fact, there was little evidence it would happen in his first season when the Latics finished 14th in their division.

In the summer of 1995 Whelan tapped his international business contacts and from Spain was recommended the names of a trio of players. He successfully recruited Roberto Martínez, Isidro Díaz and Jesús Seba – who became known as "The Three Amigos". And that's how our Wigan icon arrived at the club.

Obviously, these days Martínez is recognized as the managerial miracle worker who has kept the club in the top flight against all the odds. They are invariably among most pundits' favourites for the drop when pre-season predictions are made.

But Martínez achieved iconic status as a player, too. He was a skilful, intelligent midfielder who emerged as a skipper at several of the clubs he represented. This was quite an achievement because the Spanish invasion to a lower division club was greeted by cynicism in many places. Many people claimed the diminutive Martínez would never cope with the heavy grounds he'd have to play on in England. He was a revelation.

For six years Martínez was a cornerstone of the Wigan team. He was named in the Division Three PFA Team of the Year in his first year, and was also voted by the supporters as the club's Player of the Year. He won his first club honours in the 1996–97 season when Wigan finished as Division Three champions. He was once again named in the Division Three PFA Team of the Year, and was rewarded with a new four-year contract.

Martínez was also at Wigan when the team won the Autowindscreens Shield in 1999, which he received a winners' medal for despite being injured when the final was played. He spent six seasons at Wigan as a player, making 180 appearances for the club, with a further 47 as substitute, and scoring 23 goals.

Martínez did move on and enjoyed a roller-coaster life at other clubs before settling in at Swansea, initially as a player and later as manager. He won many admirers for the style in which he demanded Swansea play. He favoured possession football, players showing skill on the ball and displaying confidence in possession. Remember this was at a club that was in League One. He took them up as champions in his first year and established them in the Championship in his second.

Whelan, who had been a professional footballer himself, had spotted Martínez's talent and made his move. Swansea fans were outraged when their hero departed, especially as Martínez had said he would only leave South Wales if forced out. In fact, he was choosing to walk away.

But Wigan were a Premier League club and he was returning to his sporting home and a chairman who thought the world of him. There have been times when Whelan, a self-made millionaire, has publicly criticized his manager for mistakes in selection and tactics. But Whelan has always maintained he did this to provoke a positive reaction. And that's what has invariably happened. Whelan can be opinionated and outspoken but he's the boss and usually speaks immense common sense.

Even though Wigan have laboured for most of their Premier League life in the lower reaches Martínez has always asked his players to produce bright, entertaining football, and on their good days they've delivered. A glance at the size of the clubs now outside the Premier League highlights Wigan's achievements.

But the praise Martínez has been showered with has also seen a number of Premier League clubs make overtures for his services. Aston Villa were among the first, and in May 2012 Whelan announced that he had given Liverpool permission to speak to Martínez about the chance of succeeding Kenny Dalglish as their boss.

Many newspapers carried stories that Martínez was a certainty to move to Anfield. But within managerial circles the word spread that, rather than work at a potentially dysfunctional club, where there was still a debate raging about the need for a director of football and the vagaries of the wealthy American owners, Martínez preferred to stick with the multi-millionaire he knew.

Most fans would accept that the concept of a Wigan manager turning down mighty Liverpool and opting to stay at the DW Stadium was incredible. Yet Martínez did just that. But he's our Wigan icon because of so much more. The way he shifted the cultural perspective of a northern town is just part of his allure. Martínez is a charming, open, friendly guy who is a brilliant ambassador for the club.

We did consider some players as cult heroes such as the excellent midfielder Kevin Langley. He was a painter and decorator who wrote in asking for a trial and landed himself a contract. He had two spells with the Latics and remains a firm favourite even though he couldn't quite maintain his Wigan heroics when transferred to Everton and Manchester City.

But our cult hero has to be Whelan. Without him the Wigan miracle could never have happened. He was born in November 1936 and was playing in the 1960 Blackburn Rovers FA Cup final team when he broke his leg in their 3-0 defeat against Wolverhampton Wanderers. He was sold by Blackburn to Crewe and when his football career was over he showed remarkable ingenuity in developing a chain of supermarkets. Next came sportswear supermarkets and a string of deals establishing his wealth and business status. Although born in Bradford he had been brought up in Wigan and looked on the old mining town as his true home. He was galvanized to make their local football team great.

Whelan has had his critics. He will not sit back and let the big boys trample over him and his club. There is a northern bluntness to many of his observations about life in the Premier League. But Wigan fans appreciate his commitment and tenacity. In a town built on rugby league and coal mining, those are priceless qualities for the chairman of the football club.

THE FAN'S VIEW

Peter Mason: *"I remember the arrival of the Three Amigos and savouring Roberto Martínez the player. It's fantastic that he's been a successful manager with us too."*

WOLVES

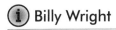 Billy Wright

 Steve Bull

When you met Billy Wright the first thing that surprised you was his size. Here was a man who had won more than 100 England caps as a centre-half, so if you had been too young to see him play you expected to find a hulking 6ft figure. Instead, he stood just 5ft 8ins tall, was slightly built, was quiet and humble. But spend just 30 minutes in his company and you realized that, while he may have been small in stature, in every other sense of the word he was a giant of a man. Wright's statue is outside the front entrance of Molineux, and rightly so. No other player better symbolizes the post-war era when Wolverhampton Wanderers were the dominant force in England and the pioneers of the European game.

With Wright as their captain they won the old First Division title three times in six seasons, but the legacy they left to the game was far greater, experimenting with the first midweek floodlit matches – friendlies against club sides from the continent that drew thousands to pack the terraces and share the excitement of a new era. Ironically, Wright's lack of inches almost meant he never got to be a footballer. The story goes that when, as a skinny 14-year-old, he first travelled from his home in nearby Ironbridge to Molineux for a trial he was told he was not big enough to make the grade. Fortunately, Major Frank Buckley, the innovative pre-war manager who laid the foundations for what was to follow, saw his talent rather than his size and offered him an eight-month trial. Within a year he was making his debut for the first team, and across two decades nobody doubted his talent again.

People who saw him said he had the gift to hang in the air as if suspended by ropes to win headers against taller, more muscular centre-forwards, and that he broke up attacks by brilliant positioning and interception, winning the ball with the most fearsome of tackles then passing it simply to the nearest team-mate.

The stats of a career interrupted by the Second World War, when he served in the army, tell only part of the story. Captain of his country in 90 of his 105 appearances, he played a world record 70 consecutive international games and captained England to three consecutive World Cup finals. For his club he played nearly 550 games, and was never booked or sent off in any of them. He was also the first celebrity footballer – the David Beckham of his day. When in 1958 he married Joy Beverley, eldest of the Beverley Sisters who were the Spice Girls of their time, the seaside town of Poole was brought to a halt by the crowds thronging around the registry office.

However great his legacy to the 1950s era he had one more contribution to the club he loved – after Sir Jack Haywood had rescued Wolves from bankruptcy in the 1980s he instinctively turned to Billy to join him on the board and bring his insight to help rebuild both the stadium and the football team. If the modern Wolves still look back to their 1950s glories, then the modern Molineux was constructed with those traditions in mind. For all those reasons Billy Wright, the tiny giant, who sadly was taken early by cancer aged just 70, has to be the club's greatest icon.

When it comes to a cult hero, however, there is equally only one contender. The once proud club had slumped to 92nd in the League just before November 1986 when manager Graham Turner paid neighbours West Bromwich Albion just £65,000 for winger Andy Thompson and a young centre-forward called Stephen George Bull.

There were those who questioned why Turner would risk the first transfer fee available to a manager on a raw kid who had only just passed his 21st birthday. Some 250 goals in 474 matches later – plus 13 England caps despite the club never quite making it back to the top flight – they had their answer.

But Steve Bull, "Bully" to his adoring fans, wasn't just an astonishing goalscorer; he was a symbol of local pride in a club reborn from financial catastrophe. A Black Country boy, born and always living in nearby Tipton, he turned down any number of chances to move to bigger clubs for more money, always insisting that his joy at playing for his club was worth far more than any contract. There is a stand named after him, and the fans still sing his name. They probably always will.

THE FAN'S VIEW

Terry O'Brien: *"When we were down Bully arrived to save us. We'll never forget that."*

WYCOMBE WANDERERS

 **Dave Carroll**

 **Steve Brown**

Steve Brown was a totally committed midfield enforcer who never gave less than 100 per cent in any game he played. He was occasionally known to give more than 100 per cent in the shape of "afters" when the referee was unsighted. That probably helped increase his popularity with Wanderers fans who grew accustomed to Steve fighting battles for himself – and most of his team-mates.

Martin O'Neill brought him to Wycombe from his home-town club Northampton for £60,000 in 1994. The deal proved to be an inspired piece of business by the Irishman.

Brown played in the 2001 FA Cup semi-final defeat to Liverpool after having been dismissed in the quarter-final win over Leicester City for pulling off his shirt to unveil a T-shirt paying tribute to his ill son, Maxwell.

Hugely respected by the Wycombe fans, Brown made 443 appearances scoring 43 goals. He endeared himself to the club by leaving the field in tears after his final game for Wycombe. Brown later worked helping to develop youth football in South-East Asia and even hosted Vietnamese reality show *Soccer Prince*.

Dave Carroll, our Wanderers icon, was a very different type of midfielder to hard-man Brown. Scottish play-maker Carroll is often cited as Wanderers' most skilful player of all time. Nicknamed "Jesus", Carroll is still regarded as the finest No. 7 in Wycombe's history. Many Adams Park regulars swear Paisley-born Carroll had the most cultured right foot outside of the Premier League. When Dave and outside-left Steve Guppy (later to play for Newcastle, Leicester and Celtic) were in the same side at Adam Park, right-sided Carroll was always thought to be the more creative player.

He played more than 600 League and Cup games for Wycombe and scored 100 goals. But those personal stats don't adequately reflect his impact with Wanderers. He created many more from pinpoint crosses and deadly set-pieces.

Carroll was a key man in Wycombe's promotion to the Football League in 1993 and his second goal in the 4-2 win over Preston in the Third Division play-off final a year later is regarded by Wycombe fans as one of the finest goals ever scored at Wembley.

YEOVIL TOWN

 **Alec Stock**　　　　　　　　　 **Warren Patmore**

Somerset-born Alec Stock is an iconic figure in his home county because of what happened on 29th January 1949. That date is etched into the memory of every Yeovil supporter of a certain age – and if you're younger you're bound to know about it too. It was the afternoon when the famed Southern League giant-killers pulled off the biggest FA Cup shock in their history.

They humbled a powerful Sunderland side, a team challenging for the League title that included the original Clown Prince of Football, Len Shackleton. The Wearsiders were known as the Bank of England club. They had spent a fortune on recruiting players, including the £20,500 British record splashed out on Shackleton.

Player-manager and captain Stock was Yeovil's inspiration in those immediate post-war years and he ensured that Yeovil used the wickedly sloping Huish pitch to their full advantage.

Stock led by example and fired Yeovil ahead against all the odds. But mighty Sunderland hit back to level through England international Jackie Robinson in the second half. The record 17,123 crowd had to wait until extra-time for Eric Bryant's winner, but that shock 2-1 win ensured that the names of Yeovil and Stock are forever remembered when remarkable Cup exploits are discussed.

What is not so often recalled is that Yeovil, away from the helpful slope, lost 8-0 in the fifth round to Manchester United at their temporary Maine Road HQ. Stock died in 2001, aged 84, but his legend as the inspiration behind Cup shocks lived with him. He was the manager of QPR when they became the first Third Division side to win the League Cup in 1967. In 1975 he was the Fulham manager when the Second Division club lost the FA Cup final to West Ham.

Our Yeovil cult hero is a prolific striker whose name became synonymous with the club. Warren Patmore was a burly, bulldozing player who achieved legendary status at Huish Park in the late 1990s as he netted a barrowload of goals.

Many Glovers fans rate Patmore as the best finisher they have ever seen, despite his reputation being less well known outside Somerset. Green and white fans of that era still recall Patmore's extraordinary celebration of his 100th Yeovil goal against Leek when he ran the length of the Huish pitch before leaping into the terraces to celebrate with some pals.

Patmore joined Yeovil in 1995 shortly after the club were relegated to the Isthmian League for the second time. But he quickly raised spirits with a four-goal blast in only his third game. And he just kept on finding the net with a total of 140 goals in his 287 Yeovil games. Another of Patmore's memorable goal celebrations came against Bolton when he scored at the Reebok. After meeting Ronnie Radford the day before the match he did a passable impression of the Hereford Cup hero's celebration. A great character, Patmore was hardly the most sophisticated footballer, but he is still revered in Somerset as one of the game's good guys.

THE FAN'S VIEW

Christopher M Johnson: *"My Yeovil icon is Terry Skiverton."*

YORK CITY

ⓘ Arthur Bottom  **ⓗ Barry Jackson**

Barry Jackson was a York City legend who just couldn't leave Bootham Crescent. In fact he loved the place so much that when his playing days were over and he was wondering what he could do he bought a sweet shop across the road from the old ground so that on match day he was still part of the buzz around the Minstermen. From such deeds cult heroes are made.

But Jackson wasn't some sad old-timer clinging on to former glories. He gave 14 years loyal service to City and made a club record 539 appearances. He was born at Askrigg in North Yorkshire. He shot up in his teens and was a gangly youth player. It was Sam Bartram, the former Charlton goalie and City manager, who signed Jackson in 1956 and explained how he would be converted into a powerful centre-back. Bartram's vision worked to perfection.

Barry played in two promotion-winning sides of 1959 and 1965. For most of his career he was City skipper. And despite being at one club all those years he was only dropped from the team once. That came after 474 games and when he was approaching the veteran stage.

In January 1970 he was sent off at Scunthorpe and was banned for eight weeks. Ironically, he was replaced by Barry Swallow, who then went on to carve out his own lengthy career as City's new defensive rock. It was time for Jackson to move on. He had a testimonial in February 1970 and then he joined non-League Scarborough for a short spell.

Arthur Bottom is our York City icon. The legendary striker died in April 2012, aged 82. Arthur scored 105 goals in 158 appearances for the club. Bottom began his football career in his native Sheffield, playing for the local YMCA team and then joining Sheffield United. He joined York in the 1954–55 season when City, then playing in the Third Division North, reached the FA Cup semi-finals and faced Newcastle United. He scored an equalizer in the first game that ended 1-1. But Newcastle won the replay 2-0 and went on to lift the trophy at Wembley. Nonetheless, Bottom scored eight FA Cup goals in that campaign and in his debut season as a whole he notched 39 goals.

The following season he scored 31 League goals, 33 in all competitions. That still stands as a club record for League goals.

You'll note there's been no attempt by the author to make fun of the York icon's surname. After all, York fans send an electronic newsletter around the world called

"There's Only One Arthur Bottom." Indeed.

THE FAN'S VIEW

Andy Long: *"I never saw him but my uncles insist Arthur Bottom was really the tops."*

ACKNOWLEDGEMENTS

This book is dedicated to my family and all the friends I've made through my life and career in football.

I extend special appreciation to literary agent Richard Havers for pulling all the elements of this challenging work together. I also owe a massive vote of thanks to my colleagues Brian McNally, Ralph Ellis, Ken Gorman and Richard Lewis. Their knowledge and inspiration made them a joy to work with and bounce ideas off.

This book wouldn't have happened without the support of Alison Phillips, my editor at the *Sunday Mirror*, and the encouragement of Fergus McKenna, head of the *Mirror* publishing team.

The research for the pictures included was conducted by the wonderful David Scripps. He's a kind and patient man. Thanks also to proofreader Rebecca Ellis.

Finally, we asked *Sunday Mirror* readers and members of the Football Supporters' Federation to share with us their views about their club icons and cult heroes. They deluged us with nominations. We are truly grateful.